PENGUIN BOOKS

TRADITIONAL AFRICAN AND ORIENTAL MUSIC

OTTÓ KÁROLYI arrived in England in 1956 as a refugee from Hungary. Born in Paris he spent his early childhood in France before returning to Budapest in 1939. It was there that he began his musical education, continuing it in Vienna and London. He has a wide range of teaching experience from school teaching to university work. Currently he is Senior Lecturer of Music at the University of Stirling, where he also lectures on literature and fine art. He particularly likes to contribute to interdisciplinary courses. His publications include *Introducing Music*, *Introducing Modern Music* and *Traditional African and Oriental Music*, all of which are published by Penguin, *Modern British Music from Elgar to Peter Maxwell Davies* and *Modern American Music – from Charles Ives to the Minimalists*.

He has been living in Scotland for the past twenty years with his wife who is a psychotherapist.

Traditional
AFRICAN
and
ORIENTAL
Music

Ottó Károlyi

PENGUIN BOOKS

PENGUIN BOOKS

Published by the Penguin Group
Penguin Books Ltd, 27 Wrights Lane, London w8 5tz, England
Penguin Putnam Inc., 375 Hudson Street, New York, New York 10014, USA
Penguin Books Australia Ltd, Ringwood, Victoria, Australia
Penguin Books Canada Ltd, 10 Alcorn Avenue, Toronto, Ontario, Canada m4v 3b2
Penguin Books (NZ) Ltd, Private Bag 102902, NSMC, Auckland, New Zealand

Penguin Books Ltd, Registered Offices: Harmondsworth, Middlesex, England

First published 1998
10 9 8 7 6 5 4 3 2 1

Copyright © Ottó Károlyi 1998
All rights reserved

The moral right of the author has been asserted

Typeset in Monotype Bembo and Monotype Gill Sans
Typeset by Rowland Phototypesetting Ltd, Bury St Edmunds, Suffolk
Printed in England by Clays Ltd, St Ives plc
Music setting by Barnes Music Engraving
Illustrations by Oxford Computer Illustration

To Benedikte

Contents

Preface ix

Acknowledgements xiii

CHAPTER ONE I
African Music *Introduction / Rhythm / Melody / Harmony / Instruments / General Considerations: religion; language, poetry and music; drama, dance and music; improvisation; music and musicians in the community*

CHAPTER TWO 55
Islam and Music *Introduction / Rhythm / Melody / Harmony / Instruments / General Considerations: religion; Qur'an recitations; the call to prayer; the Prophet's birthday; hymns in praise of the Prophet; Sufi worship; postlude*

CHAPTER THREE 95
The Indian Subcontinent *Introduction / Rhythm / Melody / Harmony / Instruments / General Considerations: religion: Hinduism, Buddhism, Sikhism, Islam; qawwali; dance and music; ragamala paintings*

CHAPTER FOUR 143
China and Tibet *Introduction / Rhythm / Melody / Harmony / Instruments / General Considerations: religion: Confucianism, Taoism, Buddhism; Peking opera; Tibet; dance in China and Tibet; epic song*

CHAPTER FIVE 181

The Far East *Introduction* **Japan** *Background / Rhythm / Melody / Harmony / Instruments / Instrumental and theatrical ensembles: Gagaku, Bunraku, Kabuki and Noh; General considerations: religion: Shinto, Buddhism in Japan, Zen* **Indonesia: (i) Java; (ii) Bali** *Background / Rhythm / Melody / Instruments / Theatrical ensembles and music / Bali*

Afterword 247

Select Bibliography 249

Discography 257

Notes 261

Index 264

Preface

Listening to non-Western music in concerts, on the radio, television or CDs has become by now an accepted part of our musical experience. The encounter with the musical cultures of other nations is no longer restricted to occasional world fairs or pioneering travels. Modern technology has facilitated communication and interaction between continents to an unprecedented level of speed and efficiency, especially since the end of the Second World War. Today we are all aware, or should be, that there is, for example, African, Chinese and Indian music, not just in anthropological terms as curiosities, somewhat strange and removed from us, but rather as a living reality of equal interest to the music which we are accustomed to in the West. Yet in spite of the growing popularity of non-Western music, the general tendency is still one of passive acceptance. One is entertained and stimulated by fascinating sounds and rhythms but without bothering too much about the underlying principles which give non-Western music its marked coherence and characteristic profiles. One of the two main aims of this book is to offer readers background information that will enable them to gain some insight into what is going on and why, in both technical and cultural terms, when they hear music of non-Western cultures. The other aim is, of course, to do some justice to a subject which is manifestly one of the great expressions of mankind. As there is no human life without language, similarly there is no human life without some evidence of music making. Animals do communicate, but it is mankind which has evolved languages as a complex system of intercourse. Animals also make meaningful sounds, some very attractive and sophisticated, but it is mankind which has evolved the art of music. As such, music is revelatory of the human psyche whether in its individual or social manifestations. The understanding of the signs of music is of paramount importance if we are to overcome the all too human tendency of thinking ourselves superior to those cultures which we do not comprehend. Since the publication of Edward W. Said's book *Orientalism: Western Conception of the Orient* in 1978, any Westerner who ventures on a topic in this field must be acutely aware that it is an entry into dangerous territory, where the likelihood of making blunders, however well meaning, is enormous and perhaps inevitable. Let us hope that in spite of the possible stumblings, the direction of the journey towards its goal, which is to gain a basic understanding of other fellow human beings' musical traditions beyond our own, will not be lost. As with learning a language, there is a minimum which it is necessary to grasp in terms of technicalities before one can start to have the joyful feeling of understanding and communicating. It is hoped that this book will provide that foundation.

In order to help the reader find information in a relatively easy way, each chapter follows a similar structural pattern: a map and background information, followed by the discussions of rhythm, melody, harmony, instruments and customs. The bibliography and discography at the end are to enable the reader to explore beyond the introductory nature of this book.

It is hoped that this layout will allow readers to follow their interests in an easily findable format. Anyone with, for example, particular interest in rhythm will know from the onset that this topic appears in the third section of each chapter. Thus the book can be read and studied chapter after chapter or across chapters according to specific topics.

To avoid any misunderstanding and possible disappointment, it must be made clear at the onset that this book aims to introduce the traditional music of five diverse regions in terms of their main characteristics and general approach to music. Detailed ethnomusic-ological regional differentiations concerning separate states or districts within states and largely Westernized modern developments are touched upon only when relevant to the main thrust of the argument.

Acknowledgements

My warmest thanks must also be expressed in print to those who have helped me significantly with their generous support in terms of encouragement and practical advice and help. These were: my wife, Benedikte Uttenthal, to whom this book is dedicated; Bill MacDonald and Gàbor Schàbert, both loyal friends and inspiring savants; Alastair Rolfe of Penguin Books, for his enthusiastic and patient professionalism; and Margaret McMenaman, for her endless typing and retyping of the MS.

I should also like to acknowledge the many authors, all listed in the Bibliography and Notes, from whose outstanding works I have learned a great deal about non-Western cultures. But, above all, I should like to express my gratitude to the fine musicians in all the countries discussed in this book. It is their music making which has for decades enchanted and enlightened me.

Finally thanks are due to the illustrators of this book, Barnes Music Engraving and Oxford Computer Illustration who succeeded in making presentable my rather clumsy sketches.

Should there be any acknowledgement overlooked in terms of copyright the author and publisher will be pleased to make good any errors or omissions in future editions.

CHAPTER ONE

African Music

*Introduction / Rhythm / Melody / Harmony /
Instruments / General considerations: religion; language, speech, poetry
and music; drama, dance and music; improvisation; music and musicians
in the community*

When the drumbeat changes, the dance changes.   HAUSA PROVERB

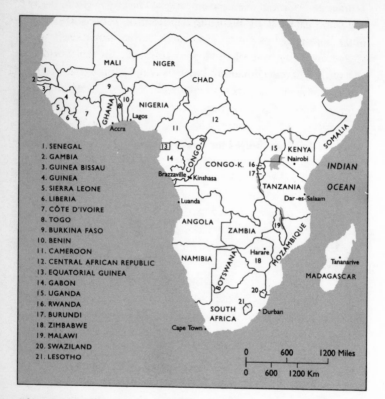

1. SENEGAL
2. GAMBIA
3. GUINEA BISSAU
4. GUINEA
5. SIERRA LEONE
6. LIBERIA
7. CÔTE D'IVOIRE
8. TOGO
9. BURKINA FASO
10. BENIN
11. CAMEROON
12. CENTRAL AFRICAN REPUBLIC
13. EQUATORIAL GUINEA
14. GABON
15. UGANDA
16. RWANDA
17. BURUNDI
18. ZIMBABWE
19. MALAWI
20. SWAZILAND
21. LESOTHO

Africa South of the Sahara

Introduction

A common attitude in discussing Africa in the West is to think of it as a homogeneous entity, absorbable in one glance, as it were. Apart from being one of the largest continents in the world and with vastly different climates and ways of living, it is also characterized by a multitude of languages (about 1000). As language affects music in terms of intonation, rhythm, et cetera, the possible differences and variations are enormous. Moreover, the fact that North Africa is under Arabic and largely Muslim influence further adds to the complexity of the huge continent's musical tapestry. Detailed accounts of each region, state and tribe would be an undertaking well beyond the scope of an introductory book on non-Western music. In the same way as it is possible to distil some characteristic musical features when discussing the nature of Western music in spite of its complex and diverse manifestations – such as the Northern and Southern styles, Central European style, national styles, individual styles, marked preoccupation with harmony et cetera – it is also possible to observe and distil certain tendencies in African music. In this chapter it is the musical practices in Africa south of the Sahara which will be primarily considered. North Africa will be referred to in the context of Islam.

To start with there are two fundamental points to come to terms with when discussing African traditional music. Firstly, there is no written but only an aurally transmitted tradition; secondly, music is largely functional. These will now be discussed in turn.

Aural tradition

African music is based on an aurally transmitted tradition which is vividly practised to this day, but, apart from Coptic Christian (Ethiopian) church music, it has no written history. Research and collecting of music go back to the late nineteenth century, and the first actual recording of African music belongs to the early twentieth century when the pioneer Peter F. White made his collection in Togo in 1905. Although there are few sources, there is clear evidence of a long-standing musical culture in Africa. These sources come from a wide variety spanning millennia: from Egyptian engravings, from Herodotus, from the illustrations of African instruments in Michael Pretorius's famous book *Theatrum Instrumentorum* (1620), from the bronze carvings of instruments and musicians from Nigeria dating from the late sixteenth as well as the seventeenth centuries and from various fascinating anthropological accounts of the use of the bow – both as a weapon and as a musical instrument – to list the most famous. The lack of written (notated) documentation of African musical tradition, however, makes it extremely difficult, if not impossible, to ascertain a historical perspective. Modern research largely relies on archaeology and on the recording and analysis of aural history as practised in this century. The picture is further complicated by historical factors, as in the case of North Africa, where the Arabic Muslim world dominates (for example, Algeria, Egypt, Libya, Morocco, Mauritania and Tunisia). Southern Africa on the other hand has been influenced by settlers from Europe (for example, Botswana, Zimbabwe, Lesotho, Namibia and Malawi). Moreover, well until the end of the colonial era (1960) African peoples lived in distinct units of population clusters of different sizes and political power. The homogeneity of these groups, as Professor J. H. Kwabena Nketia has remarked in his seminal book *The Music of Africa*, was undermined by 'population movement that followed territorial expansion, wars, famine, and other crises' and these gave rise to mixed population. 'Sometimes branches of one group migrated to another location, thus splintering the group: for example, the Sandawe, an offshoot of the so-called click-speaking peoples of southern Africa, now live in Tanzania.' He then continues, 'The establishment of territorial boundaries during the nineteenth century ignored the composition of the indigenous population, introducing similar complications. For example, in eastern Africa, the Luo are found in both Kenya and Tanzania, while members of the so-called cattle-culture complex are scattered throughout Uganda, Kenya, Sudan and Somalia.'[1] Such diversifications and interactions have, of course, left their mark on African music. Indeed, in our age of rapid transition, the justifiable fear which one might have about the future of African and other non-Western musical traditions is that they are in great danger of losing their identity and relevance in an urbanized environment and of being swept away by the CD-based pop culture.

Functional music

One must stress the fact that until quite recently African traditional music was predominantly functional, that is it was and often still is part of the community's daily life. It is not art music, in the Western meaning and practice of the word, to which one listens possibly in a concert performance engulfed in private reveries. In Africa, to this day, music is largely performed not just by professionals, but by the whole community at various significant events, such as weddings, funerals and rites of passage. Music is thus practised by active partici-pation, however humble that may be, by, say, rhythmically clapping hands or stamping, rather than by just listening to it. As such it is interwoven with extra-musical activities and events and is part of the complex texture of life which, in its own way, it signifies. Social interaction is thus enhanced by music. Its importance is made manifest within the context of its successful impact on a social occasion. For this reason the role of musicians in African communi-ties has social importance. Hence in some cases, but by no means generally, there is respect and even leniency towards professional musicians. As Alan Merriam wrote in connection with the Baongye of Congo-Kinshasa, 'The fact of the matter is that without musicians a village is incomplete; people want to sing and dance, and a number of important village activities simply cannot be carried out without musicians. The villagers are unanimous in stating that musicians are extremely important people; without them, life would be intoler-able.'[2] As the past is seen to live in the present and the present is the *raison d'être* of every given moment, preoccupation with the past for its own sake is rather alien to the African's way of thinking about art. In fact, some languages (for example, Bamana) do not even have a word for art as such. With music it is the spontaneity of the now, founded on the aurally transmitted tradition as modified by the living, which links the past with the present. Whereas in the West listeners sit and listen to, say, sixteenth-century choral music for its own sake with a historical awareness – often at the cost of neglecting the present, sometimes perhaps even negating it – Africans recall the aurally transmitted past and practically mould it into the present. The emphasis is on the now of music making, not on reproducing an authentic style of a bygone age. What was felt irrelevant, and therefore not cultivated until quite recently, is historicism. What have been maintained and cultivated to a high degree of accomplishment are spontaneity and elemental vitality, which give a quasi-improvised immediacy to the music played.

Dance and music are two closely related art forms, as rhythm is one of the main elements of both. For this reason in some African languages there are no separate words for music and dance: the two are seen to be indivisible. The close interaction between body and mind is visibly manifest in dance, and in an abstracted form it is there in music. In a way dancing is rhythm made physically visible. One could, moreover, postulate that a good dancer not only dances to rhythm but contributes to the rhythmic expression by adding rhythmic patterns not necessarily articulated by the music itself. In his essay 'An Aesthetic of the Cool: West African Dance', R. F. Thomson stated, 'Africans unite music and dance, but play apart; Europeans separate dance and music but play together . . . West Africans perform music and dance apart the better to ensure a dialogue between movement and sound.'[3] The physical is not curtailed in African music; on the contrary, it is cultivated within both the sacred and secular context of their social interaction. Whereas Europeans, largely due to the Christian preoccupation with sin and guilt, are somewhat inhibited when it comes to physical expression, not even the missionaries succeeded in suppressing the African's rhythmic sense of expression and freedom, if not defiance. What is left unbroken in the spirit and integrity of Africa is manifest in its music and dance.

Taking it with a pinch of salt, one could venture to say that it is in the twentieth century that Europeans started to regain their relations with their bodies, as it were. The reasons for this development are manifold. Three seem to stand out: the slow breakdown of the influence of the church, the sexual revolution and, finally, non-Western influences. Apart from a few exceptions, such as the nineteenth-century waltz craze, Western music tended to gravitate towards abstraction and the cerebral. It is in this context that a commentator on African art, H. L. Gates, so poignantly said in connection with Picasso's *Les Demoiselles d'Avignon* (1907) that 'Europe did not discover Africa, but rather that it has rediscovered itself through African art.'[4] In musical terms, Stravinsky's *The Rite of Spring*, with its 'pagan', 'non-Western' rhythmic power, first performed in Paris in 1913, could justifiably be substituted by the painting of Gates's quotation. No wonder that an unprecedented public scandal followed its first performance in 1913. It seems that at the tail-end of the twentieth century we have come a long way. The problem facing non-Western civilizations is how to salvage, preserve and, if possible, maintain their great musical cultures, which are in danger of being lost in the same way as the folk music traditions have been largely lost in the West. It remains to be seen whether Africa, and the Orient for that matter, will have the strength to transcend the all too tempting lure of Western popular culture while undergoing profound changes in its social structure and its view of the world, and be able to create something authentically contemporary without abandoning its roots. It would be yet another tragedy if Africa were to lose its musical integrity by adopting an international-hotel 'folk' style in terms of music for the entertainment of guests. The fact that in Mali the dancers use two masks – one for the tourists and one for 'real' local use – is very telling.

Rhythm

It is a general view that African music is rhythm centred and that rhythm is to African music what harmony is to European music. This has been contested in favour of a more complex picture which includes all four main elements of music: rhythm, melody, harmony and timbre. And yet it is perhaps worth underlining that rhythm is fundamental to all music and in the final resort, in terms of comprehensibility and structure, it is more important to music than pitch even. This assumption can be tested by making a practical experiment by looking at a familiar selection of pitches (notes) which together make up the melody of the British national anthem.

Fig. 1

Now let us have the same pitches, but without the characteristic rhythmic pattern in 3/4.

Fig. 2

Contrary to Fig. 2, in Fig. 3 it is now the rhythm which is correct but the pitches are wrong. The result is that the anthem is still recognizable in Fig. 3 by the coherence of its rhythmic structure, despite the fact that the pitches making up the melody are wrong, whereas the sound produced by Fig. 2, where the pitches are that of the anthem but the rhythm is not, is scarcely recognizable as 'God Save the Queen'.

Fig. 3

This simple exercise gives us a salutary experience in recognizing the cohesive structural importance of rhythm. Rhythm is the very nerve system of music. With it and through it, it is possible to understand and communicate. The popularity of percussive instruments and the drum ensembles of Africa offers us a heightened significance of rhythm as a vehicle of expression in its own right. With rhythm we articulate motion and time. In the case of the Ewe people in Ghana the word rhythm is not used but rhyme is. Rhythm is seen in a broader sense as related to life and described as such in appropriate contexts. As Kofi Agawu states in his study of Ewe rhythm, 'The absence of a single word for "rhythm" in Ewe suggests that rhythm refers to a binding together of different dimensional processes, a joining rather than a separating, an across-the-dimension instead of a within-the-dimension phenomenon.'[5] Accordingly he then proceeds by describing the rhythm of Ewe society in its daily manifestations, of which music is only one among many rhythmic events of Ewe life.

It is assumed that the reader has a basic understanding of rhythmic organization. Should this not be the case, it is hoped that the brief explanation in Fig. 4 will be of some help.

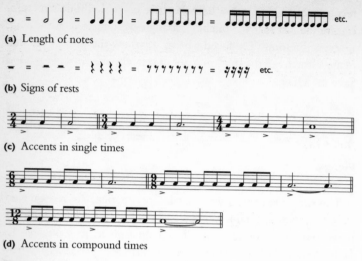

(a) Length of notes

(b) Signs of rests

(c) Accents in single times

(d) Accents in compound times

Fig. 4

The sign > indicates the stress (pulse) on the main beat. Of course there are several other variations both in terms of note values (one can have, for example, 2/16 in a bar) and in accentuating beats at places other than the strong beats. It is in this field that non-Western musical traditions have evolved their most strikingly acute awareness and sophistication. Let us now turn to the examination of those types of irregular rhythmic patterns which break away from the predictability of regular beats.

Rhythmic displacement

Rhythmic displacement occurs when, instead of accentuating the accepted strong beats, one accentuates the weak beats (see Fig. 5).

Fig. 5

Irregular times

As the name indicates irregular time is based on the nominator being not 2, 3, 4, but 5, 7.

Fig. 6 (a)

Here too it is possible to alter the accents as, for instance:

Fig. 6 (b)

Or, indeed, to introduce rhythmic displacement as well.

Variable metres

The basic idea behind variable (or additive) metres is to increase (or decrease) the nominator of time signatures. See, for example, Fig. 7.

Fig. 7

Syncopation

Although this form of off-beat pattern could belong to rhythmic displacement, for the sake of a particular feature it is discussed here separately. Syncopation proper occurs when two beats are split into three pulses of which the second is the longer note value, while the first and third note values surrounding it are half of the second, as in Fig. 8.

Fig. 8

Having established some fundamental rhythmic principles, all of which are used by African musicians, we will now examine a few characteristically African rhythmic practices.

African hemiola style

It was the American musicologist and ethnomusicologist Rose Brandel who, in her book *The Music of Central Africa: An Ethnomusicological Study*, introduced the term 'African hemiola style' in connection with African rhythmic practice. Although the hemiola was used in Europe during the Renaissance and the baroque period, as well as by some nineteenth-century composers (for example, Schumann and Brahms) and, of course, had a comeback in the twentieth century, it is a strikingly common feature of African music. Its essence is based on the relationship of the 'long' and 'short' 2:3, or its reverse 3:2. That is, for example, two dotted semiquavers followed by three semiquavers or vice versa. It is the combination of 2 and 3 (or 3 and 2) which makes this ingenious rhythmic pattern so fascinating, whether it is applied in its horizontal or vertical forms. For a horizontal example, see Fig. 9.

Fig. 9

In other words, it is a combination of the compound duple with the simple triple times. In order to illustrate further this rhythmic pattern in a less rigid form than the example in Fig. 9, here is one from the Nyasa of Tanzania (see Fig. 10).

Fig. 10

This style is not exclusively an African tradition; indeed, it bears a relationship to the rhythmic styles of the Middle East and India. In general, however, as opposed to Western music, African and Oriental music shows a marked preference for asymmetric rhythmic groupings.

Sub-beat orientation

Further highly complex rhythmic variations (patterns) can be made when the general thinking is not so much main-beat orientated, but rather sub-beat or pulse orientated. Let us suppose we are in quadruple time. This time-signature represents two main beats, that is one on the strong beat (down beat) and the second on the weaker third beat. The reason for this is because the 2 and 4 patterns in rhythm are related.

Fig. 11

Let us examine a rhythmic pattern played by five musicians. In Fig. 12, the first example illustrates the exact subdivisions, the second starts playing around, as it were.

Fig. 12

The rhythmic permutations in playing just in ⁴⁄₄, let alone in other time values, are quite considerable. For African musicians rhythm is the main organizing force which not only holds together the music they play, but can be the music itself, or, as is often the case, can be dance and music, as in this context the two can hardly be separated.

Their ability to hear music not only in terms of the common beats, but also in subdivisions (offbeat, as it were) displays musical sophistication and an instinctive musical logic of a high degree.

Polyrhythm

One could postulate that real polyphonic music is also polyrhythmic, as, in order to create contrasting independence between two or more simultaneously playing parts, contrasting rhythmic patterns are essential. It is rhythmic ingenuity rather than melodic ingenuity which makes music contrapuntally interesting. The example in Fig. 13 illustrates polyrhythmic thinking as well as the vertical application of the hemiola style.

Fig. 13

Polyrhythmic downbeats

By choosing two drummers it is possible to see what is understood by this term in practice (see Fig. 14).

Fig. 14

These types of rhythmic organization call for an instinctive sense of musical numeracy, as it were, an inborn as well as a practised ability to comprehend rhythmic structuring, or what has been aptly termed the African's 'metronome sense'.

Ostinato rhythm

Under this term we touch upon another characteristic tradition, the persistent repetition of a rhythmic pattern. Although this technique has been known and used in the West since at least the thirteenth century and revived in earnest by such twentieth-century composers at Bartók, Hindemith and Stravinsky, it is in African and Oriental music, especially in dances, that the ostinato rhythm is practised to this day. The reasons for this are manifold. The most important reason must be its trance-inducing characteristic, which can be employed in the context of both sacred and secular music. Fig. 15 draws attention to the fact that there are two ostinatos played (multi-ostinato).

It should be noted that rhythm possesses two characteristic attributes. On the one hand it represents order and structure; on the other hand it can induce trance and ecstasy. The use of the ostinato is one way of inducing the latter. It is in this context that the perceptive remark in Marghanita Laski's book *Ecstasy* is so pertinent: 'I believe that of all the more common triggers to ecstasy, music would be the most rewarding to study in any attempt to find a relation between the qualities of triggers and effects produced.'[6]

Tempo

Tempo (speed) in music is affected by many things, such as moods for example: whether the music is contemplative or aggressive, happy or sad et cetera. Accordingly the speed of music may be slower or faster. In general, however, African music tends to be on the fast side, as the most popular unit is quaver notes or eighths. Quaver notes are the basic pulses which make up the crotchet or dotted crotchet main beats (see Fig. 16).

etc.

Fig. 15 Wanyamwezi, Tanzania (Helemia, Tabora district. African Music Society GD 1311).

Fig. 16

This being so, it is fair to assume a tendency towards faster, more rapidly moving tempi. In terms of metronome marks, this means ♩ = 120 upward, and for ♩. = 80 upward. There are, of course, exceptions to this general rule, as is the case, for example, in south-east Africa, where some tempi can be unusually slow.

Melody

In its meanest definition a melody is a succession of upward- and downward-moving pitches (notes). But this definition, although correct to a certain degree, is not satisfactory when we think of music which affects our emotions. Melody is obviously more than an impersonal reference to a succession of pitches. That essential extra is easy to feel, but rather difficult to describe. Nevertheless, there are some significant characteristic aspects. For example, there are the ways in which the pitches of a melody may move, that is whether the pitches are moving in narrow steps or wider ones and whether the range of pitches is longer (many notes) or shorter. The expressiveness will depend on the skill of the combinations. Descending melodies are more natural, like gravity, than ascending melodies, as upward motion can be seen to be more stressful and dramatic. In general, however, one encounters a balance between the two directions. Personal, if not national, characteristics may be expressed by subtle and persistent variation of these tendencies. In the West, it is a debatable but strongly held view that the ability to create significant melodies is the very essence of musical artistry and a sign of individual creative genius. The West's preoccupation with harmony leads melody to be seen as part of the composer's overall harmonic thinking, and the horizontal and vertical aspects of music are thus strongly related. This harmonic view of music is debatable because music may also be more rhythm orientated and its melody therefore subordinated. In African music, rhythm can in itself be the music. Here one might be confronted not with a scale pattern of an octave, as is mostly the case in Western Europe, but with patterns of two, three, four or five notes. The melodic possibilities of, say, three notes will be limited to such a degree that, rather than speaking of a melody, it would be more accurate to speak of a motif or melodic motif. This melodic motif of African music is likely to be repeated several times and then rhythm plays an equal, if not leading, role. Indeed, a melodic motif may have a strong metric connotation, especially when in combination with other vocal or instrumental parts, and, as such, melodic and/or rhythmic motifs are fundamental to polyphonic structures. The illustrations in Fig. 17 have been chosen according to their range of notes to give an impression of some African melodic expressions.

The selection of melodies in Fig. 17 is of indigenous expressions.

(a) Three notes

(b) Four notes

(c) Five notes

(d) Six notes

(e) Diatonic octave

Fig. 17

None of these scale patterns, however, is more important than the others. There are, of course, regional tendencies, as, for instance, in the south of the Sahara, where the relatively small range of melodic structure is more frequent, but by and large any of the structures presented in Fig. 17 can be and are used.

Singing and instrumental playing are regarded as related activities. Singers are often instrumentalists as well. Nevertheless vocal music (both in solo and ensemble forms) can be regarded as an expression in its own right. The spontaneity of expression is made apparent by the often speechlike (recitative) style mixed with the song, as if the word were helping to find the music and vice versa. Pygmy performers often start with wild shouts. Out of these inarticulate articulations slowly the music is born, as if a journey were to be taken from chaos to order and from the personal to a communal harmony. There are theories that music and speech have a common origin, but they are as debatable as all the other theories on the origin of music, such as Darwin's idea of the imitation of 'lone cries during the mating season' or Rousseau's suggestion of 'speech as a form of song'. These are fascinating and even illuminating, but unproven and probably unprovable, theories. An interesting observation which strikes one concerning art in general, and music in particular, is that music seems to have the power to direct the highly subjective and personal towards the objective and universal. As Professor M. Schneider so aptly put it, 'It is easier to sing a love song than to speak a declaration of love . . . An idea set to music is more formal, more general, or more ambiguous than the same idea expressed in words alone because it is subject to a regular rhythm. In language something of the same kind occurs in the proverbs which, for the same reason, are so popular with . . . peoples.'[7] 'A melody is a series of tones that makes sense', as Victor Zuckerkandl defined it in his book *Music and the External World, Sound and Symbol*.[8] Or, as St Augustine understood music to be, 'ordered form'. Our gestalt of the world reveals itself not only in our pattern deciphering, but perhaps even more significantly, in our pattern making. Thus those who negate music as an irrelevant art form in their lives are not only negating an aesthetic experience (in the Western meaning of the word), but they are also neglecting to learn how to comprehend a major medium for pattern making and its significance for both the individual and the community. Music is one of the few master-keys at our disposal which can enable us to enter the world of other civilizations and cultures, let alone enter into understanding our own. Anton Ehrenzweig, a believer in the strong relationship between music and speech, wrote in *The Psychoanalysis of Artistic Vision and Hearing* that

It is not unreasonable to speculate that speech and music have descended from a common origin in a primitive language which was neither speaking nor singing, but something of both. Later this primeval language would have split into different branches; music would have retained the articulation mainly by pitch (scale) and duration (rhythm), while language chose the articulation mainly by tone colour (vowels and consonants). Language moreover happened to become the vehicle of rational thought and so underwent further influences. Music has become a symbolic language of the unconscious mind.[9]

In the light of African music, where speech, melody, rhythm and dance interact so strongly, the above observation seems to be most apt, especially if we consider the fact that music in Africa, including song, was seldom composed for its own sake, but rather created in a functional context, as an essential part of social interaction, which may be sacred (ritualistic) or secular. It is in its ritualistic manifestation that the 'unconscious mind', if not the supernatural, comes into operation in a marked way. Thus a melody should be valued as a document of a culture which it represents. For this reason John A. Sloboda said in his fascinating book *The Musical Mind*,

Music, perhaps, provides a unique mnemonic framework within which humans can express, by the temporal organization of sound and gestures, the structure of their knowledge and of social relations. Songs and rhythmically organized poems and sayings form the major repository of knowledge in non-literate cultures. This seems to be because such organized sequences are much easier to remember than the type of prose which literate societies use in books.[10]

In turning to examine in some detail the harmonic procedures in African music, we return to the vertical aspect of music already encountered in the discussion of rhythmic polyphony.

Harmony

When two or more pitches (notes) are sounded together we talk of harmony. In the West the most complex systems of harmonic thinking have evolved (for example, modal, tonal, diatonic, chromatic, atonal and serial atonal) and have been conscientiously cultivated. In Africa this is not so. Rather than force the issue in terms of Western practices, what is offered here is a discussion of a number of common cases when harmony of one kind or other is clearly manifested in traditional African music.

Consecutive octave

Singing or playing an octave apart in parallel does not constitute real harmony though there is an harmonic implication in the overtones. It gives, nevertheless, colouristic differentiation and reinforcement to the parts (voices). This is something which naturally occurs when, for instance, a man and woman are singing together.

Fig. 18

Consecutive fourth and fifth

The splitting of the octave either upwards (c–g = fifth, g–c = fourth) or downwards produces a hollow sound quality which is most effectively used in Africa. For example, the Anlo Ewes are particularly partial to consecutive fourths.

(a)

(b)

Fig. 19

Consecutive third

In terms of sound quality this is perhaps the most immediately pleasing to Westerners as it has formed the Western harmonic predilection since the Renaissance. Here too the splitting of the fifth into two (c–e–g) gives what is known in the West as a major third and gives the character of a major triad. The consecutive use of the lower part (c–e) gives a series of major thirds, or when it is the upper half (e–g) minor thirds.

Fig. 20

Consecutive triads

When all three notes (c–e–g) are used consecutively, one gets a sonorous passage of consecutive thirds and fifths (triads).

Fig. 21

These are the most popular harmonic combinations. There are, of course, other, less frequent, consecutively used harmonic intervals, such as the spicy second and seventh (c–d, c–b), or the mellow sixth (c–a). Much rarer is the combination of the ninth.

Hocket

An interesting technique which is popular in Africa, and practised particularly by both the San and the Mambuti Pygmies, is what is known as 'hocket'. The Latin word *hoquetus* (or old French *hoquet*) means hiccup. It was popular in the thirteenth and fourteenth centuries in Europe, but was then largely dropped until its revival in the twentieth century. The technique is characterized by breaking up the melodic flow into interrupted (hiccupped) fragments between two or more voices in Fig. 22.

As can be seen (heard) this technique may affect the rhythm, lineality and verticality (harmony) as well as the colour (timbre) of a melody. The monothematic polyphonic implication is made obvious by Fig. 22(a), (b), (c) and (d). A fascinating illustration of the style, played by an African ensemble, is also given here. Note the clashing seconds as well.

Fig. 22

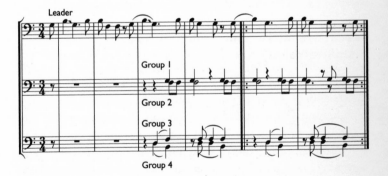

Fig. 23

It is hoped that the harmonic custom discussed above – of singing in consecutive intervals – has given the reader some idea of the vertical aspect of traditional African music, where one finds a varied use of diatonic, pentatonic and modal forms of melody with this harmonic procedure. This harmonic style did not evolve, however, into a comprehensive system of harmonic practice.

Instruments

Although such useful musical terms as idiophone, membraphone, chordophone and aerophone were established by C. Sachs and E. M. Hornbostel in the first half of this century and since then have been used often by musicologists, they show little sign of gaining popular currency. Therefore the more familiar references such as percussive, string and wind instruments will be used throughout this book for the main headings and the less familiar terms will be given in brackets and as subheadings. Perhaps in this way they may become more readily absorbed. Africa has a vast number of musical instruments; to list them all here would turn this book into an encyclopaedia of musical instruments. In each of the following main sections only the most important and characteristic instruments are discussed. In the bibliography the reader will find suggestions for further exploration.

Percussive instruments (idiophones and membraphones)

There are two main groups of percussive instruments. Firstly there are the idiophones, where the sound created by the rhythm making comes from beating, scraping and shaking naturally sonorous materials. The other group of percussive instruments is the membraphones. They are what is generally known as drums. These are characterized by stretching a skin (membrane) over a bowl, gourd or anything which may act as a resonator when the skin is stretched on it.

Idiophones
(a) The most obvious ways of producing rhythmical sound effects are clapping, beating the body, stamping or using stamping sticks. Indeed, the stamping stick is the forerunner of the conductor's baton.
(b) Another type of sound can be produced by rubbing together the rough parts of sticks, bones or other material such as, in modern times, the notched surface of a washboard.

(a)(i)

(a)(ii)

(a)(iii)

(a)(iv)

(b)(i)

(b)(ii)

Fig. 24

(c) Shaking sea-shells or bones of various sizes attached to the body, often to the legs, like the ankle jingle of South Africa, which is made of nuts, can considerably enhance the rhythmic movements of a dancer. Rattles made in various ways, such as by filling the insides of a dried gourd or clay container with stones, sand or other small material and by adding a handle to it, can produce very interesting effects.

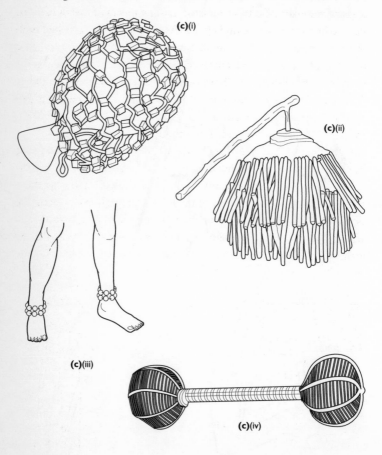

Fig. 24 – *continued*

(d) The African *mbira* (sansa) is a plucked idiophone (or lamelo-phone when the keys are made of metal) made of a board to which a selection of graduated strips of wood or metal are fixed. This is not unlike a keyboard. For this reason it is also known as a 'hand piano' or 'African hand piano'. The 'keys' can number between five and forty-five. Manuals from five to twenty-two are, however, the most commonly used. The 'keys' may be fixed to a box resonator or placed inside a gourd resonator. To this resonator, rattling pieces of metals can also be attached for greater sound effects. As the tongues are plucked with the thumbs, the sansa is sometimes also called a 'thumb piano'. The tuning of sansas is by no means fixed as there are some which are tuned to five (pentatonic), six (hexatonic) or seven (heptatonic) notes. Though sansas are also known outside Africa, it is a characteristically African instrument. Its peculiar sound is made even stranger when each tongue is wrapped with wire. This produces a buzzing effect.

(e) Slit drums Slit drums are made of wood or bamboo which are hollowed out through a slit along one side, hence the reason for the name. They can be made in any size and are mainly used for signalling and, to a much lesser extent than in the Far East, for ceremonial occasions. The simplest may be made of a hollowed-out tree trunk which is hit rhythmically with a stick. Many are also skilfully carved for good measure.

(d)

(e)

Fig. 24 – *continued*

(f) Bells There are three basic types of bells:

(i) pellet bell, in which a freely moving pellet is put inside the cavity of a closed bell;

(ii) clapper bell: in this case the clapper is attached inside the bell. By swinging it, the sound is produced by the clapper hitting the inside of the bell. Another version is when the clapper is fixed outside the bell and strikes it on the outside;

(iii) struck bell, where the sound is produced by the player using a separate striker. In Africa all three are used, but mostly the clapper and the struck bells.

(g) Gong Apart from in Ethiopia (in the Coptic Church), the gong is not an instrument of significance in Africa.

(h) Xylophone The xylophone on the other hand is a common African instrument. Its origin, however, is likely to have been outside Africa, perhaps brought via Madagascar from Indonesia hundreds of years ago (note that the language of Madagascar is Malayo-Polynesian). A xylophone is made by cutting up bars of wood of different length, thickness and density. These three attributes will define whether the pitches are low or high (the longer, thicker and denser the bar the lower will be its pitch, and vice versa). Xylophones of all sizes are widespread all over Africa. Of the two main types of xylophone, the *non-fixed-key* and the *fixed-key* types, the non-fixed key is the more rudimentary as it rests on a tree trunk without resonators. This type is used in the Congos, Central Africa, Uganda, et cetera. The second type, with fixed keys, is characterized by fixing each slat to a frame and reinforcing their sound by fixing a resonator under each of them. This type may be suspended and held from the shoulder, but the most popular version is the one with a frame placed on the ground. The resonators can be made of gourds, but also of tin cans. The African's ingenuity in making instruments from all sorts of *objets trouvés* seems to be inexhaustible. The number of slabs (keys) may range from a small number to twenty. Usually the player uses two mallets. Although a fine solo instrument, it is often played by two or more players. Moreover, xylophone bands

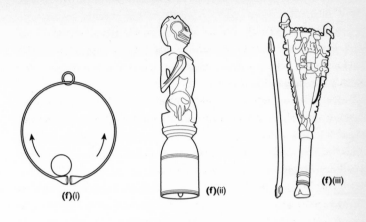

(f)(i)

(f)(ii)

(f)(iii)

(g)

Fig. 24 – *continued*

can perform with three to thirty xylophones of various sizes. This ensemble style is practised in both central and southern Africa, but above all in the eastern part of South Africa, notably among the Chopi. The name for these ensembles is *timbala* (timbala band). The local root name for the xylophone varies. For example, in the northern Congo it is called *padingbwa*; in the southern Congo its name is *marimba* or *malimba*.

As it is still used in some parts of Africa we might as well include here the lithophone. This is in a way an even simpler instrument than the non-fixed-key xylophone, as it is a set of carefully chosen sonorous plates of stones of various sizes and thicknesses which are then hit with either other stones or a stick.

Membraphones

Drums, as was already stated on p. 26, are classified as membraphones. Their main physical characteristic is of a skin or membrane stretched over the opening of a resonating body or holding frame. There are several ways of classifying drums. The most satisfactory method is to label them according to their body shapes. Thus drums are:

(a) cylindrical;
(b) conical;
(c) barrel;
(d) waisted;
(e) goblet;
(f) long.

Drums can have one or two membranes, that is on one end of the drum or on both ends. Accordingly they are called *single-headed* or *double-headed* drums (see Fig. 25(c)(i) and (ii)). The sound is created by the vibration of the stretched membrane. The tuning is controlled by altering the tension of the stretched membrane (the playing head). In Africa the lacing of the stretched skin or membrane may be shaped in I, Y, W, or X patterns (see these patterns in Fig. 25(a)–(d).

The sound of a drum may be achieved by beating the membrane

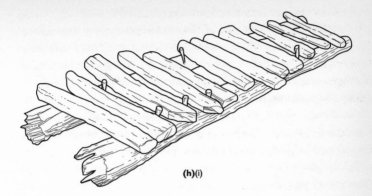

(h)(i)

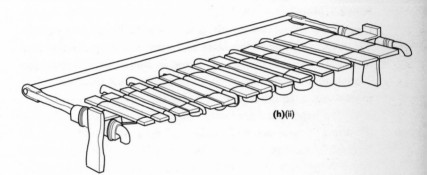

(h)(ii)

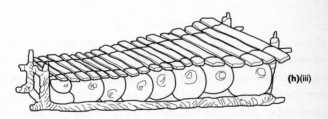

(h)(iii)

Fig. 24 – *continued*

with the hand(s), stick(s) or by friction. Note that the ends of drumsticks can also be padded (see Fig. 25(i)(iii)).

Drumming is perhaps one of the most characteristic expressions of Africa, so much so that, even when there is no drum available (a rare occasion), women create makeshift drums by stretching their skin aprons over pots. This is still a custom in eastern and southern Africa (for example, in Uganda and South Africa). Thus the material for making a drum may be a clay pot, gourd, calabash or, most importantly, wood. The wood is either carved out or wood strips are cut and held together, barrel-like, with iron bands.

All the drum types referred to so far are widely used across Africa in one way or other. There are, of course, local preferences – for example, the *waisted drum* can be found in eastern as well as western Africa. Those of eastern Africa, however, are likely to be single-headed: the *Uganda drum* with its densely woven stretching strings, which gives a knitted appearance to the instrument, is characteristic of eastern Africa; it can be also found in Burundi and Kenya; the Tanzanian wooden *hand drum* is played with one hand or with a leather thong. In other parts of Africa hand drums may be beaten with two hands. And for better effect, jingles may be attached to the drum; to do so is most popular in Guinea, Mali and Senegal. In Nigeria, for example, the player may carry his drum by using a strap which is put over his left shoulder and he strikes the drum with a curved drumstick; alternatively, as in South Africa, the player carries his instrument with a strap placed over his neck. This leaves both his hands free to play on both sides of his double-headed drum; Congolese drummers often play a pair of conical drums which are fixed to a holding frame. As can be seen the diversity and variations of making, holding and playing drums are very numerous. Ensembles may range from two players to fifty or more, as is the case in Uganda when the festive *bwole* dance is performed.

Finally, we turn to a peculiar drum type known in many parts of the world, the *friction drum* (h). This is an instrument which more or less looks like a drum, but instead of hitting it with hands or sticks, a sounding stick is pushed through the centre of the stretched

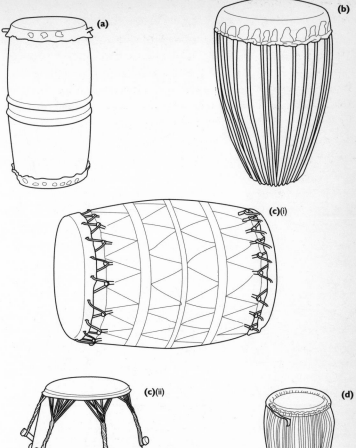

Fig. 25

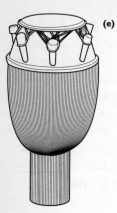

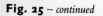

Fig. 25 – *continued*

skin or membrane and, by moving it up and down or rotating it around, friction, and therefore sound, is created. A similar effect can also be produced by rubbing the membrane of a drum with a wet hand or by using a rubbing stick or a bundle of wet corn stalks. These ways of playing friction drums can be found in Ghana, Zambia and South Africa. The friction drum is used, for example in Côte d'Ivoire, in order to imitate the panther, an animal which is associated with both intelligence and strength. Both men and women can be drummers, but here too there are variations in customs. For instance, the big kettledrum called *ngoma* in Venda is mostly played by a woman with one stick. It should also be noted that in some parts of Africa, as in the south of Ghana (Anlo Ewe), drumming, clapping, dancing and singing are seen to be integrated. A change in any of these activities will affect the unity of the whole. Accordingly a change in one will mean a change in all the above activities.

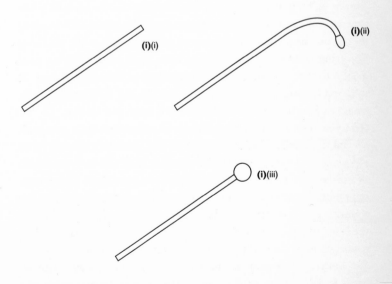

Fig. 25 – *continued*

String instruments (chordophones)

The string family consists of a vast array of instruments, many of which are not used in traditional African music. The most important string instruments in Africa fall into six categories: musical bow, lyre, harp, lute, fiddle and zither. To discuss these we should first start with perhaps one of the most ancient string instruments of all, the musical bow.

(a) Bow A bow can serve two purposes at the same time: it can be a weapon to shoot an arrow or an instrument on which to play. Indeed, it is believed that the musical bow, which is made by connecting a string to the two endings of a flexible stick, is likely to have originated from the hunter's bow. The stretched string when plucked or scraped will produce sound. This sound can be reinforced by attaching a resonator to the flexible stick. This is usually half a gourd, but it can be an empty tin can on which the bow is simply rested. An instant resonator can be achieved by holding the end or near the end of the bow in the mouth while plucking the string. The compound musical bow, as its name suggests, goes a step further by increasing the number of stretched strings of different lengths and, therefore, the pitches. All these types can be found in South Africa as well as in the Congo and Kenya.

(b) Lyre The lyre has a most distinguished history which goes back several thousands of years in time. In fact, there is evidence of its existence in Sumerian art of about 2800 B C. Basically the lyre consists of a three-part frame which is then fixed to a soundbox. The strings, which can be three or more, are stretched from the crossbar to the soundbox over a 'bridge'. There are two types of soundboxes for the lyre: the square (box-shaped) and the round (bowl-shaped). The round shape is the most popular in Africa, but in Ethiopia, to this day, both types are made and played. In size, lyres vary from relatively small to large. One of the largest, the *obukano* from Kenya, also known as the 'double-bass of East Africa', is still manageable enough to be held under the left arm.

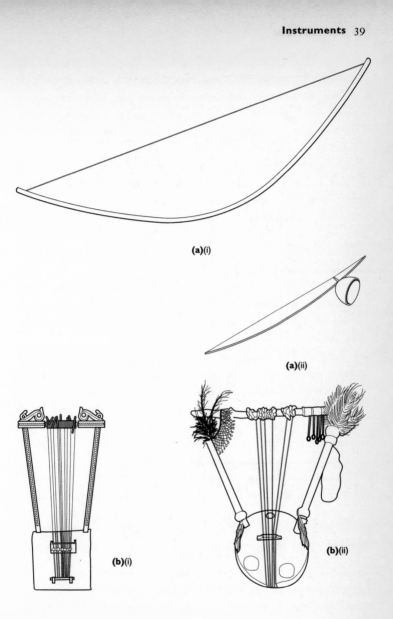

(a)(i)

(a)(ii)

(b)(i)

(b)(ii)

Fig. 26

(c) Harp The harp too has a distinguished history, as it was known in ancient Egypt, Sumeria and Persia, which is assumed to have been the place of origin of this noble instrument. What interests us here are the 'simple' or 'folk' harps still in use in Africa and eastern Asia. The principle of the harp's construction, not unlike the lyre, is that the strings are attached to the soundbox, but instead of coming from a crossbar, they are stretched at an oblique angle from a neck or mast at one end of the soundbox. The harp's head, that is the place where the soundbox and the angled mast are fixed, is often beautifully carved in Gabon, West Africa. Both the lyres and harps are mostly used to accompany singing. The lyre, however, is also associated with magical healing powers and for this reason it is utilized for medical purposes.

(d) Lute The type of lute to be found in Africa is called the 'harp lute' for the obvious reason of its being somewhat of a mongrel: a combination of the lyre and lute. It is more likely to be found in West Africa.

(e) 'Fiddle' The 'fiddle' or 'folk fiddle' is still commonly played in many parts of Africa (for example, Mali, North Africa, Ethiopia and south-west Africa). The 'fiddle' can have one (monochord) to four strings and is a bowed instrument. The bows may be curved or straight. The playing position of the instrument varies from the player holding it vertically, against his chest, to holding it, not unlike a violin, between the left shoulder and chin.

(f) Zither A zither is a string instrument characterized by covering the width and length of the resonating body with a layer of strings. It is usually plucked though it can also be played by hitting the strings with a pair of sticks. Zithers of all kinds and shapes can be found in many places of Africa as they are valued as fine accompanying instruments.

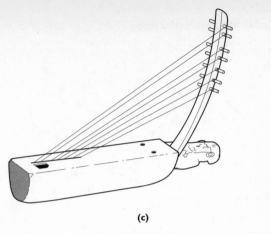

(c)

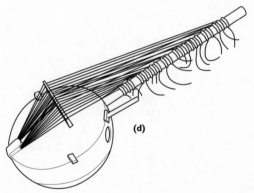

(d)

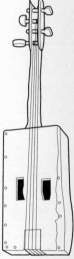

(e)

(f)

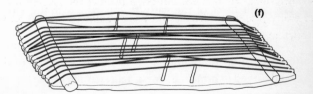

Fig. 26 – *continued*

Wind instruments (aerophones)

In comparison to the considerable number and variety of percussive and string instruments to be found in Africa, the range of wind instruments is relatively small. The most likely which a visitor would encounter in Africa are flutes, trumpets, horns and buzzers.

(a) Flute Simple flutes are made from various materials, all of which naturally offer a bore (for example, bamboo, cane or the upper part of a gourd) or from a material like wood which enables the maker to carve a bore. A flute may be held vertically and, therefore, played from the top end (end-blown flute), that is the place where the mouthpiece is cut. Or, if the mouthpiece is at the side end of the flute, it is held horizontally in transverse position. The finger holes affecting the pitches can be as few as two holes but, by and large, three-to-six-finger-holed flutes are the most common. Flutes can be played solo, duo or in large ensembles in combination with voice, drums, lyre or other available combinations. When played in duets flutes are often considered to symbolize the male and female in a relationship. Accordingly the female flute is often smaller in size. Fulani shepherds in West Africa are reputed for their skilful playing of single flutes.

(b) Trumpet What interests us here is not the trumpet as we know it from modern bands and orchestras, but what could be called the 'simple' or even 'early trumpet'. Like so many African instruments the simple trumpet is made from natural material (bamboo, horn, wood et cetera). These materials can also be combined: for example, wood with gourd, or wood with horn. The sound of these, as is the case with most of the early trumpets, is startling rather than pleasant. And they are, after all, meant to startle, as they are primarily used for ritualistic and magical purposes. In the Congo, among the Babeme, a trumpet ensemble consists of four trumpets of different sizes and carved in human likeness, representing the father, mother, son and daughter. There may be some significance in the fact that the trumpet representing the daughter is held horizontally while the rest are held vertically.

(c) Horn The horn is often linked with the trumpet on account of its similar sound-producing technique. (In each case the sound is generated by the vibration of the player's lips.) There is, however, a major distinction to be made. A simple trumpet is more or less straight and cylindrical, while the horn is curved and conical. In Africa, horns are made from animal horns with finger holes and often fine decorations are also carved on them. Like the simple flutes they can be either end-blown or side-blown, but the end-blown is the most common. The long Kakaki horn (or trumpet) is made of three detachable parts for easy transportation and is characterized by its long tube (of up to two metres). Sometimes these horns are fitted with double horns at their ends. They have been known since the sixteenth century in the Sudan. They are still in use, especially by the Yoruba in south-west Nigeria, but also in north Cameroon and northern Nigeria. As can be easily guessed, they are mainly used for signalling.

(d) Buzzer It is likely that we have all had the experience in our childhood of making a sound by attaching something (a piece of card or a nail) to the end of a string and whirling it round over our heads at different speeds. The result is an eerie buzzing or even roaring sound. By making sounds in this fashion, we continue a tradition which goes back to the Stone Age. The sounds thus produced may enable the player to imitate the sound of wind or thunder and are used sometimes to evoke spirits.

Another way of producing buzzing or humming effects is by making those toylike gadgets where a buzz-disc and a piece of string are employed. The idea of the buzz-disc is to generate vibration in the air by spinning a disc between a wound-up doubled string. By skilfully stretching the twisted string the disc will continue for a while to untwist rapidly and then twist again thus producing a buzzing sound. These simple, but most effective, sound makers are to be found in South Africa.

Finally, it is not far-fetched to say that African instruments, even when they are not played but are just resting in a silent state, have a meaningful presence. Their shapes, types and potential functions

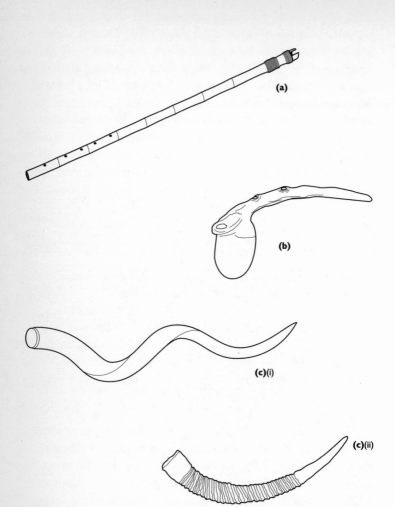

Fig. 27

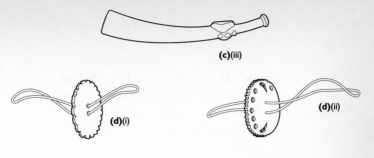

Fig. 27 – *continued*

represent associations not only in terms of female/male (for example, drum/drumstick), but also in terms of signifying the spiritual world. Instruments are thus masks among other masks to be used for evoking spirits and for evoking the Other from both within and outside the individual as well as the community. For example, the *mbira* of the Lemba, in the Transvaal, South Africa, with its hemispherical gourd resonaters, twenty-two keys and the string tied round the gourd, represents more than a much favoured instrument. The gourd is the womb of a woman; the frame, women who are giving a hand to the birth; the sound-hole is seen as the deflowered girl; the keys are the men seated in a python's belly, which is believed to help women to become fertile; the plucking of the keys is an act of creation which leads to the sound which symbolizes the birth of a child.

General Considerations

The final section of this chapter on African music will be devoted to topics where music plays an integral part. These are: religion; language, poetry and music; drama, dance and music; improvisation; music and musicians in the community.

Religion

African religion is a combination of various adopted religions, such as Islam (to be discussed in Chapter 2) and Christianity (Catholic and Protestant), superimposed over the regional and tribal 'traditional' religions. In this book preference is given to the use of the term 'traditional' rather than to the often-used terms 'pre-literate' or 'primal' or even 'primitive' in attempting to define religions which have not developed the complex superstructuring of Christianity, Islam and the religions of the Far East. Traditional religions function on a small scale and without religious writing. Beliefs are passed on by oral means from generation to generation, like music. Over eight hundred ethnic groups in Africa confront one with a bewildering variety of customs and beliefs. When a minority religion, a 'traditional faith', is superimposed on by a large-scale Messianic and imperialistic religion, what often happens is not so much the abandonment of the old indigenous religion, but rather that the two coexist, albeit in a modified way. This is what is called 'syncretism' or 'mixed religion'. The Nandi people in Kenya, for example, are largely Christians, yet they still practise the traditional initiation rites side by side with the worship of Christ. Thus the Christian priests, whether they like it or not, are working in conjunction with the elders of initiation, diviners, medicine men, rain makers and the like. In musical terms a fine example of 'syncretism' is the famous performance of *Missa Luba* by Les Troubadours du Roi Baudouin under the direction of Father Haazen, where the Christian Mass sung in Latin is mixed with the traditional musical idioms of the

Congo. In the context of tribal existence, life is linked in the continuous realization of rituals; life itself becomes largely a ritual, both in the sacred and secular meanings of these terms. From birth, puberty, initiation into adulthood, marriage, war, illness and other afflictions, to death, all are marked by ritualistic activities. In these communities the whole concept of existence is, in a sense, religious and therefore ritualized. In one form or other traditional music in Africa is part of this ritualistic celebration and lament of life. As Francis Bebey put it in his perceptive and passionately written book *African Music: A People's Art*:

Once we have grasped the importance that life holds for the African, his music becomes much easier to explain and understand. Birth and rebirth are the key words in the simplest of cycles. Music is born with each child and accompanies him throughout life. Music helps the child triumph in his first encounter with death – the symbolic death that precedes initiation; it is reborn with the child who is now a man and it directs his steps along the path of law and order that has been laid down by the community.

On that path, music and truth become one; order and rhythm become one. Musicality is no longer a mere word, but becomes a series of acts. Hence, the real disappointment of the foreigner arises when he vainly tries to grasp a melody, chord, or movement without seeing the music in its entirety. No matter, for African music goes blithely on its way with all of its vices and virtues and a total lack of concern for its own future. It is precisely this latter aspect of the African's philosophy that should merit our attention at the present time, a time when practical considerations are more urgent than musicological theories.[11]

Language, poetry and music

Linguists speak about 'tone language' when the meaning of a word is made intelligible by the relative pitch at which a syllable is uttered. Although in music the interpretation of words is relatively flexible, it is nevertheless quite remarkable how often higher or lower pitch levels and accentuations in speech will correspond to similar treatment in music, especially when setting a text to music. We have already touched upon the fact that the use of sounds for signalling purposes is a highly developed skill in Africa. Thus the sound effects sent by a signaller are instantaneously comprehended and translated to a verbal, practical meaning. As was pointed out by G. Herzog in his essay 'Canon in Western African Xylophone Melodies', the rhythmic and short melodic phrases of a Jabo xylophone player in Liberia can convey, by purely musical means, not only general information, but even subversive and satirical utterances about events or individuals.[12]

By and large, African languages are prone to use what is called 'comparative constructions', which may seem quite bewildering to an outsider. For instance, the saying among the Djonga, in South Africa, 'that which makes the dogs bark' in connection with the fresh grass in spring (*zilambyana*) is hardly comprehensible at its face value. It signifies a lean period when food is scarce and the spring grass is a reminder that this is the period when dogs bark out of hunger. With this way of thinking, we enter the domain of poetry. Whether in terms of language or of music, the African ear is attuned to these subtle ways of both verbal and musical conceits. Moreover, as Kwabena Nketia stated:

African traditions deliberately treat songs as though they were speech utterances. There are societies in which solo poetic recitations, both spoken and sung, have become social institutions. Instances of choral recitations have been noted, as well as the use of heightened speech in musical context . . . furthermore, the possibility of enhancing musical expression through the choice and usage of the prosopic features of speech is not ignored. The use of rapid delivery of texts, explosive sounds or special interjections, vocal grunts, and even the whisper is not uncommon.[13]

As African music has evolved through the characteristic intonations and rhythmic onomatopoeias of African languages, music and speech are closely related. Indeed exhorted poetic speech interacts with music.

Drama, dance and music

On p. 6 we have already emphasized the important and strong relationship between music and dance. It was stressed that the two art forms are closely related as they are both based on rhythm. When the performers jointly start communicating shorter or longer extra-musical ideas, and when the action goes into miming and enacting episodes taken from various communal or individual events, we are confronted with a combination of drama, dance and music or, more briefly, 'dance drama'. Dance dramas can be performed on both sacred and secular occasions. Accordingly, there are dance dramas for festivities and for funerals. An illuminating description is given of a dance drama in connection with a hunter's funeral in J. Goody's book *Death, Property and the Ancestors*, where he writes:

When a hunter is dead and the funeral is well under way, some six men under the leadership of the elders of a clan sector go to the house where the last death of a member of that group took place. There in the byre are kept the horns (*kpiin iile*) of the larger and dangerous animals killed by the dead ancestors. These horns are gathered up and borne in slow procession to the accompaniment of a hunting whistle blown by the leader, the most senior member of the sector present at the time. When the procession arrives at the funeral, the points of the horns are thrust into the earth in front of the stand. Other hunters present at once jump up and begin to dance, simulating the stalk of a wild animal, the drawing of the bow, the release of the arrow, and occasionally breaking out in victory hallos. Anyone who wishes to show that he has killed more dangerous animals than the deceased can seize the horns and dance with them holding them above his head.[14]

Among rituals, the one dedicated to death, the 'dirge' or lament, is one of the most widespread and forceful traditions of mankind. In certain parts of the world this is more emphatically ingrained into both the collective and individual conscience. The tradition of the dirge is markedly maintained and practised in Africa. It seems that individual as well as communal suffering leaves deeper and more lasting impressions than happiness does. This truism is strongly reflected in the arts. To give a European example, it is significant that the dirge plays such an important role in the folk music tradition of Central European countries (for example, Hungary and Romania). This tradition is strongly reflected in the art music of these countries as well. Note, for instance, Béla Bartók's lifelong preoccupation with the dirge in his own compositions. Lament is a universal expression of humanity. But so is defiance, the metamorphosing power of hope. As the Senegalese poet Birago Diop put it:

> Those who are dead are never gone:
> They are in the brightening shadow
> And in the shirkening gloom.
> The Dead are not beneath the Earth:
> They are in the quivering Tree,
> They are in the groaning Wood,
> They are in the flowing Water,
> And in the still Water,
> They are in the Hut, they are in the Crowd:
> The Dead are not dead.[15]

Improvisation

Improvisation is the art of 'bringing out', 'realizing' the musical potential in terms of rhythm, melody and harmony of a motif, phrase, complete musical sentence, or even larger formal units, such as binary form. There are two types of improvisation as far as its originating material is concerned: either it is based on an already existing model or not. The one with a pre-existing, and often familiar theme, is the most likely material on which improvisation is based. As African music tends to be founded on the repetition of short phrases – that is, the melodies and rhythms are characterized by being repeated short motifs rather than complex large units – the immediate comprehensibility and memorability of short repeated phrases enable the improviser(s) to elaborate on, if not deviate from, the original theme. In a sense, improvisation is closely related to variation technique. This is so whether one talks of African or any other musical cultures. As traditional African music is not written down but preserved and passed on by memory, the tendency to improvise on a rote learned pattern is the rule rather than the exception. But in some parts of Africa where strict rules may govern a musical performance, the possibility of improvisation would not only be minimal, but seen as improper. *Akandinda* (free-key xylophone) players of Uganda do not improvise, but the *jongo* (music and dance played on happy occasions) players and dancers of Ghana, on the other hand, pride themselves on their improvisational skills. This may include the final section of a funeral which may be seen to be a happy occasion as the departed is now in peace and metamorphosed. The same can be said about the virtuosi *mbira* players of the Shona people of Zimbabwe.

Music and musicians in the community

One of the many striking aspects of African traditional arts, including music, is the lack of preoccupation with the individual as genius. The genius is there all right, but without the cult of the individual. A work of art created by an individual (all works of art are first conceived by a single person, whether folk art or not) finally manifests itself as part of a shared functional statement of the community. The singular is submerged into the communal. In other words, the whole concept of the idolized individual in art, as cultivated in Europe since the Renaissance, was until quite recently alien to the African way of relating to art. The changes which have been taking place, especially since the 1950s, are entirely due to 'modern' developments and Western values and influences on Africa.

Traditional music in Africa is mainly focused on ritualistic and social events which are shared in communities of similar ethnic and linguistic groups, in the same way as, say, the British stick together in Spanish holiday resorts. It is rare to go beyond one's borders for the sake of an alien event. Solo musical activities such as singing, playing an instrument for its own sake, like listening to music for its own sake, are not uncommon, but it is the performing with others in small or larger groups during social occasions which is the most characteristic musical activity across Africa. Moreover, although it is true that most musical activities are linked with events such as birth, initiation, marriage and so forth, some tribes may not necessarily always call for music for every social occasion. Customs are as many as the ways of making, tuning and playing instruments. In some cases the 'royal drums' are hidden, not to be seen by the uninitiated, in other cases they have restricted performing timetables: drumming in the night; drumming during the mourning period (this is not unlike the Christian bell ringing in remembrance of the departed); drumming and singing while executing certain work (work songs). These are seldom, if ever, performed out of their practical context.

Obviously both men and women can be musicians and participate in music making. There are, however, specific instances when women have their own roles. For instance, laments are invariably 'performed' by women. During initiation ceremonies (puberty rites) for girls, it is mature women who would, of course, be involved with the girls' initiation. Significantly, the drums, which are usually played by men, on these occasions are played by women. As was pointed out by K. Oberg in *African Political Systems*, women who were chosen to be a king's wife were 'taught . . . to dance, sing and play the harp'.[16] It has already been stressed that in Africa music is largely a communal and functional activity. Musical professionalism, nevertheless, rests in the hands of specialist musicians (in Mali, Senegal and Gambia called *griots*) whose role is to perform at religious or social occasions. It is generally agreed that in order to be a good musician one has to start early and that craftsmanship is largely a matter of practising, granted that there is talent in the first place. Specialization in instrumental playing usually runs in the family, in the same way as there are other skills which may be passed on from fathers to sons or mothers to daughters. 'The ways of the ancestors' do matter. In this case too, attitudes also differ greatly. Instruments may be used by anyone who can play them. Conversely, they may be jealously guarded by the owner as something very personal. A good musical instrument may, in some cases, be seen as comparable to a young woman whom one may wish to marry. 'One would not want anyone to handle such a personal and blessed thing,' stated a Zimbabwean *mbira* player, Simon Mashoko. To the question of what the musician's status is in Africa, the answer is as ambivalent as anywhere else in the world. We have seen on p. 5 that music and musicians may be highly esteemed and venerated, but equally, they are often judged as drunkards, lazy, morally questionable and altogether troublesome misfits, who are nevertheless on occasions invaluable.

Finally, a warning. The image of people in Africa frequently bursting with song and dance belongs to the Western film industry. It is a crude and naïve interpretation of traditional culture as seen by an urbanized world which believes itself superior on untenable grounds.

Islam and Music *Introduction / Rhythm / Melody / Harmony / Instruments / General considerations: religion; Qur'an recitations; the call to prayer; the Prophet's birthday; hymns in praise of the Prophet; Sufi worship; Postlude*

God hath men who enter Paradise through their flutes and drums.

MOHAMMED (*c.* 570–632)

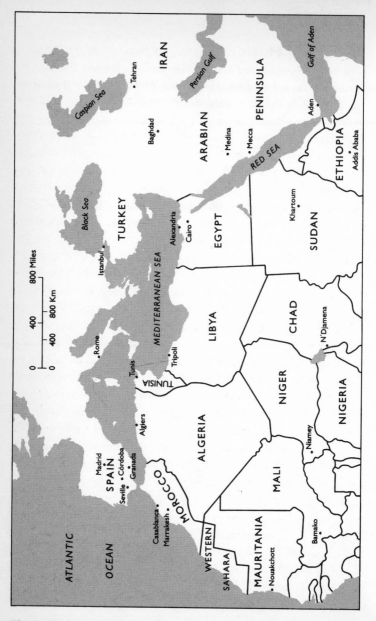

The Middle East and North Africa

Introduction

For a Western reader unfamiliar with the world of the Middle East (or Near East), one of the many confusing aspects of its nature is that although it is relatively easy to grasp in terms of its location (see Map 2), the vastness of its diversity as expressed in terms of its linguistic and ethnic complexity (i.e. Semito-Chamatic, Arabic, Uralo-Altaic, Turkic, Indo-European and Persian) creates formidable barriers for those who do not make the daunting effort of familiarizing themselves with these languages. The Muslim religion, which is by and large hardly understood and therefore looked upon with fear and hostility in the West, further adds to the emotional and intellectual blocking which usually takes place when confronted with something so unfamiliar. The Muslim religion, which is furthermore largely associated with the Arab world, goes well beyond its 'home territories', strongly affecting many parts of the world with its ideology and, of course, also affecting the arts in general and music in particular. In this chapter we will be discussing primarily the musical styles and techniques of the Middle East and North Africa, as their musical cultures share characteristic tendencies distinct from that of the West in a marked and broadly homogeneous way. These tendencies may be summed up by stressing that they are based on modality, a technique of quasi-improvisational style based on the *maqam* (a mode or scale), and on a dominatingly 'linear' or 'monodic' approach to music. Like the music of Africa, Arabic music is also largely aurally transmitted.

In contrast to African music, however, the Arabic musical tradition does have a distinguished practical and theoretical written history to this day, but most importantly covering roughly the periods from the beginning of Islam (AD 622) to the fall of Granada in 1492. These Islamic interpretations of music are largely divided between the study of sound as a scientific phenomenon and music as an artistic expression. It is also significant that the sacred text of the

Qur'an is not sung, but recited. A Western listener may interpret the beautiful 'musical' rendering of the holy text as music, but Muslims prefer to avoid confusing exhorted recitation style with making music, as music could be seen as an act of profanation of the Qur'an. It seems that there is an inherent ideological suspicion about music (*musiqa*) *per se* as opposed to the more objective scientific study of sound (*sawt*) as practised under the guiding inspiration of the Qur'an, which is seen to be a guide to everything in Muslim lives, including the arts. As an art form, music may be seen to be placed far down in the hierarchy of the arts, yet in reality it has a well-documented history in Arabic literature. Indeed, in music, the Arabic world has preserved one of its most sustained and authentic expressions, with perhaps the least changes during the twentieth century. In Arabic music we encounter not only characteristic elements of a great living musical culture, but also an unbroken continuity of a musical expression entirely authentic to the Muslim world.

Nevertheless the Muslim orthodoxy's rather hostile attitude towards music is based on seeing music as a sensuous art form which has to be kept under some control, like women are. Islamic religious music is thus strictly divided into what is admissible and what is not on moral grounds. Some of the highly operatic sacred compositions in the West would be judged as incongruous and unacceptable by an orthodox Muslim. It is for this reason that Muslim orthodoxy looks upon the highly sensuous style of the dervish and Sufi musical traditions as objectionable. In summary, Arabic music is characterized as being monodic, modal, *maqam*-based and with a marked prefer-ence for the human voice. Thus purely instrumental music, apart from in Persia, is secondary in music making. Yet the early Arabic descriptive literature on instruments shows an enthusiastic interest in them. Although the sacred and secular traditions influence each other, Muslim orthodoxy keeps an eye on music because of its sensuous nature and tries to maintain the purity of the chanting (*filawa*) or reciting (*tajwid*) of the Qur'an.

General historical survey

Pre-Islamic stage

This period takes us up to AD 622, that is to the time of Muhammad's departure from Mecca to Medina. We know that in the tribal Arabian peninsula and in the Yemen vocal music flourished. One of the most popular song types was the Bedouin *huda* or song of the camel-drivers, which is said to have had a rhythmic pattern miming the walk of camels. Some believe that this song was also related to a lament known as the *buka*.

Battle songs of a dark character were also popular. These, although mainly sung, could be accompanied by instruments such as the *mizaf* (lyre), *qussaba* (flute), *duff* (drum), as well as the *wan* (harp). The instruments were often played by women, as their role as singers, dancers and instrumentalists was prominent. It is likely that from the popularity of the 'singing slave girls' (*qaynas*), the role of the female entertainer as performing musician emanated in the Arabic world.

The Islamic period

From anecdotal evidence comes the story that one day when the father of Aisha (the last wife of Muhammad), Abu Bakr, visited Muhammad, he was found asleep, though two girls were singing and playing the tambourine. Hearing Abu Bakr's indignation, the prophet, uncovering his head, said, 'Let them sing, as it is a feast day.' Unfortunately the Qur'an does not stand either for or against music. This ambiguity by omission gives a field-day to interpreters of whatever bias. Another well-known occasion dates from the Umayyad period (a dynasty of rulers who first spread Islam, AD 661–750). Jamila, a famous singer on her pilgrimage to Mecca, was accompanied not only by fifty female singers, but also by poets of the period such as el-Ahouas and Ibn Atiq. On her arrival she was welcomed with more musicians and the poet Omar Ibn-abi Ali Rabia. During a three-day festivity there was a competition of music in which the most noted composers and singers of the time, such as Ibn Missja, Ibn Surayi and Ma'bed Rathma participated. Jamila herself was in charge of a performance consisting of fifty lutenists and female singers. Ma'bed, one of the founders of a renowned school of music of the period in Baghdad, established his method of teaching based on aural tradition. When he died in AD 743 he was honoured by the Caliph of Baghdad, Umayyad al-Walid II, who personally assisted at his funeral.

The time following the Umayyad period, known as the Abbasid period (AD 750–1258), was significant in the history of Arabic music. Ibrahim Ibn al-Mahdi and his son Ishak, for example, had the greatest reputation in Baghdad and beyond. They were the precursors of the Arabic music which we know today. The Caliph el-Ouathec complimented Ishak by saying that if he had not had such a great reputation as an artist he could have been a Chief Magistrate! When Ishak died in AD 850 the Caliph al-Mutawakkil said that with his death he lost one of the best aspects of beauty in his reign. His influence spread to North Africa and eventually to Andalusia.

Music as a profession was now slowly taken over by men, above all by the notoriously immoral group of effeminates known as the *mukhannathum*, who were associated with prostitution. These transvestites, together with slave girls, were responsible for making music. In the main they were not of free-born Arab descent, but were converts to Islam, and this added to the suspicion with which music was increasingly viewed. Indeed, because of the licentious associations of music and musicians, music has not only been looked down upon on occasions, but has been disapproved of altogether by orthodox Islamic law-makers even to this day. Divorcing the cantillation of the Qur'an from music has its roots in those times. Though Islam acknowledges the pleasure music can give, it was nevertheless classified as 'forbidden pleasure' (*malahi*). The theologians based their hostility towards music on what is called 'traditional tales' or conversations and sayings (*hadith*) of Muhammad as authenticated by theologians. This 'tradition' formed the basis for all four schools of Islamic law.

Both Byzantine and Persian music were most popular at that time and influenced Arabic musical traditions, but without disturbing the Arabic character. Arabic music in turn itself exercised its influence on Persia. Indeed, Yunus al-Katib (d. AD 765), a singer and writer of music in Medina, was of Persian origin. It is through his description of Medina's musical life as quoted in al-Isfahani's (d. AD 967) book that we can gain an insight into the musical life of that place. From the tenth to thirteenth centuries Arab theorists, confronted with the conflict between profane and sacred aspects of music, made an attempt to solve the problem by arguing in favour of the idea of spiritual power, of the power of music to mutate, which can transform its sensuous, profane aspects into the purely spiritual, that is to sacred manifestations. It was argued that the realm of the sacred can be attained by a metamorphosis, as it were, which is one of music's strengths. This is a highly perceptive Sufi interpretation of music's power and regenerative attributes. In Western music too, we encounter similar preoccupations and symbolic solutions, as is the case in the late medieval and early Renaissance practice of the 'Parody Mass', where a secular theme (love song) could be used for the *cantus firmus* of a Mass (for example, Dufay, 'Se la face ay pale' and 'L'homme armé'). One of the most frustrating aspects of al-Isfahani's monumental (twenty volumes) *Great Book of Songs* (*Kitab al-aghani al-kabir*) is the complete lack of musical illustrations. However, he readily compensates the reader with detailed descriptions not only of poets but also of composers, instruments and theoretical aspects of music, covering about four hundred years of activities from the seventh to the tenth centuries. It is a mine of information covering Arabic musical activities and thought.

Equally frustrating is the lack of musical illustrations in the famous book of al-Farabi (AD 872–950), *Great Book of Music* (*Kitab al-musiqa al-kabir*). On the other hand he gives detailed descriptions of scales and rhythmic patterns.

It was jealousy among colleagues which in the ninth century forced one of the most gifted musicians, Zirjab, to flee from Baghdad to Granada, where the Umayyads ruled after their downfall in Arabia in AD 750. Zirjab's move to Spain was a blessing to both Arabic and Spanish music as it established the Andalusian school of Arabic music.

In this context it is by no means an exaggeration to speak of the School of Zirjab as Granadan because it became as much of a centre of culture for the Umayyads as Baghdad was for the Abbasids. The musical tradition of the Andalusian golden age did not stop with the fall of Granada in 1492, but carried on in the Maghreb with hardly a change to its musical language.

Islamic influence on African music

Islam's influence in the African style of music making, as seen in Chapter 1, affected not only the Hamitic and Negritic areas of North Africa, but also West Africa and some parts of the borders of the Sahara. As is often the case, two traditions can and do live together side by side. But cross-fertilization of indigenous elements in terms of singing (melody) and rhythm shows the mixing of styles.

For example, whereas in African music the accompaniment of a singer would likely be several drums or ostinatos played on melodic instruments, as in Central Africa, the Arabic (Muslim) influence would manifest itself by using instead heterophonically one or two accompanying instruments such as a drum or a bowed string instrument. By and large, Islamic music is monophonic rather than polyphonic. Under Islamic influence African polyphony is that much less prominent.

In terms of instruments Islamic influence can be noticed in African musicians' adoption of double-reed instruments. The black African singers moreover had adopted the Muslim style of a tense nasal voice quality as well as the ornate style of vocal execution. As William P. Malm pointed out:

Interesting if ambiguous mixtures on separation of two musical cultures are found at the terminals of the Sahara caravan routes. The Wolof of Senegal and Gambia, for example, show such a mixture: they use both cylindrical and pot-shaped single-headed drums in groups to produce African polyphony for their secular dances, but when their holy man sings Muslim hymns (*hasida*), a small kettledrum called a *tabala* is used along with an iron beater; together these produce single rhythms much more akin to the music of the rest of the Muslim world.[1]

These types of mixtures of styles are characteristic not only of the fringes of the Sahara but everywhere when the two musical traditions meet.

Ottoman domination

The Muslim Turkish empire ruled over the best part of the Middle East as well as territories in Europe from the fifteenth to the twentieth centuries. This empire, comparable with the Habsburgs in the longevity of its power, reached its peak in terms of power in the sixteenth century, when it conquered Egypt and Syria, Hungary and vast territories in the Middle East and North Africa. The Arabs, however, continued to cultivate their musical traditions even under foreign rulers, although Baghdad, Cairo and Damascus lost their importance in favour of Istanbul. Ultimately stagnation took over where once flourished great cultural and scientific life. The change from the Ottoman rulers to European colonial imperialism did not help the situation either. One might well question the value of the 'inevitable' influences of Europe on Arabic music during this century.

The two major traditions of the Muslim world, those of the east (Egypt, Persia, Lebanon, Syria and Iraq) and of the west (Morocco, Algeria and Tunisia) had evolved during the Umayyad and Abbasid periods, as we have seen. The North African tradition was less affected by either the Persian or Ottoman influences, thus representing a fascinating survival of the musical tradition of Moorish Spain and the north-west side of Africa. Popular and art (court) music have interacted and fed off each other; this is a universal tendency in the histories of music, whether in non-Western or Western musical cultures.

Rhythm

In the music of the Islamic world rhythm can vary from the simplest
to the most complex patterns. One of the most influential theorists
was Safi al-Din (d. 1294) who, in his treatise, established modes of
scales and rhythmic cycles. He emphasized two rhythmic cycles: one
was to divide a circle into as many numbers of sections as there are
time units; the second was based on poetic metres. This worked in the
following ways: the syllables *ta* and *na* equalled one time unit each; the
syllables *tan* and *nan* were equal to two time units. By and large, Arab
theorists shared the view that time should be divided into short and long
units and that there are strict as well as free ways of organizing time.

Strict rhythmic unit

A strict rhythmic measure or bar represents a rhythmic unit of
regular beats in numbers of two, three, four and their compound
variations. As we have seen in Chapter 1, these units can also be
irregular, that is five or seven beats in a bar. Strict rhythmic pulsation
is usually associated with dance music or is influenced by dance.

The rhythmic patterns with bars or measures in Arabic music are
named *wazn* (measure). These patterns are also referred to by other
names such as *usul*, *mizan* and *darb*; they consist of regular reiteration
of two or more beats. The subdivisions can be either equal or
unequal as, for example, an equal pattern of three beats for each of
the two beats would be 3 + 3 while an unequal pattern could be
4 + 2 or 2 + 4. Musicians memorize these patterns by using
onomatopoeic syllables, such as *dum* for a beat played on the centre
of the drum, or *tak* when the player hits the edge of a drum. The
dot . is the rest sign for both *dum* and *tak*. Thus · · · · equal four
beat rests for the player. If two beats are of the same stress they will
be either both *dums* or *taks*. When the second beat is weak it is
called *mah* after a *dum* beat or *kah* after a *tak* beat. Two examples of
the method, one in 3/4 the other in 4/4, are shown in Fig. 1.

Fig. 1

Thus the two sonorities, the heavier *dum* and the lighter *tak*, and a few satellite sonorities are enough to produce a wide range of rhythmic patterns.

The rhythmic sonorities of the two basic beats are fundamental in establishing the characteristic metre, whether this is done in the Arabic Middle East and North Africa or in Turkey. The long occupation by the Ottoman Turks of Arab as well as non-Arab countries has left its mark and produced a cross-fertilization of ideas, whether in music or otherwise. The way in which the Turks organize rhythm – for example, their *aksak* pattern based on 9 beats: 2 + 2 + 2 + 3 – bears a resemblance to the Bahraini 8-beat pattern 3 + 2 + 2 + 1, known as *sant*. Both show a similar preoccupation with the idea of combining 2 and 3. These rhythmic patterns, as expressed in repeated cycles, give rhythm to the *maqams* (melodic modes) used by Arab musicians as the fundamental material for the elaborate unfolding of their music.

Free rhythmic organization

Free rhythmic organization is a highly personal handling of time structure. In essence it is a way of performing music in such a way that the actual beats do not appear in a fixed, regular and predictable way, but appear instead as long and short irregular patterns (for example 5:2). Obviously there is a tendency towards asymmetric thinking and rubato playing. This type of music making particularly suits solo performance, as the soloist is not restricted by the consideration of others. What is gained is infinite poetic subtlety in expressing temporal nuances.

Language has its musical rhythm and poetry all the more so. Arabic music is closely linked to the rhythm of its native poetry.

It is revealing that rhythmic patterns such as 13/8, 14/8, 17/8 and 21/8 appear quite frequently in Arabic metric structuring. Music and poetry were bedfellows for a long time before music evolved its own independence and separated from poetry. Rhythmic patterns such as 2/4, 3/4, 4/4 and 6/8, 5/8, 7/8 and many others infinitely more complex established themselves as rhythmic modes of music. These rhythmic modes, named *dawar* in Egypt and *taqm* in Syria, may vary both in length (one, the Syrian *darb al-fath*, consists of 176 beats!) and in quality. They are played repeatedly throughout a composition, whether entirely or partially. In the Arab Near East a large number are in practical use; on the other hand in the Maghreb (that is northern Africa, for example, Morocco) only a few stereo-typed modes are in frequent use. These symmetric, asymmetric, free and strict patterns show the relationship of music, dance and poetry.

Music is obviously an integral part of both dance and poetry, as rhythm is the very nerve centre of all three art forms. Moreover, both dance and music are non-verbal, ordered contemplation of time and space. In this context a piece of music can be seen as a transient evocation of the infinite. It is perhaps at this point that the secular and sacred aspects of music meet. The Sufis' approach to music seems to indicate a profound understanding of these aspects of music. Indeed, they use music in order to send themselves into a trance from where they believe themselves to be in direct communication with Allah.

Melody

In the Islamic world, vocal music is the foundation of all music. As everywhere else in the world melodies are theoretically explained as being founded on scales and scale systems. The Arabic scale system is immensely complex and its theoretical roots go back to such theorists as al-Kindi (796–873), al-Farabi and Sati al-Din. These classic masters enlisted twelve *maqamat* (singular: *maqam*), which were seen as the main scales, and six subscales. These became the fundamental scale patterns of Arabic music. Before going further it is appropriate to deal here with a crucial pitch and notational problem: in Arabic music the use of less than 1/2 (or even lesser) tones as well as augmented intervals (for example, augmented second) are common characteristics. These can be played on string instruments, but the piano is quite inadequate for this type of music. As Arabic music is not based on a tempered system, unlike in the West, these changes of interval give a *maqam* a particular colouristic nuance and emotional subtlety to an Arabic listener which is likely to be all but lost on a Western listener, who may even think that the melody performed is out of tune. In Western musical notation these sounds are indicated in the ways shown in Fig. 2.

♯ = sharp ; ‡ = half sharp ; 𝄪 = 3/4 sharp ; ♭ = flat ; ⅍ or ┼ = half flat ; 𝄫 = 3/4 flat

Fig. 2

In many ways the *maqam* is more than a scale, more than a skeleton as it were, as it predetermines the potential base for an instrumental improvisation (*taqsim*) or for a solo vocal form, such as the one based on the text *ya layli ya ayni* ('Oh my night! Oh my eye!'), which gives the name *layali* for this vocal form. These quasi-improvisations founded on a chosen *maqam* are perhaps one of the most characteristic phenomena of the Arabic musical world. Another characteristic is the tendency to treat the melody with greater organizational control while the rhythm is relatively free. As opposed to the one octave scale in the West, the *maqam* pattern is usually spread to two octaves. *Hijaz*, in Fig. 3, is a common and strikingly 'exotic' sounding *maqam* for a Western ear. Some of the flats and sharps could be half sharps or flats, but in order to enable the reader to play them on a piano

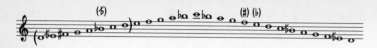

Fig. 3

they are notated as ♭ and ♯. The possible differences are indicated in brackets.

Every *maqam* has its own tone centre as well as its satellite secondary centres around which all tones gravitate. For instance, Fig. 3 can be reduced to its main nucleus thus:

Fig. 4

D–F♯–G (see also: a–c–d, e–g–a; together these three clusters form seven notes out of fourteen notes of the ascending part of the *maqam*).

The frequency of emphasis on notes such as d, g and a indicates tonic, subdominant and dominant functions. The c, on the other hand, functions as a modal seventh and/or part of a cadential pattern.

There is no definitive list of the existing *maqamat*, although the French musicologist R. d'Erlanger listed well over a hundred in 1949, but the most popular in use today is likely to be about twenty *ajnan* (*jins* = genre; plural: *ajnan*).

Obviously the *maqamat* display various specific moods or mood associations, such as masculinity with the *maqam rast*, femininity with the *maqam bayati*, love with the *maqam sikah*, sadness with the *maqam saba* and, with the one illustrated in Fig. 3, a distant landscape evoked in the *hijaz*.

Arabic music and form

We have already touched on the variation technique when we discussed the instrumental *taqsim* and the vocal *layali* on p. 67. It is now time to consider larger musical structures. There seem to be two distinct styles recognized which form a convenient division: eastern Arabic and western Arabic, each representing the styles of two groups of countries mainly including Egypt, Iraq, Lebanon and Syria in the east, and Algeria, Morocco and Tunisia in the west, the last three representing the still-living tradition of the Moorish Spain of Andalusia. The eastern style is mainly improvised by solo per-formers or by a small ensemble of generally no more than five players. These singers or instrumentalists display virtuoso technique and tend to be professionals. Apart from employing the variation techniques as applied to the *taqsim* and *layali*, they employ an Arabic version of the suite, called *nubah*. The origin of the *nubah* can be traced back to the Abbasid period. It consists of eight highly varied sections or movements which are performed in reverse order of rhythmic difficulties, that is, from the complex towards the simple modes. The rhythmic modes are either performed in strict or free styles.

The *nubah* of the western Arabs now practised in the Maghreb states came there via the Arab refugees expelled from Spain at various times, but above all at the end of the fifteenth century with the fall of Granada. Indeed *maghrib* in Arabic means 'place of sunset' as opposed to *mashriq* which means 'place of sunrise'. This clearly underlines the geographical locations of the two prominent styles under discussion. As Habib Hassan Touma pointed out: 'in the current musical practice of North Africa, there are at least three distinct *nubah* styles, all of which have been handed down by the great masters of Andalus. In Tunisia can be found the old style of early Seville; in Algeria, that of Cordoba; and in Morocco, that of Granada and Valencia.'[2]

In contrast to the eastern *nubah*, the western *nubah* consists of five sections of movements and each of the sections opens up with an instrumental interlude. A popular musical structure is based on the pattern of the stanzas of a poem sung as part of a *nubah* performance, similar to what is known in West European culture as the rondo form: Ab Ac Ad A. However, in practice it is more likely to be substantially elaborated with repetitions and extra episodes. Thus the pattern given above, when repetitions are included, will be: AAbbbAAcccAAdddAA . . . The above pattern is a relatively simple one. Much more complex patterns are also possible, but the one illustrated here gives a fair idea of the principle involved.

There are, of course, many more distinct forms in use in Arabic music, but those referred to so far are a sufficient introduction to the main tendencies in Arabic musical form. To conclude this section, here is the closing section of a call to prayer (*adhan*) from Syria.

Fig. 5

Harmony

It has already been stressed that the most characteristic features of Arabic music are monophony and heterophony (see p. 62), the use of melodic and rhythmic modes both being closely linked with the Arab language itself and, of course, poetry. To these one should add a most sensitive and highly decorated melodic line as well as the use of characteristic instruments, to be discussed under their separate heading in this chapter. Contrary to the marked preoccupation in the West with harmonic procedures, Arabic music has paid only modest attention to harmony. The few references one can find speak of 'the harmony of notes', that is pitches following each other in harmonious succession as in a melody. Harmony proper, however, is the art of combining two or more pitches simultaneously, that is the vertical and not the horizontal aspect of manipulating sounds. This aspect of music, until quite recently, was neglected by Arab musicians. The types of harmonic combinations are nevertheless as follows: octave, fifth, fourth, major and minor thirds and seconds. These appear as temporary decorative melodic and rhythmic diversions in an otherwise linearly thought-out and dominatingly monophonic compositional process. The musicologists' term heterophony may be of some use here, as it describes a style of composition in which two or more performers (either singers or instrumentalists) are performing the same melody but with occasional modifications and elaboration, thus deviating momentarily from the main melodic line and creating a sense of polyphony and harmony. The term heterophony originates in Plato's *Laws* where he warns that the diversity of the performances on the lyre may 'not be suitable for the education of the young' (because of their enervating sensuousness). The example in Fig. 6 illustrates the characteristic nature of heterophonic style of so much ensemble playing in Arabic music.

A closer look at the example in Fig. 6 reveals that the two parts are largely in unison, yet the lower part produces occasional melodic and rhythmic embellishments which touch on two-part harmonies based on the simultaneous sounding of minor and major thirds, minor seconds, a perfect fourth and even a major sixth and minor seventh in a truly heterophonic style. This is a monothematic polyphonic style which appears not only in Arabic music but also in Japanese, Javanese and Balinese music.

Fig. 6

Instruments

As with so many other topics, it was Arab scholars who laid down the foundation of a classification system for musical instruments in the tenth century under the by now familiar headings: percussion, bowed, plucked and wind instruments. In Arab countries it is, to this day, the small ensembles which are the most popular. The most notable exceptions to this trend are the large orchestras popular in Egypt, Iraq and Morocco, where there have been references for many centuries to orchestras numbering a hundred musicians. Today radio, television, the theatre and film music have developed a taste for large orchestras, but at a cost, as they are markedly hybrid. They mix traditional instruments with Western instrumental forces as well as mixing the Arabic and the Western musical styles. Good examples of this mixed style can be heard in Egyptian film music. Let us now turn to the discussion of the most important and popular musical instruments used in Arabic music.

Percussion instruments (idiophones and membraphones)

Idiophones

(a) In Arabic music, as in African music, the clapping of hands either on its own or together with drumming is one of the most effective and natural ways of creating percussive sonorities.

(b) Small or larger *cymbals* (crotals) are also used in ensembles or by dancers. They are popular in Turkey, Morocco and in Maghreb locations in general.

(c) Among the jingles it is the *Turkish crescent* which is perhaps the most notable. It became an important instrument in the military band of the Turkish Janissary (the élite troops of the Ottoman sultans).

(d) Bells are used all over the world. Camel bells are used in Somalia, but equally popular are the Egyptian bells.

(e) Gongs, as we have seen in Chapter 1, are not popular in Africa nor are they popular in Arabic countries.

(f) An unusual 'drum', if one can call it such, is the *sand drum*, which is made by digging a tunnel in the sand and, having created two holes at each end of the tunnel, the linking bridge part is then beaten rhythmically by the hands. This creates a rather muffled stamping sound. This practice has been noted in Ethiopia.

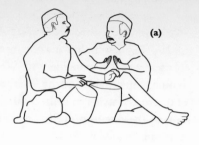

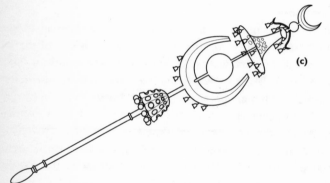

Fig. 7 Idiophones

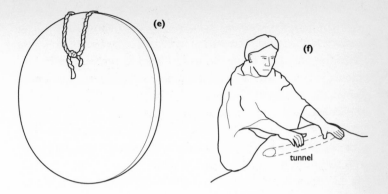

Fig. 7 Idiophones – *continued*

Membraphones

(a) One of the most common types of percussive instruments in the Middle East is the *frame drum*, better known as the *tambourine*. It consists of one or sometimes two stretched skins over a light and shallow frame which is usually shaped into a circle although square-shaped tambourines are also in existence. A really good instrument is covered with fish skin. Most tambourines are, however, covered with goatskin membranes as they are cheaper. According to Arab musicians, the tambourines made in Cairo and Damascus are among the best. In different parts of the Arab world the tambourine is named in various ways. For instance, in North Africa it is called *tar*, in Turkey it is also called *tar*, but in Iraq its name is *daff zinjari*. The sound of a tambourine is often enriched by fixing in and around the frame a series of up to ten pairs of cymbals.

Moreover it is traditional to decorate the frame lavishly with mosaics.

(b) The *duff* is a large tambourine with a shallower frame and only five pairs of cymbals. It is mainly played by women dancers, as its primary function is, to this day, to accompany female dancers.

In the context of large tambourines, the *bandir* and the *mazhar* should also be noted, as they are very popular. The *bandir* is characterized by having two snares fixed underneath the stretched skin. The *mazhar* has no cymbals attached to it; instead it has a set of iron-ring chains fixed inside its frame. Both these instruments are used for ceremonial religious occasions such as funerals or Sufi sect ceremonies. As such they are sanctioned for religious purposes, unlike many other instruments, and are particularly used by the Sufis.

(c) The *waisted drums* of both Iraq and Turkey are characterized by their elegant bodies. They are usually held under the arm and played with fingertips hitting the stretched skin.

(d) *Goblet drums*, or *darabukkah* drums as they are known in Islamic countries, are less graceful than waisted drums, but they are even more decorated with painting or inlaid work and traditionally are made of clay. They are played in the same way as waisted drums. *Darabukkahs* are very popular in the Arab world; no festivity can be without them. They are mostly played by men, though in the context of folk music activities, women can also play them.

(e) The *naqarat* (singular: *naqarah* or *naqara*) is the predecessor of the timpani (kettledrums). Made of clay or copper, the kettledrums come in pairs, representing the main beat (*dum*) on the right hand and the second beat (*tak*) on the left hand. They are made in different sizes from small, to be held by one arm (left), to large sizes, to be carried on processional occasions on the backs of camels or donkeys. More often they are placed in front of the player, who sits cross-legged on the floor and uses cloth-covered beaters.

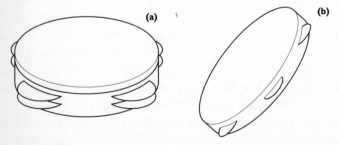

Fig. 8 Membraphones

(c)(i)

(c)(ii)

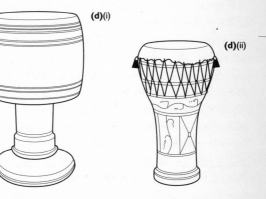

(d)(i)

(d)(ii)

(e)

Fig. 8 Membraphones – *continued*

There are, of course, several more percussive instruments which could have been illustrated here, like the double-headed drums, but those discussed here are sufficient to illustrate the most frequently used percussive instruments which the reader is likely to encounter.

String instruments (chordophones)

The family tree of stringed instruments consists of five basic types: lyres, harps, lutes, bows and zithers.

(a) Lyre The lyre was a popular instrument in ancient Egypt, where it was used from about 2000 BC. By now, however, we largely associate this instrument with ancient Greek culture, with the image of Apollo and his lyre and Orpheus charming the gods with his playing, though the lyre actually survives in parts of Africa, particularly Ethiopia, and, interestingly enough, in Siberia. To this day the two types of lyre, bowl- and box-shaped, are still in use.

(b) Harp The harp again brings us to ancient Egypt as well as to Persia where the *angle harp* dating about 2000 BC was used. Its complex modern descendant found its way into the repertoire of the symphony orchestra.

(c) Lute The characteristic of the lute (*ud*) is that it consists of a belly-shaped body and a neck. The strings are stretched from the lower part of the belly to the upper part of the neck. Further characteristics can be observed from their backs, which can be either rounded or flat; the neck length can be either short or long. Lutes used in the Middle East, like the *ud* in Iraq and Syria, are short-necked, but the *tar* in Iran as well as the *saz* or waisted *tar* in Turkey are long-necked instruments.

The lute is essentially an Arabic musical instrument. It embodies its musical culture more than any other instrument. The whole Arabic tone system is based on it. For this reason, among the Arabs the lute is referred to as the 'sultan of the instruments'. What the violin or the piano is for the West the lute is for the Arab world: the most precious instrument of all.

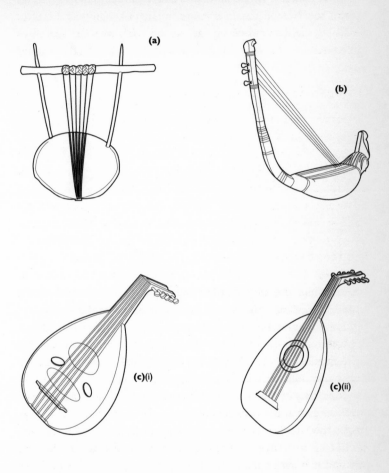

Fig. 13 Chordophones

The old lute (*ud qadim*) had four strings tuned in fourths, but in the ninth century, Zirjab extended it to five strings. These strings in turn represented the four temperaments of man and the fifth, added by Zirjab, symbolized the human soul. Modern tuning of this instrument is based on tuning five double strings in the manner shown in Fig. 9.

Fig. 9

The instrument's compass is therefore as shown in Fig. 10.

Fig. 10

The strings are still plucked with the quill of an eagle feather, but a modern version is made with the much less romantic plastic.

There are several variants or relations of the lute much in evidence in various parts of the Arab world. These instruments are, for example, the *kwitrah* of Algeria and Morocco, the *nash atbar* of Syria or the mandolin-like *buzug* of Lebanon and Turkey, which show the popularity of this type of string instrument in the musical life of the Near East and North Africa.

(d) Guitar The guitar, like castanets, is likely to have been introduced to Europe by the Arabs via Spain. It is easier to play than the lute and it became one of the most popular instruments in Spain and beyond.

(e) Fiddle The folk fiddle, above all the *spike fiddle*, is part of the musical tradition of the Middle East and North Africa. It is believed that the spike fiddle originated in Persia. The one-stringed spike fiddle is to be found in Africa (Mali and Ethiopia) but also in Iraq, Syria and Turkey. Some of these instruments may have two or three

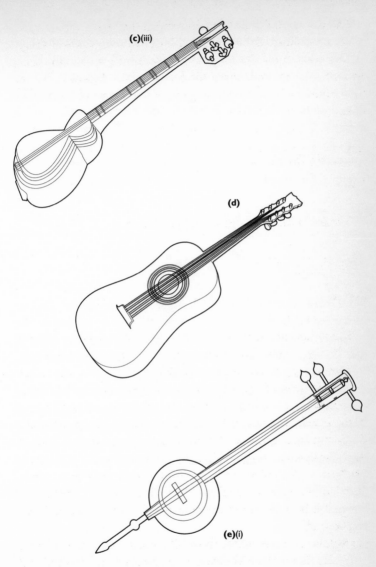

Fig. 13 Chordophones – *continued*

strings and may be referred to as *rabab* or *rebab* in Islamic countries
and are usually played with curved bows. On the whole the *rabab*
has a short neck and its distinguished history leads to the early fiddles
such as the medieval rebec, *lira da braccio* and, eventually, to the
violin family as we have known it since the late sixteenth century.
Kamanjah is the Arabic name used for the European violin, which
is likely to have originated in the Near East. The reason for men-
tioning it here is because it is also popular in modern Arabic
ensembles. Its tuning, however, is different from its European
brother. The way the *kamanjah* is tuned is shown in Fig. 11.

Fig. 11

(f) Zither The plucked board zither's ancestor is the Turkish
qanun and has been known since the tenth century. Its brother, the
dulcimer, which is a zither struck with two beaters, also came to
Europe via the Middle East in the eleventh century, probably from
Persia and Iraq, where it is known as *santur*.

The strings are tuned diatonically and their number varies between
sixty-three and eighty-four. They are usually tuned in groups of
three, that is, each neighbouring three strings will have the same
pitch. Therefore a zither with sixty-three strings will have twenty-
one pitches to play on. The usual range of the zither is shown in
Fig. 12.

Fig. 12

The zither is the most popular instrument for rendering traditional
Arabic music after the lute and drums.

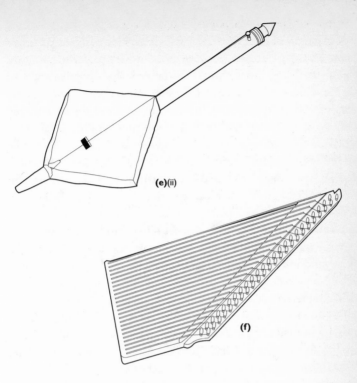

Fig. 13 Chordophones – *continued*

Wind instruments (aerophones)

We have seen that, in spite of regional variations, the Middle East and North Africa are largely dominated by the cultural tradition of Islam. Instruments such as the lute, zither, spike fiddle and drums are characteristic representatives of a musical profile belonging to Arabic civilization. Obviously the Arabic tradition of wind instruments will also reflect their predilections and long-standing customs.

(a) End-blown flute The end-blown flute, known as *nay* (its Persian name is the one mostly used in the Arab world), is open at both ends and is made of bamboo or cane. Its range of pitch is determined by the length of the instrument, which may have five or six finger holes. By using the over-blowing technique the player can produce sounds covering more than three octaves. It is popular in rural regions of Iraq, Jordan and Lebanon and naturally favoured by shepherds and shepherdesses. In art music, however, the *nay* is played only by men. It is played with the non-stop breathing technique based on the performer's use of his cheeks by which he keeps the air under control for a considerable length of time. In the Maghreb and Turkey the *nay* is also used in sacred music, as it has an important role in trance-inducing musical activities as practised by the Dervish orders.

(b) Folk-clarinet The folk-clarinet is likely to have originated in Egypt. It is a characteristic single-reed instrument. The reed is attached to a cylindrical tube. Often the cane pipe is doubled and, at the end of each pipe, a cowhorn is affixed. This doubling or even trebling of pipes for greater versatility is quite common in Arab countries.

(c) Shawm The *shawm* family is the ancestor of the oboe. They are double-reed wind instruments, that is two double blades of cane are bound together and fixed into the top of the instrument. The player blows through the gaps between the two blades, which causes them to vibrate and thus generate sound. The sound of a *shawm* is rather harsh and buzzing. The Turkish *shawm* (*zurna*) represents the characteristic form of the instrument in the Middle East. Another striking feature of the Turkish variant of the *shawm* is that it has a miniature plate-like mouthpiece and the body of the instrument may be covered with leather.

(d) Bagpipes Bagpipes are reed instruments which can be either single or double. A peculiar aspect of reed instruments in the Arab world is that there seems to be a preference in some regions for single, in others for double reeds. For instance, double reeds predominate in Iran, Turkey and North Africa while the single reed is favoured in Iraq, Jordan, Lebanon and the Arabian peninsula.

They are characterized by having an air bag which is inflated either by the player directly blowing air in or more likely by bellows which are pumped under the player's arm. Because of the air-reservoir the player can play uninterrupted on the melody pipe while the drone pipes (those pipes without finger holes) produce their characteristic drone sound. The Arabic bagpipe is further characterized by fixing a cowhorn at the end of the melody pipe(s) in the same way as we have seen with the clarinet. It is an open air, folk instrument which is to this day in evidence above all in Turkey, Iraq and North Africa (for example, Tunisia).

Apart from their military use, horns and trumpets do not figure prominently in Arabic music. Their role, if used at all, is restricted to festival processions during Ramadan (the month of fasting).

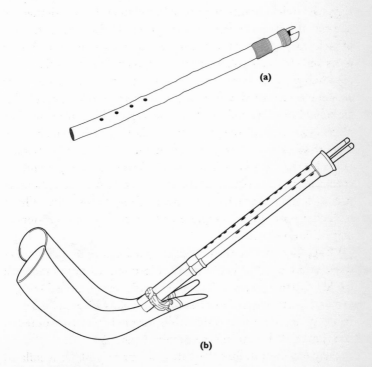

(a)

(b)

Fig. 14 Aerophones

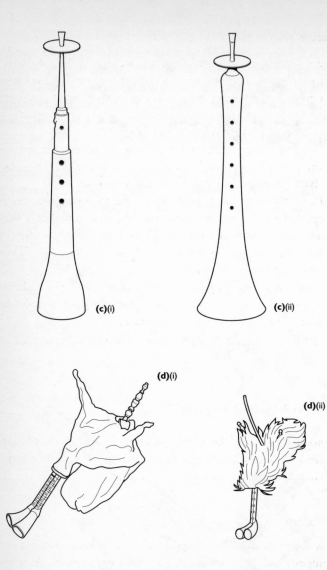

Fig. 14 Aerophones– *continued*

Ensembles

These instruments are generally played either solo or more likely in a small ensemble as, for example, a clarinet or oboe with the backing of a drum. Larger ensembles may comprise three wind instruments (*shawms*), a pair of kettledrums as well as an extra drum, which may be cylindrical in shape, like the *tabl baladi*.

The three most important art music ensembles are the *takht* (podium or seat), *jalghi baghnadi* (also known as the *tchalgi Baghdad* = the Baghdad ensemble) and the *Andalusi ensemble*.

The *takht* ensemble is made up of the following instrumental forces: one end-blown flute, one lute, one or two violins, a zither, a tambourine and a goblet drum. These instruments are often also joined by a male or female singer soloist as well as a small vocal ensemble of four or six voices.

Jalghi baghnadi is a popular ensemble of Iraqi origin. In addition, in place of some of the above instruments, the *jalghi baghnadi* may include a spike fiddle as well as a dulcimer.

The *Andalusi ensemble* prefers to include a bow-necked lute and a viola.

General Considerations

General considerations: Religion, Qur'an recitation, the call to prayer, the Prophet's birthday, hymns in praise of the Prophet, the naming of God, the whirling Dervishes.

Religion

It is hardly possible to comprehend a civilization without some familiarity with its language, religion, history and culture. As religion is such an all-embracing aspect of the Arab world, it is of paramount importance to touch upon it here in the hope that it may help

towards a better understanding of one of the world's three monotheistic religions. It evolved from the same root as Judaism and
Christianity. The name 'Islam' comes from an Arabic root word
meaning 'commitment' or 'surrender'. To a Muslim, 'Islam' is life
in submission to the will of God (Allah). The followers of Islam are
called Muslims, who all share the fundamental belief that 'There is
no god except Allah and Muhammad is the Messenger of Allah.'
These words are known as the *shahada*. Muslims profoundly believe
that their faith is sufficient for all spiritual and religious needs of not
only the Arab people, but the whole world beyond. Thus, like
Christianity, it is a missionary religion. The worldwide community
of Muslims is called the *ummah*. They trace their origin to the
Prophet Muhammad, who was born in AD 570 in Mecca. From
the beginning of creation Allah sent his messengers to earth in order
to help people to understand and follow the right path. The first of
these prophets was Adam, the last was Muhammad. When Muhammad was forty years old he went to the hills for his regular contemplation. It was then that Allah's message was received by him via
the angel Jibril (Gabriel), calling him to preach Allah's own final
words for the guidance of people everywhere. These words were
written down through dictations based on oral and written sources
after the death of Muhammad in AD 632. These sources are what
form the Qur'an ('Recitation' or 'that which should be read'), the
Muslim holy book. It contains the infallible words of Allah which
must never be changed. It has to be recited in Arabic which is the
sacred language of the Qur'an and which is where the Arabic
language achieved perfection both in content and expression. Next
in importance to the Qur'an is the *Hadith* (tradition) which is the
record of the activities and actions of the Prophet Muhammad and
the early history of Islam. The Hadith contains what is called the
sunna ('examples'), which are to guide Muslims and are a standard
to be followed by all Muslims. The Qur'an and the *sunna* together
offer a comprehensive guide (*shari'a* or law) concerning life and
one's conduct. The *shari'a* is 'the science of all things, human and
divine'. There is no real distinction between the sacred and secular,

spiritual and material, or personal and communal. Allah's purpose is all-embracing, and humanity is to take part in the realization of his creative will as his representatives. There are two groups within Islam: the Sunni, who believe in the consensus of the community in propagating the *sunna* (custom), and the Shi'ites who prefer to follow exemplary teachers (imams). The Shi'ites represent about only 10 per cent of the Muslim world but they are, all the same, a considerable ideological and practical force.

Qur'an recitations

How does music in general and religious music in particular fit into the world of Islam? We have already touched upon the fact that in the history of Arabia several Islamic scholars and theologians were hostile to both sacred and secular music on the grounds that singing and performing music were far too sensuous activities and that the moral standing of the musicians themselves was questionable. Such a scholar was, for instance, Ali al-Dunya of the ninth century, who condemned most instrumental and vocal music, and even listening to it, on moral grounds. Others, however, defended music, for example, Abu Hamid al-Ghazali in the twelfth century. No agreement was ever reached and consequently the status of music remains to this day somewhat ambiguous but the orthodox are quite hostile towards it. In order to dissociate the Qur'an from the dubious nature of music, as seen by some of the law makers, a compromise solution was found by never referring to the presenter of the Qur'an as a singer (*mughanni*), but as a reader (*qari*) or reciter (*tali, muqra, murattil, mujawwid*). The practical reality, however, is that the reciting of the Qur'an represents a most distinct vocal style requiring a good voice and refined musical skill as well as a profound understanding of the intonation and pronunciation of the Arabic language. Although the recitation of the Qur'an must be clearly separated from any connotation with secular singing, it is nevertheless based on the *maqam* scale patterns which are, as we have seen, the foundation of secular Arabic music. Every Muslim learns the complex reading rules of the Qur'an without necessarily 'singing' it. The professional reciters, however, receive their religious and musical training in Qur'an schools. Reciting the Qur'an in public calls for a mastery of technique, a good voice and artistic integrity in the service of the holy text which must not be obscured by subjective individualism.

There are several occasions when sacred music is involved in Islamic worship. The most important of these are the call to prayer (*adhan*), the Prophet's birthday (*mawlid*), in praise of the Prophet and his family (*na't*), the naming of God or spiritual concert (*dhikr*).

The call to prayer (*adhan*)

Muslims are required to pray five times daily – at daybreak, noon, mid-afternoon, after sunset and early in the night. The prayer (*salat*) can be said alone, in company or in the mosque. The congregational prayer which takes place is at noon on Fridays. What concerns us here is the beautiful tradition of calling the Muslim to prayer five times daily by the *mu'adhdhin* (*muezzin*) who used to climb up to the minaret to do so vocally. The call to prayer is called *adhan* in Arabic. The *muezzin*'s office became a most important and respected function in the practice of Islam. During the Ottoman empire they even formed their own guild. The regulations for performing the *adhan* are similar to those for reciting the Qur'an, that is clear pronunciation and projection of the text, the melody being based on the use of the *maqam* principle. Sometimes the word *imam* (leader) is used, as an imam is the leader of prayer in a mosque. But it is the *muezzin* who goes up the minaret in order to call to prayer. These are two distinct functions.

The Prophet's birthday (*mawlid*)

The celebration of Prophet Muhammad's birthday is a tradition which goes back to the ninth century, if not to earlier times, although the oldest *mawlid* text known is from the twelfth century. The musical performance of the birth of the Prophet calls for a solo voice and is also backed by a male chorus who sing in unison *maqam*-based melodies. The texts incorporate poetry, hymns and prayers together with the charming custom of blessing those taking part in the festivity.

Hymns in praise of the Prophet (*na't* or *madih*)

The first *madih* or praise was written by Hassan Ibn Thabit who was the scribe of Prophet Muhammad. From that evolved a fruitful tradition of poetry, song writing and performing. A Sufi poet named al-Busiri wrote a large poem of 182 verses which he named *Al-burdah* (a reference to the clothing of the Prophet). This poem became the model for all subsequent praises. Again, performance of these praises is by a solo singer and a male chorus, who also accompany themselves with drums. The dialogue, as it were, between the soloist and the choir may involve the soloist in improvising, elaborating further on the melody, which is based on the *maqam* tradition.

Sufi worship

The naming of God (*dhikr*)

This is music closely linked with Sufism (*suf* = wool; *sufi* = wearer of woollen cloak, mystic). Sufism arose within Islam during the eighth and ninth centuries. The main purpose of Sufism is to achieve mystical union with Allah through ecstatic worship. In order to reach this goal, trance-inducing music and dance are not only allowed but encouraged. In addition to singing and dancing, the *dhikr* involves a characteristic breathing technique enabling the performers to rhythmically pronounce God's name or its equivalent, *hu* (He), as well as his attributes. This is performed with ever increasing ecstasy, leading to its climax, the *hadrah* (God's presence), when the participants are with increasing tempo repeatedly pronouncing the words 'Allah!' or '*Hu!*'. The singing style is an amalgamation of the contemplative with the ecstatic, requiring virtuosic performing ability. It is a profoundly communal ceremony to be shared by all, as even listening to music, that is ecstatic listening, is also a legitimate part of Sufi worship.

The Whirling Dervishes

The Dervishes are an off-shoot of Sufism, a brotherhood which was founded in the twelfth century and then spread throughout Islam during the period of the Ottoman empire to the Balkans and North Africa. The Mevlevi circle-dance is danced as part of a larger ceremony which includes recitation from the Qur'an and hymns as well as songs and instrumental ensemble playing based on the *maqam rast* (g a b♭ c' d' e♭ f g').

The dance is characterized by the dancers having their hands held out to the side with the right hands turned upwards and the left hands downwards, while in their long white dresses (consisting of jackets and long skirts) they whirl in two circles around a central solo dancer who then breaks the circles in order to join the rest, who form themselves into one circle. It is one of the great ecstatic dances in the world, which during its long history has been in turn banned and reinstated.

Postlude

At present we are witnessing a conflict between one of the great musical cultures of mankind and the modern Western light music industry. The pop song craze is in direct contrast to the tradition-bound practice of Arabic music. Radio programmes are dominatingly pop-oriented, whether in Baghdad or Cairo. The world seems to be unable to live in mutual respect and peace, yet it seems to be united in listening and dancing to the amplified sound of pop from Tokyo to New York. One wonders to what such a common base might lead. Already in 1950 Bernhard Lewis, in his book *The Arabs in History*, clearly saw the situation when he wrote:

In these problems of readjustments the Arab people have a choice of several paths; they may submit to one or other of the contending versions of modern civilization that are offered to them, merging their own culture and identity in a larger and dominating whole; or they may try to turn their back upon the West and all its works . . . or finally – and for this the removal of the irritant of foreign interference is a prerequisite – they may succeed in renewing their society from within, meeting the West on the terms of equal co-operation, absorbing something of both its science and humanism, not only in shadow but in substance, in a harmonious balance with their own inherited tradition.[3]

The Indian Subcontinent *Introduction / Rhythm / Melody / Harmony / Instruments / General Considerations: Religions: Hinduism, Buddhism, Sikhism, Islam; Qawwali; dance and music; Ragamala paintings.*

Once a King asked a Sage:

KING: O sinless One! Be good enough to teach me the methods of image-making.

SAGE: One who does not know the laws of painting can never understand the laws of image-making.

KING: Be then good enough, O Sage, to teach me the laws of painting.

SAGE: But it is difficult to understand the laws of painting without any knowledge of the technique of dancing.

KING: Kindly instruct me then in the art of dancing.

SAGE: This is difficult to understand without a thorough knowledge of instrumental music.

KING: Teach me then, O Sage, the laws of instrumental music.

SAGE: But the laws of instrumental music cannot be learned without a deep knowledge of the art of vocal music.

KING: If vocal music be the source of all arts, reveal to me, then O Sage, the laws of vocal music.

INDIAN TALE.

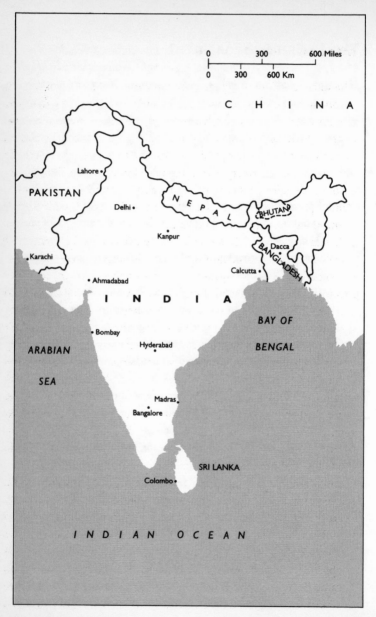

The Indian Subcontinent

Introduction

The vastness of India – 3,287,590 sq km with a population of 882.5m – confronts the outsider with a bewildering variety of languages, religions and customs and with one of the oldest civilizations on earth, which has impressed its influence well beyond its shores. Around 3000 BC the people living near the Indian river – originally known as Sindhu river – were named Hindu by the Persians on account of their inability to pronounce the s sound. It is this name, Hindu, passed on via Greece to the rest of the world, which came to mean anything pertaining to India.

It was here in the Indus valley (in what is now Pakistan) that India's first civilization flourished. Its disintegration by 1750 BC weakened its standing against the Aryan tribes who invaded the country between 1500 and 1200 BC. The Aryans eventually settled and developed cities along the Ganges valley. Their language, Sanskrit, became the language of the country for 2000 years and their Vedic religion the foundation of Brahminism. By the sixth century BC two religions, Buddhism and Jainism, emerged and established themselves. The first Hindu empire was established in the fourth century BC under the Maurya dynasty. By the third century BC more than two-thirds of the Indian subcontinent was under their rule. In time, Mauryan domination also disintegrated, but by the fourth century AD, the north was again united under a new dynasty, the Gupta dynasty. One of the most far-reaching events, however, came when, from around the tenth century AD onwards, Islam began its invasions of India and from the thirteenth to the nineteenth century ruled over a major part of India, which profoundly affected the Hindu and Buddhist states. The first Muslim sultanate was established in Delhi in 1129. In AD 1526 the Mughal empire was established under Babur – a descendant of Genghis Khan – who became the emperor of India. His dynasty ruled until 1858. During this time two major forces emerged which led to the eventual downfall of the Mughal rule: the first was the Hindu Marathas, who in the late seventeenth and eighteenth centuries made attempts at upsetting the fortunes of the Muslim Mughals; the second was the increasing Western, above all British, presence in India which finally helped the defeat of the Mughals, but at a cost to the Marathas, as they became subjugated to British rule. A further consequence of these events was the grotesque imposition of British values on the complex Indian society structured in a caste system. The largely upper-caste Indians, to give them credit, eventually turned against the rulers and after a long struggle succeeded in gaining independence in 1947. The Muslim League insisted on a separate Muslim nation. This was realized by separating the Indian empire into Pakistan, Bangladesh and India as we know them today.

What is striking is that, despite all these momentous events in its long history, India succeeded in cultivating and preserving its unique voice in the arts in which music (*sangita*) plays a major role. In Indian culture, music refers not only to the art of sound, but also to dancing, singing and playing an instrument. These are all incorporated in the Indian word *sangita*. It is also closely related to myth, religion and philosophy. The special position held by music in Hindu thinking is based on the belief that sound had an important role in the creation of the world. The god of the male creative force, Shiva, among several other attributes, is closely associated with music and dance. Indeed, one of his best-known images is as *Lord of the Dance* (*Nataraja*). In his right hand he traditionally holds a drum (*damru*), which is both the symbol of creation and the instrument through which the end of the cosmic age is announced. Shiva danced his dance of creation to the rhythmic beats of the drum. Thus, one of the most fundamental components of both music and dance, rhythm, is seen as having paramount importance. Hindus speak of two types of sound, one audible and the other inaudible, that is, abstracted sounds like the Pythagorean 'music of the spheres'. Accordingly they refer to struck (*ahata*), sound, which is audible, and unstruck (*anahata*), inaudible sound. The unstruck sound can only be heard by those who have achieved consciousness to such a level that they became one with the cosmos. They can hear the unchangeable numero-musical patterns which are the basis of existence. One could argue that in Indian culture the secular and the sacred are closely linked or at least tend to overlap. A telling contemporary evidence of this relationship is in Ravi Shankar's autobiography, where he tells us that every musical training session began with worship. It should also be noted that one of the most important Hindu symbols is the sacred syllable *Om* (or *Aum*). This is the sound of God, the origin of all sounds. Music, thus seen, has a religious connotation.

The folksong or village music tradition in India is likely to have developed as a need for non-sacred music, in contrast to sacred music, which was largely performed by priests. But even in folk music the subject matter is often 'sacred', being concerned with marriage, birth, death or with references, in the form of legends, to the deities, as is the case in the folk music of Bengal in East India. Even the subject of profane love is often embedded in religious references, in which Shiva or his female counterparts, Parvati and/ or Devi are evoked. The classical musical tradition of Indian music was cultivated in various courts up and down the country. Indeed, Indian classical music was for and practised by an élitist milieu. All artists were employed by maharajas in whose courts music was not only cultivated but preserved more or less without modifications through several generations. The art of music making was often passed from father to son. When the Muslims established themselves in North India this custom soon became the norm. Increasingly performing music and dance was left to professional families and their students. Monotheistic Islam did not share the Hindu belief in music's divine origins and its happy relations with a host of gods and goddesses. What was seen by the Hindus as spiritual and a way of self-realization was seen, at best, by the Muslim orthodoxy as entertainment usually practised by inferiors. Consequently the social standing of musicians became more restricted in Muslim India. Fortunately, rulers like opulence and, in time, in the Mughal courts there evolved one of the great Hindu-influenced Islamic art traditions.

By the sixteenth century two classical music cultures were

distinguishable in India – Hindustani in the north and Karnatic in the south. They are both based on the same rules and systems, but with differences in detail. In summary, from its earliest sources, the historical development of music in India broadly falls into the following main periods: the *Vedic* (second – according to some, fourth – millennium BC to second century AD); the *Classic era* (second century AD to the Islamic invasions of *c.* tenth century); the *Islamic period*, which reached its climax with the Mughal era and saw the division of Indian music into the southern and northern styles (eleventh to eighteenth centuries); *British colonization*, leading to the modern era (eighteenth to twentieth centuries).

Vedic hymns

Written in archaic Sanskrit about 1500 BC, the Vedas (divine knowledge) consist of four main collections, comprising hymns, rituals, sacrificial worship of gods, et cetera. The style of the musical content is similar to the Christian tradition's chant, whether Gregorian or otherwise. Being a sacred Aryan source of wisdom, it was cultivated by the élite of the caste structure introduced by the Aryans in order to secure their own supremacy.

The correct intonation of these Vedic hymns was of supreme importance, as any deviation from the sacred rules was believed to upset the stability of the universe. The performance of the Vedic hymns falls into two styles: *Rig Veda*, which employs a limited range of notes (basically three), and *Sama Veda*, where a much wider range of notes (up to an octave) were and still are used by Brahmins.

Classical era

Most of the fundamental theoretical works on which Hindu music is based were created during this period. One of the oldest books written on art is the *Bharata Natya Shastra* (*Bharata's Dramaturgy*), allegedly written by a legendary figure, Bharata, who may have lived any time between the second century BC and the third century

AD. His book is venerated as the most important source on Indian music, dance, drama and aesthetics. It was not until 1950 that an English translation of it emerged through the dedicated scholarship of Manomohan Ghosh. The basic tenets of the *Bharata Natya Shastra* are that all arts are seen to be related to each other and that the source of all the arts is vocal music. Vocal music is seen as the most natural primal sound-producing media and therefore man-made instruments should imitate as closely as possible the human voice. Bharata stressed that the role of the arts is to induce emotion (*rasa*), to evoke certain moods and associations. Accordingly he named eight archetypal emotions with their corresponding deities and colours (for example, Shringar ↦ Love ↦ Vishnu ↦ Light Green; or Adbhuta ↦ Wonder ↦ Brahma ↦ Yellow). Later theorists agreed to add others (Rasa, Shanta ↦ Serenity ↦ Naraqana ↦ White). These states of emotion became the prototypes of Indian arts. Bharata, moreover, examined topics such as scales, modality, rhythm, tuning and instruments, and their classification into four main groups are all discussed in this remarkable compendium of learning, whose main aim was to deal with dramatic theory, but which ended up by embracing most of the arts and doing great service to Indian music.

One of the most important writings on music after Bharata's is Matanga's *Bhraddesi* (*Country Languages*) dating from the eighth or ninth century. In it the concept of the *raga* (Sanskrit for colour) is introduced for the first time together with the explanation of Tantric yoga theories.

The Islamic period

With the Islamic domination of North India began a new development in Indian music, as it was strong enough to maintain its identity whilst fusing Islamic elements into its own tradition in a superlative way. Similarly the conquerors themselves showed adaptability to a surprising degree, as the Muslim rulers not only tolerated but even encouraged Hindu arts.

Two major theorists stand out in this period: Sarangadeva (1210–47), who in the seven chapters of his book *Sangeet – Ratnakara* not only discusses theories of music, including musical instruments, but gives insights into the thinking of other theorists such as Narada of the seventh century, who, among other things, introduced the idea of male and female types of *ragas*; and Amire Khusro, who was thirteen when Sarangadeva died, was the first Muslim theorist of India. He was an all-round courtier who represents the very best of the Muslim intellectual tradition in India. He thought that Indian music was the finest of all music. He became a legendary figure and, like so many such figures, many ideas and inventions are attributed to him which one should regard with some scepticism. All the same he is likely to have been the inaugurator of the *qawwali*, a Muslim devotional song style, and the *tarana*, a fast vocal style based on using syllables, which for a long time seemed to be meaningless, but it was discovered in the 1960s that when the syllables were joined together they had mystical meanings in Persian.

There were numerous theorists and practical musicians of fame who set out to explain and illustrate further the complex nature of music and music making, but what is quite remarkable is the Mughals' own attitude towards India's art which, during their heyday, produced something of an equivalent of the European Renaissance in India. It is evident that the Mughals found Hindu culture congenial and were able to absorb it into the Muslim way of thinking with surprising flexibility in spite of the fact that the ideological differences, if not conflicts, between the two great cultures were considerable. One of the master musicians who served in the court of a most significant Mughal, Akbar (1556–1605), was Miyan Tansen (*c.* 1520–90). He was one of the most revered singers and instrumental players of his time. He was an enlightened Muslim who also worshipped in Hindu temples and gave his five children both Muslim and Hindu names. As a theorist he is largely remembered as one who codified almost four hundred *ragas* of which some were composed by him and are performed to this day. Akbar appointed him to his court and elevated him as one of the *Nara Ratna* (Nine Gems of the

Empire). His appreciation went even further when he named Tansen as the 'Monarch of Music'. In poetry he was eulogized as the 'Lord of Music'. The Mughal's enlightened despotism, which the French Renaissance writer Rabelais believed to be the only recommendable way of ruling, was carried on in the hands of the son and grandson of Akbar. The last of the great Mughals, Bahadur Shah II, was not only the emperor of India but a musician and poet, who became famous under the pen name *Zafar*. After his death in 1862 India had to wait for a long time before someone else of his calibre emerged.

The Muslim monarchs ruled over not only the North but a substantial part of the south of India as well, right down to Mysore. Yet South India firmly resisted the influence of Islam and succeeded in maintaining its own tradition, which is profoundly based on ancient temple culture and the hymn tradition associated with it. It has already been pointed out that Karnatic music is basically similar to Hindustani music, but with differences in detail. For instance, ornamentation in Karnatic music is much more abundantly in evidence than in Hindustani music. There is also a marked tendency to sharpen the melody a fraction when it rises up and to flatten it when it descends. As H. S. Power put it in his essay 'A Historical and Comparative Approach to the Classification of Ragas': 'The South Indian system on the whole tends to generalize ragas in the direction of scales while the North Indian system on the whole tends to particularize them in the direction of tunes.'[1]

South Indian pieces of music tend to be shorter with less scope for improvisation. Instrumental music is entirely secondary to vocal music and it is more of a custom to clap the rhythm during performances. All that being said, it is not the differences that are remarkable, but the similarities between the Karnatic and Hindustani musical traditions. It shows strongly shared historical and spiritual foundations.

British colonization

The Mughals were succeeded by the British, who did not possess the cultural interest and assimilating genius of the Mughals. On the contrary, apart from a few exceptional men with academic interests, the British were unable and unwilling to understand Indian art, which they considered inferior to their own. The picture has changed since then quite considerably. Apart from the Hindus' ingenious absorption of the harmonium, to be discussed under instruments in this chapter, it is hardly possible to detect anything of real value concerning music which came out of the British colonization of India. It was a time for India to consolidate its great past and achievements leading to its eventual independence and regained pride in its cultural identity.

Rhythm

In general parlance the Sanskrit word *tala* (or *tal* = measure of time) may be defined as rhythm. It could be argued that *laya* could be nearer in expressing the meanings of both rhythm and tempo. In Hindustani music, the root meaning of the *tala* is to do with hand-beating the rhythm of a composition, that is to keep the time cycles in a composition under control. As such it is now firmly associated with a way of denoting a system of rhythmic organization in the same way as the *raga* is a reference to melodic organization.

Every *tala* contains a set number of beats which can be divided up into bars or, more accurately, cycles of beat groups. For example, a *dadra* has six beats (*matras*) in each unit with a slight stress on the first beat (see Fig. 1).

| 1 | 2 | 3 | 4 | 5 | 6 | | 1 | 2 | 3 | 4 | 5 | 6 | | etc. |

Fig. 1

In order to distinguish between smaller units or subdivisions with differing accents or stresses, the following technical differentiations evolved: *tali* (stressed or clapped) and *behali* or *khali* (unstressed or empty). The *khali* is indicated with a graceful wave of the hand or, when written, with the sign 'O'. The *khali* is another way of keeping control of the rhythmic flow of a *tala*. It serves as much as a compass bearing, that is to say as a means of finding your way, as the *tali* itself. The sign 'X' ranks the sum of the first *matras* of a *tal* (see Fig. 2).

$>$ = stress

O = unstressed or empty

X = the sum of a matras

Fig. 2

A *vibhag* denotes the sections within a *tala*, thus Fig. 3 consists of two *vibhag* sections each consisting of two *matras*. Thus the *dadra tal* is shown in Fig. 3.

Fig. 3

The possibilities of structuring *talas* with various numbers of *matras* are numerous. The most popular *talas* in Indian music are 6, 7, 8, 10, 12, 14, 16. Every *tala* has its own characteristic identity based on the distribution of stresses or non-stresses. For a Western listener the examples given in Figs. 1, 2 and 3 are easy, as the basic rhythm is symmetrical and familiar. The difficulty starts when the beats are asymmetrical, as is the case, for instance, with the grouping of 7 in *Rupak tala* in Fig. 4.

Fig. 4 Tintal tala

In Western music one is also used to the idea of brief basic rhythmic patterns (for example, 2/4, 3/4, 4/4 and their compound variations, such as 6/4). In Indian music a *tala* may be of substantial length and complexity, as is the case with *Tintal tala*, which consists of sixteen beats (see Fig. 5).

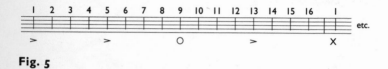

Fig. 5

By changing the pattern of a *tala*, one changes its character and therefore its original evocative power to something else. See, for example, the *Jhaptal tala* in Fig. 6(a) and (b).

(a)

Jhaptal tala

1	2	3	4	5	6	7	8	9	10	1
>		>			O		>			X

1	2	3	4	5	6	7	8	9	10	1
>		O		>		>		O		X

(b)

Fig. 6 Jhaptal tala

It should be remembered that Indian rhythm is additive, as opposed to Western rhythm, which is based on equal divisions of beats. Fig. 7 is an example to illustrate this point with the *Jhaptal tala* again.

$$\frac{2}{4} \quad + \quad \frac{3}{4} \quad + \quad \frac{2}{4} \quad + \quad \frac{3}{4} \quad = \quad \frac{10}{4}$$

Fig. 7

Both the northern and the Karnatic music share this additive approach to rhythm. The *tala* patterns are usually fixed groups of bars (*avarta*) which are then repeated again and again. For example, Fig. 8 is a *Dhamar tala* consisting of fourteen beats which are grouped in the following pattern:

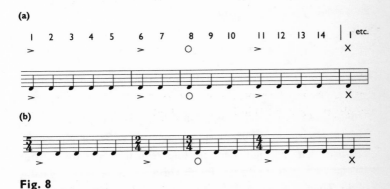

Fig. 8

It was this additive approach to rhythm which fascinated, among other modern composers, Philip Glass, who declared that his encounter with Indian music was 'a revelation'. He explained his understanding of the difference between Western and Indian thinking in terms of rhythm and time in the following way: 'In Western music we divide time – as if you were to bake a length of time and slice it the way you slice a loaf of bread. In Indian music (and all the non-Western music with which I'm familiar), you take small units, or "beats" and string them together to make up larger time values.'[2] When polyrhythmic combinations are performed the most complex textures are possible and are executed with great virtuosity.

Structurally the first unit of a *tala* cycle can be used for both the opening and the ending of a composition. In fact that is one of the main characteristics of Hindustani music. Another typical feature is that their *talas* are characteristic entities; they stand as individuals because of their pitch structure or melodic pattern. In Karnatic music a *tala* may have several variants, which, of course, adds to the complexities but also to the vast numbers of nuances between which a sophisticated Karnatic listener can differentiate.

The commonest of all the *talas* is perhaps the *Tintal*, with sixteen beats. It is believed among Indian musicians that once this pattern is mastered all the others may follow relatively easily. It consists of four *matras* per *vibhag* (section).

1	2	3	4	5	6	7	8	9	10	11	12	13	14	15	16		1	etc.
>				>				O				>					X	

Fig. 9

It would be a mistake to think this to be four times four or twice eight bars, reflecting a Western interpretation of *Tintal*. Notice, for instance, that although there are four regular groups the actually accentuated units are three; the third group is *kahli*. The very name of the *Tintal* is a compound of *tin* = three + *tal* = beat. One should also remember that the main beats are not necessarily emphasized; they represent a refined structure, not a strait-jacket.

Finally one must touch upon speed in Indian music. In India speed is specified in relative terms and was originally based on heartbeats. In both North and South India musicians speak of slow (*vilambit*), medium (*madya*) and fast (*drut*) tempi. When *ati* is prefixed to *vilambit* or *drut*, it will mean very slow or very fast respectively. In Karnatic music, however, the established *tala* tempo, that is the basic counts, are not allowed to be tampered with during a performance. Around the main beat lots of things may and do happen, such as the doubling of speed of the melody, but without disturbing the main speed of the *tala* counts. This is not strictly the case with Hindustani music. *Tintal*, like *Ektal* (twelve beats) can be played at any tempo.

Melody

The complex melodic foundations of Indian music are the *ragas*. The colloquial Hindi form *rag* is also used. The Sanskrit root of *raga* is *ranga*, which means 'colour'. Therefore *raga* refers to melodic colour or atmosphere. *Ragas* are more melodic archetypes than scales, although for the purpose of an introductory study it might be useful to look at *ragas* as a combination of notes which make up melody-like scale patterns. The pattern of a *raga* is usually presented with both its upward and downward moves (*aroha*/*avaroha* = ascent/ descent). This establishes the character of the *raga* in terms of the contour of the pitches which are used or omitted. The two examples in Fig. 10 illustrate when a melody/scale is gapless and another when the melody/scale is constructed with gaps.

(a)

(b)

Fig. 10

Each *raga* has its own individual emotional and associative meanings, which include the changing seasons and different times of the day. Thus the example in Fig. 10(a), called *Bilaval*, is a late morning *raga* and is said to be signifying joy and affection. Fig. 10(b), *Megha* (lit. 'cloud'), is also associated with joy, but on a rainy day, presumably during the monsoon rains. Although nowadays *ragas* of all kinds are played at any time for the love of it, originally they were meant to be performed only at the appropriate times. To illustrate this point, here is a charming anecdote from the time of the great Mughal Akbar, when we are told the legendary court musician Tansen sang a night *raga* (*Malakosh*: b d e f a b b a g e d b) at midday with such eloquence that he was surrounded by darkness. We are also told that on one occasion he saved himself from fire by playing the *Megha raga* (a *raga* associated with water) which immediately extinguished the flames. Anecdotes like these show how the master musicians were revered for the perfection of their performances as well as illustrating the associative nature of *ragas*. Ravi Shankar describes these associative moods with the insight of one of India's foremost performers in the following illuminating way:

Each *raga* has to have its own psychological temperament in relation to its tempo, or speed. Many of the heavy-serious *ragas* such as *Darbari Kanada* or *Asavari* should be sung or played in slow tempo. Others, such as *Adana* or *Jaunpuri*, which express a lighter mood, are best rendered in a medium or medium-fast tempo.

The performing arts in India – music, dance, drama, and even poetry – are based on the concept of *nava rasa*, or the 'nine sentiments'. Each artistic creation is supposed to be dominated by one of these nine sentiments. The more closely the notes of a *raga* conform to the expression of one single idea or emotion, the more overwhelming the effect of the *raga*. This is the magic of our music – its hypnotic, intense singleness of mood. It is now generally agreed that there are nine of these principal sentiments, although some scholars number them as eight or ten.

In the generally acknowledged order of these sentiments, the first is *shringara*, a romantic and erotic sentiment filled with longing for an absent lover. It contains both the physical and mental aspects of love and is sometimes known as *adi* (original) *rasa*, because it represents the universal creative force.

Hasya is the second *rasa*, comic, humorous, and laughter-provoking. It can be shown through syncopated rhythmic patterns or an interplay of melody and rhythm between singer and accompanist, or between sitarist and *tabla* player, causing amusement and laughter.

The third *rasa* is *karuna*, pathetic, tearful, sad, expressing extreme loneliness and longing for either god or lover. (Hindus tend to elevate mortal love into a divine love, so the beloved can be an ordinary human being or often a god, such as Krishna or Shiva.)

Raudra is fury or excited anger. This *rasa* is often used in drama, but in music it can portray the fury of nature as in a thunderstorm. Musically, it can be shown through many fast, 'trembling' ornaments, producing a scary, vibrating effect in the low tones. (But such *rasas*, far from frightening an Indian, excite in him a solemn reverence for the Divine in nature.)

Veera expresses the sentiments of heroism, bravery, majesty, and glory, grandeur, and a dignified kind of excitement. If it is overdone, it can turn into *raudra*.

Bhayanaka, the sixth *rasa*, is frightening or fearful. It is difficult to express in music through one instrument (though a symphony orchestra could do it easily) unless there is a song-text to bring out its exact meaning.

Vibhatsa – repugnant or disgusting – is also difficult to show through music. This *rasa* and *bhayanaka* are used more for drama than music.

The eighth *rasa*, *abdhuta*, shows wonderment and amazement, exhilaration and even a little fear, as when one undergoes a strange new experience. It can be expressed by extreme speed or some technical marvels that, in certain kinds of singing or playing, provoke amazement.

The last *rasa* is *shanta rasa* – peace, tranquillity and relaxation.

Some people mention a tenth *rasa*, *bhakti*, which is devotional, spiritual, and almost religious in feeling; but actually, this *rasa* is a combination of *shanta*, *karuna* and *adbhuta*.[3]

In Indian music the *ragas* may consist of up to seven pitches (*svara*). Each of these has a name (*sadj, risabh, gandha, madyam, pancam, dhaivat* and *nisad*), but in practical use only their first syllables are pronounced (*sa, ri, ga, ma, pa, dha, ni*) in a similar way to what is known in the West as the sol-fa system (do, re, mi, fa, so, la, ti, do). To be familiar with what is the equivalent to sol-fa (*sargam*) is very useful for practising singing. Each *svara* is also associated with sound and pictorial images:

sa – peacock's cry
ri – cow calling her calf
ga – goat's bleat
ma – heron's cry
pa – cuckoo's song
dha – horse's neigh
ni – elephant's trumpeting

We now turn to a crucial aspect of the *ragas* and of Indian music in general. During the performance of *ragas*, notes smaller than semitones are used in the whole work. These are microtones. The term microtone is preferable to the quarter note, as often the note performed is less or more than a quarter note. These smallest pitch nuances so characteristic of Indian music are called *srutis*. It was the thirteenth-century theorist Sarangadeva who worked out the twenty-two *srutis* within the framework of the seven-note scale patterns. This was further studied and conceptualized by such eminent figures as Bhatkhande during the first half of this century. These subdivisions are illustrated here in a useful chart (see Fig. 11).

In order to understand, but above all to hear, Indian music properly, it is essential to become familiar with the sound of these microtones and the subtleties which they represent in the unfolding of a largely improvised music. It is for this reason that some commentators on the state of Indian music have expressed their fear that the nonmicrotonal invasion of Western music is likely to be detrimental to the sensitivity of perceiving smaller note values than the semitones; this is, after all, one of the major characteristics of both Arabic and Indian music. There are over 250 *ragas* in use of which not even a few of the most popular are familiar to music lovers in the West.

What has been discussed so far applies to both Karnatic and northern Indian music. In northern India nowadays there is, however, a basic group of *ragas*, ten in number, which are called *thaat*. This codification of the North Indian *ragas* was the result of the

Western Notes	Indian Notes (swaras)	Indian Microtones (srutis)	Names of Microtones
C	SA	1	
C# or D♭	RE♭	2, 3, 4	(1) Tivra, (2) Kumadvati, (3) Manda, (4) Chandovati
D	RE	5	(5) Dayavati, (6) Ranjini, (7) Raktika
D# or E♭	GA♭	6, 7	
E	GA	8, 9	(8) Rudri, (9) Krodhi
F	MA	10	
F#	MA#	11, 12, 13	(10) Vajrika, (11) Prasarini, (12) Priti, (13) Marjani
G	PA	14	
G# or A♭	DHA♭	15, 16, 17	(14) Kshiti, (15) Rakta, (16) Sandipini, (17) Alapini
A	DHA	18	(18) Madanti, (19) Rohini, (20) Ramya
A# or B♭	NI♭	19, 20	
B	NI	21, 22	(21) Ugra, (22) Kshobini

Source: Massey, Reginald and Jamila, *The Music of India*, Kahn and Averill, London, 1993, p. 21.

Fig. 11

work of India's great modern theorist, Bhatkhande. The *thaat* system differs markedly from the Karnatic tradition, which maintained the old seventy-two *melas* (*melakarta* system) and the stupendous collections of *janya ragas* (derivative *ragas*). But the matter of which system is better is far from settled. As Ravi Shankar puts it in his autobiography *My Music, My Life*:

This system was finally classified [at this point he refers to the Karnatic system] in the seventeenth century by Pandit Venkatamukhi in his Chaturdaudi Prakashika. According to the present Hindustani system of the North, there are ten primary scales called *thaats*. Unlike the South with its uninterrupted, continuous musical tradition, the North has no one system of classification of the scales or primary *ragas*. At the turn of this century (that is 250 years after Venkatamukhi) an attempt was made by V. N. Bhatkhande to recodify the system into ten *thaats*. I myself, however, as well as a number of other musicians, do not feel that these ten scales adequately accommodate a great variety of *ragas*, for there are many *ragas* that use notes not contained in these ten *thaats*. We therefore think it is more reasonable and scientific to follow the old (seventy-two-scale) *melakarta* system of the South because it can sustain almost any *raga*, no matter how unusual its ascending and descending structures.[4]

Clearly the conflict here is between the rich varieties and individuality inherent in the old system versus the pragmatic reductionist impersonality of the *thaat* system. Ravi Shankar and his fellow musicians rightly stress the compositional presence of a real *raga* versus a mere lifeless scale pattern. In other words a *raga* is already a composition while a *thaat* is not. In Western terms, the scale of c major becomes something via, say, Beethoven, while on its own it is lifeless. A *raga* on the other hand is already a compositional expression in a way as expressed in Fig. 12(b). It is hoped that Fig. 12(a) and (b) will illustrate by musical means the problem inherent in the two systems: (a) is a *thaat*, (b) is the *melakarta* tradition as adapted to the finale of Beethoven's Symphony No. 5.

Fig. 12 (a) C major scale

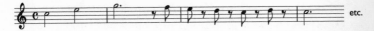

Fig. 12 (b) Finale, Beethoven Symphony No. 5

Be that as it may, the *thaats* on which all other possible variants of North Indian *ragas* are founded are:

	Ascending	Descending
Kalyan	C D E F♯ G A B (C)	B A G F♯ E D C
Bilava	C D E F G A B (C)	
Khamaj	C D E F G A B♭ (C)	
Bhaivar	C D♭ E F G A♭ B (C)	
Marva	C D E F♯ G A B (C)	
Purvi	C D♭ E F♯ G A♭ B (C)	
Kafi	C D E♭ F G A B♭ (C)	
Asavari	C D E♭ F G A♭ B♭ (C)	
Bhairavi	C D♭ E♭ F G A♭ B♭ (C)	
Todi	C D♭ E♭ F♯ G A♭ B (C)	

All these scales have their Karnatic equivalents. For example, the *Bhairavi* (*Hanumantodi*) *raga* is one on which musicians in South India practise their *alamkaras* (ornamentations). As can be seen from the following list, apart from four *ragas*, all the other *ragas* have their equivalent in Western Church modes:

Kalyan	=	Lydian
Bilava	=	Ionian
Khamaj	=	Mixolydian
Kafi	=	Dorian
Asavari	=	Aeolian
Bhairavi	=	Phrygian

In a performance of a *raga* there are certain technical features which an observant music listener may notice, but without necessarily knowing their exact functions and meanings. An instrumental performance, usually involving a sitar or sarod, a tambura and a pair of tablas, would begin with a prelude-like introductory passage called the *alap*. This gives the foundation of a piece by introducing the most important notes of the *raga*, starting from its lowest to its highest register. This exploratory introduction leads to the unfolding of the potential material with increased use of decorative or grace notes, called *gamaks*. The sections of this introductory material are punctuated by *mohras*. These are points where the music is momentarily played in strict rhythm before returning to a new section in free rhythm. The *alap* is followed by a section *jor*, a solo passage in regular rhythm played without tabla, leading to what is called *gats*, a set of improvisations based on a chosen *tal* and usually with tabla accompaniment. Finally a fast rhythmic finale with tabla completes the work. This section is named *jhalla*. To conclude we now turn to one of the most obvious aspects of Indian music making, which is the presence of the drone.

The drone has harmonic implications which will be discussed in the next section of this chapter. In this section it is only the melodic implication which will be considered. Each *raga* is accompanied by a drone. This is normally achieved by the constant sounding of the basic note (*sa*) as well as the fifth note of the *raga* (*pa*). There are three possible drone patterns played on the tambura (see the section on instruments in this chapter). These are determined by the pitch structure of the *ragas*. Fig. 13 illustrates these.

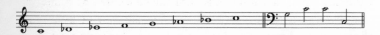

Fig. 13 (a) When the scale of a *raga* includes a fifth

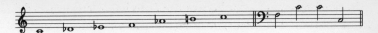

Fig. 13 (b) When the scale of a *raga* has no fifth but includes a fourth

Fig. 13 (c) When the *raga* has neither a fifth nor a fourth, the major seventh is used

The drone gives a static gravitational tonal centre to the whole composition from which melodies and rhythms move away and to which they return. The infinite and the finite, the permanent and the temporal are simultaneously evoked in a contemplative way, as contemplation is one of the most distinctive aspects of Indian life and music. As it is written in *The Dhammapada* (*The Path of Truth*), a collection of aphorisms illustrating the Buddhist moral system (*c.* third century BC):

> Better than a hundred years lived in ignorance
> without contemplation, is one single day of life
> lived in wisdom and in deep contemplation.[5]

Harmony

Contrary to the Western preoccupation with highly developed harmonic sense, Indian music is primarily concerned with melody and rhythm. Thus it is the linear, intervallic use of notes and not the vertical superimposition of notes which dominates India's musical thinking. In the largely modal and partly pentatonic world of Indian music a sense of key is not as strong as in the Western tradition. The *sa* is not a 'tonic' in the harmonic meaning of the term, consequently in Indian music harmony does not figure in any significant form. In the modal world of India one contemplates the mode and mood of a *raga*. The Western tendency towards relentless changes and juxtapositions (modulations) is entirely alien to the Indian classical tradition. There are, nevertheless, harmonic events in Indian music which are in evidence even if by accident. For instance, when a drone is played, the drone itself creates harmonies c–g, g–c, f–c, c–c or b–c, as well as those notes which are played as part of the improvised and ornate *ragas* over the drone. These pitch encounters will have their harmonic implication in both their consonant and dissonant forms. But, whereas India evolved one of the most sophisticated melodic and rhythmic musical cultures in the world, it has neglected harmony as it was not felt to be relevant to its musical philosophy.

Rhythmic polyphony and, short of a better term, colour-polyphony, that is layers of sound colours created by the individual timbres of different instruments, are, of course, part of Indian musical expressions, but polyphony of the kind one understands in the West (say, in the music of Bach) is alien to the musical tradition of India. This should be interpreted neither as a loss nor as a gain. It is just different and the musical style of India is entirely self sufficient as it is.

In the next section we will examine some of the most characteristic instruments on which Indian music is played. As the nature of classifying instruments has been discussed and established in Chapters 1 and 2, the understanding of these is from now on taken for granted. On the other hand new instruments in each category will be commented upon.

Instruments

The four types of instrument (*vadya*) as classified by Indian theorists are: *chana* (idiophones); *avanada* (membraphones); *tanto* (chordophones); and *susir* (aerophones). These will be considered in turn.

Percussion instruments (idiophones and membraphones)

Idiophones

Several types of idiophone are used in India both for pure instrumental performances and for dance. The most popular idiophones are:

(a) rattle;
(b) clapper;
(c) jingles;
(d) bells;
(e) cymbals (small and dome-shaped [*manjara*]; larger variants [*jhanj* or *kartal*]);
(f) gong;
(g) Jew's harp;
(h) *jaltarang*.

Of these, the clapper, jingles, the Jew's harp and *jaltarang* are to be described.

Clapper This is basically a substitution for body or hand clapping. The clapper is made of two or more pieces of wood, bone or shells which are fixed at one end while the other ends are left free. When these are rhythmically shaken they produce a clapping sound. They can be found worldwide. The oldest are from Sumerian and Egyptian civilizations (3200 BC). In India clappers are used in ensemble playing and in accompanying dances. In medieval and Renaissance Europe they were used by lepers in order to warn people of their coming.

Jingles The nature of jingles has already been discussed in Chapter 1. They are most effectively used by Indian dancers, who fix jingles on their legs in a similar way to and for a similar purpose as their African counterparts.

The Jew's harp Its name may be a corruption of jaw's harp. It is a simple, but sonorous instrument consisting of a metal (or wooden) horseshoe-shaped frame to which at one end a flexible thin plate is fixed, with its other end being left free. The narrower end of the Jew's harp is placed in between the teeth of the player who plucks the flexible thin plate (lamella) which then vibrates and resonates in the mouth of the player. The sound thus produced is basically a buzzing monotone, but with some possibilities in producing overtones by changing the position of cheeks and lips. This elementary small sound maker is especially put to good use in Rajasthan, where it appears in instrumental ensembles.

Jaltarang This fascinating instrument is based on the principle which some readers may remember from their schooldays when a series of milk bottles were filled with carefully worked-out volumes of water which, when struck with a stick, made sounds at various pitches. Similarly the *jaltarang* consists of a number of porcelain bowls of graded sizes into which the relevant amount of water is poured. These bowls are then struck with a pair of sticks. Alternatively the player may use his wetted fingers in order to rub the rim of the bowls giving a characteristically sonorous vibrato sound.

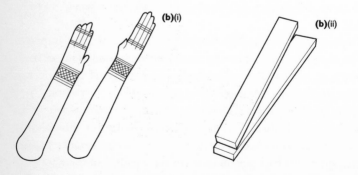

Fig. 14 Idiophones

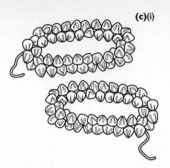

(c)(i)

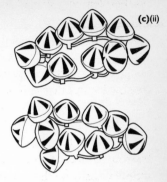

(c)(ii)

(c)(iii)

(g)

(h)

Fig. 14 Idiophones – *continued*

Membraphones

Most members of the membraphone family are represented in Indian music. Accordingly the types of membraphone instrument as discussed in Chapters 1 and 2 are the following:

(a) Barrel drums
(b) Frame drums
(c) Goblet drums
(d) Kettle drums
(e) Long drums
(f) Double drums

(a) Tabla The most popular and perhaps best-loved percussion instrument in North India is the tabla. It consists of two drums played with the right and left hands. Although it has a long history it was only permanently established in the eighteenth century and in a way it is a mongrel, derived from several types of drum, such as the *naqara* and *parkhawaj*. It is occasionally referred to as being an Arabic instrument. This is largely because the generic name in Arabic for drum is *tabl* and the tabla tradition established itself in the North, indicating Islamic influence in India. The two tablas are different in shape and size, and each with a different name: the smaller one, played with the right hand, is the tabla and the one played with the left hand is the *bayan*. They are also known as the right (*dahina*) and the left (*dugga*). For this reason the pedantically correct name is the hyphenated *tabla-bayan*. The tabla is pitched higher than the *bayan*. The notes to which the tabla is likely to be tuned are the tonic (*sa*), dominant or subdominant notes of the *raga*. This is achieved by moving the blocks held by braces around the instrument. The *bayan* is not tuned to a specific note, but is tuned to a lower sound than the one played on the tabla. The tabla is made of wood but the *bayan* is made of either clay or copper. The 'heads' on which the player plays are made of goatskin.

On the stretched goatskins are the characteristic black spots made of a paste and dried on the centre of each drum. The paste is normally made out of a mixture of iron filings and flour. Obviously the thickness of the paste will affect the pitch of the instrument (the more paste the lower the note; the less paste the higher the note). The two instruments are placed in front of the player on two cloth rings which enables the player to position them according to his convenience. A most useful memory aid and form of notation is what is called *bols*. According to this system each drum has a set of syllables indicating whether the outer rim or the inner part of the instrument is to be hit by the player. Fig. 15 should make clear the practical implication of this system:

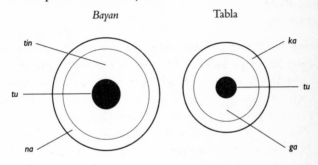

Fig. 15

When the *na* and *ga* are played at the same time or *tin* and *ga*, the word notations are *dha* and *dhin*. If the black centre is to be struck, the syllabic indication is *tu*.

(b) Mridangam In terms of popularity, what the tabla is for the North the *mridangam* is for South India. It is one of its most favoured percussive instruments; it is the classical drum of South India. Its shape is an elongated barrel, but with two heads of different sizes. In a way it is the tabla and the *bayan* in one. The Sanskrit root of *mridangam* is *mrd* (clay), yet it is usually made of wood. The heads are fixed to hoops and tightened by leather straps laced from head to head. The heads are tuned, like the tabla, by using tension wedges as well as by the distribution of the black paste. The black paste is permanent on the right hand (the smaller drum head), but temporary

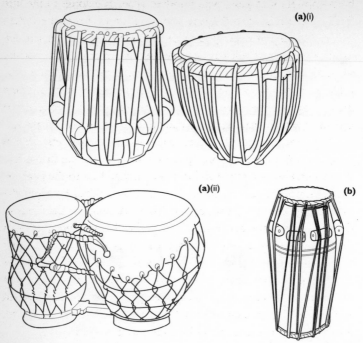

Fig. 16 Membraphones

on the left hand (the larger drum head). This is in order to enable the player to tune the larger head an octave below the pitch of the smaller head. The diameter of the larger head is almost one and a half times that of the smaller head. When played by masters, it can be a most subtle and versatile instrument.

String instruments (chordophones)

(a) Musical bow The musical bow, as we have seen, is one of the simplest stringed instruments. It is common in both Africa and Asia, but the Asian versions are relatively more refined. The resonator is often held against the body; this reinforces the resonator.

(b) Sitar The sitar is a North Indian string instrument which has been known for at least seven hundred years. It belongs to the lute family and is related to the *vina* (see p. 126) and also to the Indian zither. Although it is likely to be of Persian origin – in Persian *sitar* means three strings – it has become one of the most characteristic stringed instruments of India. Strictly speaking the name sitar is misleading, as the sitar can have between four and seven strings. These main strings, say in a seven-stringed instrument, are divided into two groups: four main playing strings and three drone, or rhythm, strings.

There are, moreover, eleven to nineteen sympathetic strings (*taraf*), which are for reinforcing the sound. The playing strings and drone strings are stretched and run over arched frets to the pegbox. The sympathetic strings run under the arched metal frets and the main bridge over a separate bridge. They are tuned to the notes of the *raga* chosen for performance. It is the shimmering quality of these unplayed sympathetic strings which gives the characteristic timbre of this fine instrument. Neither the number of strings nor the tuning is standardized. These vary according to the instrument and to the individual player's personal preference, mostly learned and passed on from their masters. One of these masters is, of course, Ravi Shankar. An example of his tuning is given in Fig. 17.

Fig. 17

The soundbox usually rests on the left foot of the player while the neck is held in position by the right knee and right forearm. The left hand is thus free to move on the finger-board of the sitar. The range of the sitar can cover up to four octaves from C upward. It should be noted that on the sitar the notes are played linearly along the string and not across (chordally) as is often the case on the guitar. This linearity of playing, and using only one or two fingers in doing so (index and middle fingers), gives a peculiar, quasi-vocal, smoothness to the instruments.

Visually, one of the most beautifully made sitars is the South Indian peacock sitar (its body is shaped like a peacock, with plumage and all).

(c) Vina Recently this became a generic term for stringed instruments (chordophones) in South India. Its equivalent is known as *bin* in North India. It may have been related to the Egyptian harp (*bint*) but, as the harp is not an instrument used in India, the *vina* is more likely to be related to the lute family. The sitar itself is often referred to as a *vina*. The particular position held by the *vina* is also because the most favoured of goddesses, Saraswati – the goddess of learning and, above all, speech and music – is herself depicted as playing the *vina*. The form of the *vina*, once seen never to be forgotten, consists of a long finger-board and two sound resonators. In South India one of the resonators has been replaced by an incorporated body and the finger-board by a wide neck. The compass

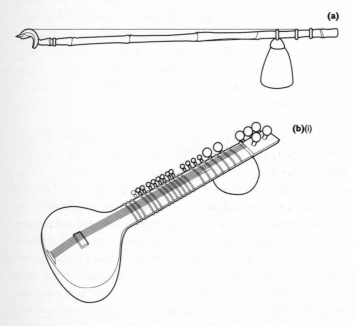

Fig. 18 Chordophones

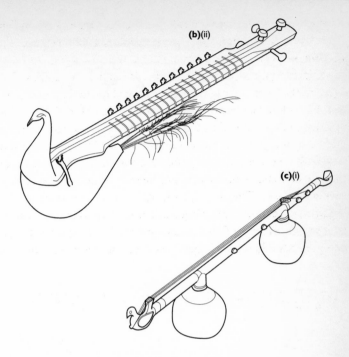

Fig. 18 Chordophones – *continued*

of the *vina* is about three octaves and it is plucked either with a fingernail or with a plectrum. The high-pitched drones are played with the little finger. When played, the upper part of the instrument, with one of the gourds, rests on the performer's left shoulder. These instruments are most lavishly decorated. Hindu legend tells us that Shiva, enraptured by his wife's beauty, made the *vina* representing her: the long neck her body; the two gourds (the sound resonators) her breasts; the metal frets her bracelets; but, above all, its subtle sound her voice. These attributes may be the reason why the *vina* is so often played by women, whereas the sitar is more popular amongst men.

(d) Sarod It is smaller than the sitar which, none the less, it resembles. It is likely that it developed from the *rabab* of Afghanistan.

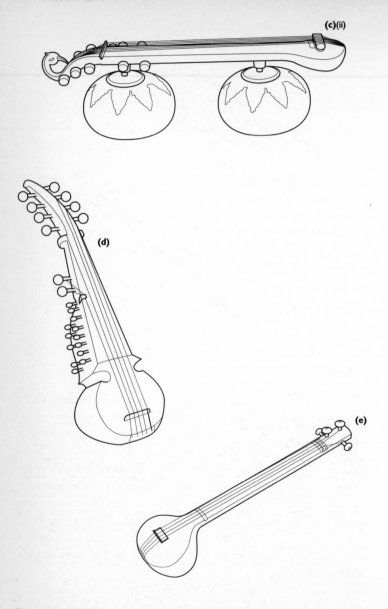

Fig. 18 Chordophones – *continued*

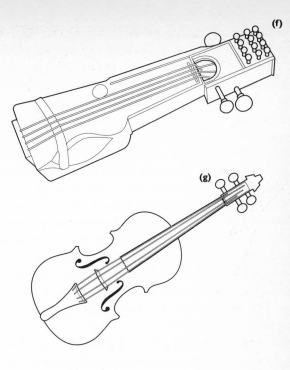

Fig. 18 Chordophones – *continued*

It consists of twenty-five metal strings: ten playing strings and fifteen sympathetic strings, which are below the playing strings. Its performance is like that of the sitar, which it matches in refinement of sound, though it has less of the shimmering presence of the overtones so characteristic of the sitar.

(e) Tambura The tambura was introduced to India during the Middle Ages from Persia. It established itself as the classical drone lute instrument of India, i.e. melodies are not played on it. In a way a simplified version of the sitar, its body is made of wood (or a gourd), often with a pot-belly and a long unfretted neck. Its four metal strings are tuned to tonic, fifth (or fourth) and two unison octaves (c g c c). The tuning is achieved by adjusting the movable ivory bridge. Held in an upright position, its body rests on the player's right thigh. The strings are stroked rather than plucked and are left vibrating (dying out), never stopped. Once the tambura is played, it maintains both its speed and rhythm. The sitar, tabla and tambura are the instruments of classical Hindustani ensemble playing with which Western music lovers are likely to be familiar.

(f) Sarangi Whereas the sitar, sarod and tambura are graceful-looking instruments, the *sarangi* is rather clumsy and sturdy looking, yet capable of a wide range of subtle, human voice-like sounds. For this reason, it is immensely popular for the accompaniment of solo singing, but also as a solo instrument. It belongs to the folk fiddle family and it is played with a bow. It has a slightly waisted body and a short neck. It contains four playing gut strings, but there may be as many as forty sympathetic wire strings. It is held vertically on the left-hand side of the player while the right hand administers the bow. In the past the *sarangi* was popular among dancing and singing girls and as such it was linked with prostitution. This picture is now changing and this ungainly, but remarkably fine, instrument is receiving the recognition it deserves.

(g) Violin The Western violin has been part of the Indian's musical life now for about two hundred years, especially in South India. It is likely that it was introduced there via Portuguese 'visitors'. Its tuning has been altered to suit the Indian system and it is often held either against the chest or vertically and not under the left chin as in the West.

Wind instruments (aerophones)

(a) Side-blown flute The flute is associated with magical if not seductive powers. For this reason it has a distinguished place in the history of Indian music and mythology. There are several statues illustrating Krishna playing the flute, demonstrating the power of both. The name commonly given to the flute in North India is *bansuri*. It is often made of bamboo (*banse* = bamboo) in various sizes and with different hole arrangements, of which the most common are shown in Fig. 19.

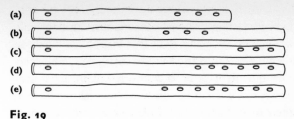

Fig. 19

(b) Tiktiri This is the Sanskrit name of a double clarinet popular in the Indian subcontinent and Sri Lanka. It is a pastoral instrument made notoriously well known by snake charmers, who play on it in front of a basket in which a snake is curled up. The desire to enhance the capability of a wind instrument led to the doubling or even tripling of the pipes. The *tiktiri* consists of two cane pipes which are fixed into a gourd which acts as a blow pipe (i.e. not unlike a bag in a bagpipe). The right pipe has up to eight finger holes; the left, with three or four holes, is used as a drone. Like most instruments, the *tiktiri* has many other names, for instance in South India it is known as *magudi*, in Sri Lanka as *tumeri*.

(c) Shahnai This is an oboe-like double-reed instrument, but with finger holes rather than mechanical keys. The advantage of the finger holes is that the player is able, by the direct manipulation of his fingers, to produce microtones. As its name suggests (*shah* = king, *nai* = flute in Persian) it is a highly valued wind instrument used on festive occasions, such as weddings. When played in pairs, one will be the melody instrument, the other will play the drone.

(d) Harmonium This instrument is a portable organ introduced, among other things, by the British. It was an instrument meant to be used for Christian indoctrination via hymn singing, an absurdity in the midst of Indian culture. No wonder that a commentator on Indian music, B. Chaitanya Deva, referred to it as 'the bane' of Indian classical music. Although one may agree with the sentiment expressed by Deva, another, more complimentary, view does justice to the accommodating spirit of India. The way in which India succeeded in absorbing this colonialistic intrusion is to the credit of India's musical integrity – they turned this incongruity into a melodic and drone instrument to such an extent that many would believe that it is an authentic traditional Indian instrument. As often occurs in history, the conquerors have been conquered. This instrument is most effectively used in North India and above all in Pakistan where it became a fundamental part of Muslim devotional music, the *qawwali*. A strange cocktail, but it works, and works with the integrity and unconquerable dignity of its adoptive ancient cultures.

(e) Horn Splendiferous sounds are produced on the various horns made in India, Sikkim and, of course, in the neighbouring countries such as Nepal and Tibet. But neither the horn nor the trumpet

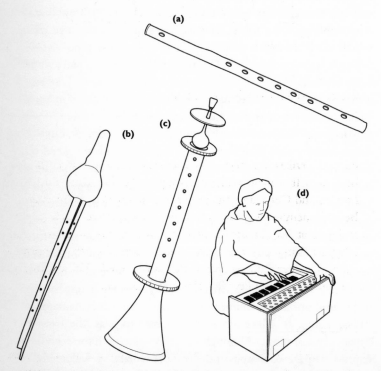

Fig. 20 Aerophones

characterizes the musical styles of southern or northern India. The other instruments which we have discussed, on the other hand, do.

Let us conclude the instrumental section of this chapter with a diagram of the seating arrangement of the classical Indian ensemble: the sitar, tambura and the tabla.

Fig. 21 Seating arrangement

General Considerations

Religion

In every civilization religious worship and music are closely linked. In India's five main religious groups – Hindu, Buddhist, Sikh, Muslim and Christian – the presence of music is in daily evidence. Before touching upon some of the ritualistic activities it is important to have, at least, a broad understanding of the nature of these religions. Familiarity with the Christian forms of worship is assumed and in Chapter 2 the Muslim faith was discussed. We now turn to the nature of Hinduism, Buddhism and Sikhism.

Hinduism

Hinduism is the religion of India: 83 per cent of the population are Hindus. Hinduism, however, is not easy to define, as it has neither a founder nor a specific creed. It has scriptures, of which the oldest is the *Rig Veda*. In about 1500–1200 BC, the priests of the conquering Aryan tribes composed hymns to their gods. These were committed to memory and passed on orally until they were written down in about 900 BC, to become the sacred book of Hinduism. There are 1028 of them, representing one of the world's oldest religious literatures. There are other subsequent Vedas, such as the *Sama Veda*. This consists of verses mainly taken from the *Rig Veda* for use in chanting; there are also the *Yajur Veda*, an instruction book written in prose for those involved with sacrifices, and the *Atharva Veda*, written in verse on the subject of magic cures of diseases as well as for bringing triumph in warfare. The *Brahmanas* are something of a supplement to the Veda scriptures. The *Upanishad*, on the other hand (600 BC), although based on the Vedas, is philosophical instead of ritualistic and introduced the doctrine of reincarnation. In addition the great Hindu epics, the *Mahabharata* (*c.* 300 BC) and the *Ramayana*, explain the essence of Hinduism. Finally the *Puranas* are versified texts in which Hindu mythology is told. In reading these works an essential principle emerges: the doctrine of reincarnation, that is after death the soul passes continuously into another body until, through good actions (*karma*), one is released (*moksha*) from the continuous wheel of rebirth. In spite of so many gods, Hindus are monotheist: they believe in Brahma, 'the Absolute', who rules over the world, aided by lesser gods. One worships lesser gods in numerous festivities, but Brahma (the creator) is above and beyond worship. The ritualistic activities towards these lesser gods, expressed in terms of festivals, are considerable in number and in all of them music, in one way or other, plays an important part. The recitation of Vedic hymns is a closely studied activity by specialist priests, involving detailed knowledge of intonations and rhythmic stresses. For instance, the *holi festival* held in the beginning of spring is associated not only with the crowds singing and dancing but with carrying phallic symbols and squirting each other with coloured water and powder. The *temple festival* with its yearly processional activities calls for processional sound effects. So do such festivities as the *Desera festival*, which is held in honour of the goddess Durga (in Vedic myth the name given to Siva's wife is Parvati; the name Durga is actually the giant whose cut-off head she holds in her hand), or the *Divali festival*, which is a four-day-long festival celebrating the New Year with oil lamps and fireworks. These are all part of a rich expression of life-enhancing communal celebrations.

Buddhism

If Hinduism is monotheistic with several gods in secondary roles, Buddhism is a religion without a principal God. Gautama Siddhartha (*c.* 563–483 BC) was an Indian prince who, at the age of twenty-nine, abandoned his family and the luxury of his life in order to pursue asceticism. After six years of self-imposed austerity he concluded that that way of existence was unlikely to lead to enlightenment, which he was determined to achieve. This he found alone, within himself, as he was seated one day under a banyan tree in Bihar. He spent the rest of his life teaching the principles of this experience of enlightenment in Benares, where he founded the Buddhist order of monks, and in other places in North India. The Sanskrit title with which he is remembered, Buddha, means the *Enlightened One*. The teachings of Buddhism are based on scriptures called *Tripitakas* (three baskets) and other collections of scriptures. The *Tripitakas* contain topics dealing with monastic disciplines and doctrines, theories concerning the self, rebirth and general theo-philosophy. The oldest Buddhist text is the *Dhammapada*, which contains the 'Four Noble Truths' and the 'Noble Eightfold Path' as well as advice on self-discipline and moral values. Of the two main forms of Buddhism, *Theravada* and *Mahayana*, Theravada is not only the oldest, but also teaches an élitist doctrine whereby only Buddhist monks can aspire for salvation from this world's suffering. *Mahayana* is more liberal and includes everyone who makes the effort towards salvation and eternal bliss (nirvana). There is a proviso though, as it is said it is because in his previous life he has been a monk. Ideologists think of everything. Needless to say, most Buddhists adhere to Mahayana principles not only in India, but also in China, Japan, Korea, Nepal, Tibet and Vietnam. South-East Asian countries such as Burma, Cambodia, Laos, Sri Lanka and Thailand adhere to the principles of Theravada. Strangely, in Buddha's own country, Buddhism is a minority religion (1 per cent of the whole population). There are more Christians in India than Buddhists. Nevertheless there are about five hundred million followers of Buddha in the world today, and in the Buddhist temples ancient ceremonial music is performed daily by monks, showing a profound recognition of the symbolic power of sound.

Sikhism

There are about 10 million Sikhs living in India, of which 90 per cent live in the Punjab. They are a relatively small community, yet their impact is inversely proportionate to their numbers, as they are renowned for their outstanding abilities as soldiers, farmers, workers in the transport industry as well as in sport and so forth.

The origin of Sikhism can be traced back to Guru Nanak (AD 1469–1504), who spent his childhood in a village not far from Lahore. His achievement is that he succeeded in formulating a coherent synthesis between Hinduism, Islam and Tibetan Buddhism as expressed in the following main beliefs:

(i) there is only one God;
(ii) all human beings are equal;
(iii) all religions should be accepted;
(iv) men and women are equal;
(v) it is good to serve others.

These are noble principles for which Sikhs are even willing to die, as was the case with the legendary Guru Tegh Bahadur (1664–75), who was executed by a Mughal emperor for defending the rights of Hindus to worship as they like. The three further principles which should govern Sikhs' lives are:

(i) *nam japna* (the remembrance of God);

(ii) *kirat karni* (honest living and hard work);
(iii) *vand chhakua* (caring for those people who are less fortunate than oneself. An important Sikh word is *sewa* = service given to others).

For these eight admirable principles the Sikhs had to pay dearly during the Islamization of North India, as the Muslims did not share their liberal attitude. In more modern times the partition of Punjab was a disaster for the Sikhs, and India is to this day far from being fair to the Sikh community.

It was the fifth guru, Guru Arjan Dev (1581–1606), who collected the writings of his four predecessors, adding Hindu, Muslim, as well as his own writings, and compiled them into what is known as *Guru Granth Sahib*. Another Mughal emperor unsuccessfully tried to convert the guru to Islam and he was then tortured to death.

This venerable book, sometimes referred to as *Adi Granth* (*First Collection*) contains the sacred *Words* as revealed in the *shabads* (hymns). The whole of the collection is written in poetry and can be either recited or sung. Often professional musicians are engaged to perform these stanzas with great skill. These singers are called *regees* and the performance of the text is referred to as *kintan*. There are numerous festivals in which the Sikhs celebrate the birthdays of various gurus as well as the martyrdom of others. During most of these festivals they like arranging competitions not only of a sporting nature but also of poetry, public speaking and music.

Qawwali

Sufi ideology and its musical rituals were already introduced in Chapter 2, which is entirely devoted to Arabic–Islamic music. Here we are to introduce one of the most remarkable musical expressions of Islam in the Indian subcontinent, above all in North India and Pakistan. The term *qawwali* denotes professional musicians who perform in ensembles which are led by one or more solo singers. It also refers to the Sufi song itself. The exalted mystical poetry sung by the singer(s) backed by an ensemble usually consisting of drums, hand-clapping and harmonium(s), is entirely devoted to the worship of Allah and to the desire to enter into spiritual communion with him. These sacred performances are spiritual songs which involve not only the players themselves but the listening community as a whole, who follow a thousand-year-old Sufi tradition of what is called *Mahfil-i-sama*, the Assembly of Listeners or Gathering for Listening. Music is thus a vehicle which helps participants (listening to music is not seen as passive, but as an active individual and communal experience) to be transported to a state of divine ecstasy, where ultimately a union with God is aimed for. Indian Muslims recognized the value of the Hindu tradition of music and dance and the Sufi *qawwali* tradition developed by incorporating them with Islamic worship. In this way it was possible to foster the conversion of Hindus to Islam. Often during these sacred performances the participants leave their seats and start dancing in a state of trance and give offerings to the musicians. *Qawwali* is a male-dominated activity, but women are also part of the experience as participants in the Assembly of Listeners, though they do not come forward in order to take part in the trance-induced dancing. On occasions when they do start dancing, they mostly remain separated from the men. Although this 'performance' of the *qawwalis* can be seen by a Westerner as an artistic event, it should be remembered that for the Sufis this is a primary 'method of worship' and not entertainment.

The style of the performance is based on improvisation and on the trance-inducing repetitions. The texts of the mystical poetry are of Indo-Persian origin and invariably in praise of God, the prophet or saints, and are sung in either Farsi, Hindi or Urdu. The nature of the exalted texts can be illustrated with the following quotation from one of the late Nusrat Fateh Ali Khan's performances (a renowned *qawwali* performer):

> King of Kings
> One without peers
> One is He
> There is no God but He.

The performance usually follows a pattern which is succinctly observed by R. Qureshi in her seminal book on the subject, *Sufi Music of India and Pakistan*:

The vigorous drum accompaniment on the barrel-shaped *dholak* is reinforced by handclapping while the small portable harmonium, usually in the hands of the lead singer, underscores the song melody. A Qawwali song normally begins with an Instrumental Prelude on the harmonica; then an Introductory Verse is sung as a solo recitative without drums, leading directly into the song proper: a mystical poem set to a strophic tune and performed by the entire group of Qawwalis.[6]

Dance and music

During the course of this book the close relationship between dance and music has been pointed out. In India there are numerous literary and archaeological sources giving evidence of the practised reality of dance and its relationship with music, that is, above all, rhythm. It is sufficient to remind the reader of the rich Indian tradition of painting and sculpture in which the two disciplines are depicted. Apart from the varieties of folk-dance traditions reflecting the diversities of the Indian subcontinent there are five dances which are considered to be classical: *bharato-natyam*, *kathakali*, *odissi*, *manapuri* and *kathak*. References to the nature of these dances are to be found in Indian literature, treatises and in mythology. For instance, in Sanskrit literature, the *Mahabharata* and *Ramayana*, detailed descriptions are given to the dancing Krishna and Shiva. We learn that Shiva first played on a small drum (*damru*) and that he danced his dance of creation to the rhythm of his drum. Dance is impossible without rhythm. Thus in India the primacy of sound and rhythm are understood and venerated as symbols of creation. There are two contrasting dance styles – pure dance (*nritta*) and programmatic dance (*nritya*) – in which a story is told or a specific mood is expressed. In both cases rhythm and sound are indispensable. We have seen (p. 100) that Bharata in his treatise on dramaturgy (*Natya Shastra*) incorporated both dance and music as well as laying down aesthetic and philosophical principles which are still in evidence today, but the first treatise on dance is attributed to Nadikesvara (*c.* third century AD, not verified), who in his *Abhinaya-darpana* discussed postures, hand and feet movements. It should be borne in mind that the classical tradition of art in India is founded on philosophical and spiritual/theological thought. An aesthetic experience in India has a threefold implication: to project states of emotion, be it permanent or transitory; to give a flavour of existence (*rasa* = flavours); and to evoke a state of bliss (*rasvastha*). These principles are applied to all the arts whether this be architecture, painting, sculpture, dance or music. But dance has a privileged place in Indian art, as it is thought to combine most of the arts in one. The body of a dancer is seen as a personification of structures; indeed a dancer is an animated sculpture. Accordingly the human body consists of two basic sections: the major section contains the limbs, head and torso; the minor section is that of the face. Western readers may recall that in Renaissance art much emphasis is given to anatomic detail, above all to muscles. In Indian art the emphases are on stereotyped bone structure and joints. It is in this context that the importance of the *nritta/nritya* divisions reveal their significance. In *nritta*, sculptural abstraction dominates the dancer's movements, while *nritya* calls for the total expressive artistry of the face, on which the whole range of stylized moods and feelings is expressed. The interaction between *nritta* and *nritya*, the structural/sculptural, and the dramatic/emotional provides the peculiar characteristic nature of Indian classical dance. Dances may fall into male and female categories, but on occasion, when the subject touches upon a universal topic, such as love, a dance which conveys this sentiment may be danced by both sexes.

Dasi Attam, or as it is nowadays referred to, *Bharata Natyam* (Dance of India), is a classical dance which was originally danced by female temple dancers. To call it the Dance of India is misleading as it is a dance predominantly danced in South India. South Indian Dance would be a more accurate name. It is one of the purest dances in which the principles discussed above, concerning *nritta* and *nritya*, are executed together with the most elaborate rhythmic feet movements, which are further emphasized by the dancers' ankle bells. The seven sections of this classical dance include the recitation of Sanskrit verse as well. In many ways this dance could be classified as dance drama, like other Indian dance dramas, such as the *Kucripudi Yaksu-gana* or the *Kutiyattam*. The accompaniment to these dance dramas usually consists of drums, cymbals and singers/reciters, but other instruments, especially in South India, such as the *vina*, violin, flute or clarinet can also be part of the performance. The poetic texts are also spiced, as it were, with the Indian solmization as well as rhythmic mnemonics. The most characteristic Indian sculptured dance posture appears in the *Odissi* in the temple at Orissa, where the dancer has her thighs and feet turned outward and knees slightly bent; this is called the *chowk* position. Or the equally well-known position, the *tribhanga* in sculpture or the *bharigi* in *Odissi* dance, in which the dancer takes the posture of number eight with the torso and head turned to one side. In the Ajanta cave temples of the first century BC, the wall paintings demonstrate the posture of the *tribhanga* as well as the Buddhist artist monks' inspired tribute to dance and music. It is a great monument to faith turned into art and has a hymn-like quality. These and other dance postures have been immortalized in the sculptures of many Indian temples, of which perhaps the most famous, at Chidambaran, is dedicated to Shiva Nataraj (AD 600). During the period from the seventh to the fifteenth centuries AD a considerable number of major temples depicting dance and music were built, which are mines of information for researchers of today. Again, the instruments chosen for the accompaniment of the dances in the semi-religious Odissi are a drum, cymbals, a flute and, on occasions, also the *vina* or violin and a singer.

The *Kathak* is a classical North Indian dance influenced by court dances of Persia and introduced to India by the Mughals in the fourteenth century. The instrumental accompaniments are rich in sonorities as they may include sitar, sarod, tambura and tabla as well as a singer. It must be remembered that as the drum is closely connected with Shiva, the Buddhists' influence affected not only neighbouring countries such as Tibet, but also the whole of East Asia, where drums play a major role in ceremonial and ritualistic musical activities.

Ragamala paintings

During the Mughal period, from the sixteenth to the nineteenth centuries, there flourished a style of largely miniature painting usually referred to as *ragamala* (garland of modes or *ragas*) paintings. The three most representative schools during this long period were Deccan (sixteenth to seventeenth centuries), Pahavi (seventeenth to eighteenth centuries), and Rajput (eighteenth to nineteenth centuries). The principle of this type of miniature painting was to make visible the verbal imagery of a poem as well as to translate into pictorial form the mood of a *raga*. We have discussed the individual nature of the *ragas*, each representing a definite state of mind and emotion, and how they are also associated with the seasons and time of day. Accordingly one can speak of a 'morning *raga*' or 'evening *raga*' and so forth. The symbolic nature of music was also applied to visual art; after all, visual art in itself is symbolic. If life is an illusion (a Hindu and Buddhist view), a painting is therefore an illusion of the illusion. Colours were given specific symbolic meanings, for instance, brown = erotic; yellow = marvellous; red = furious. Musical notes of the *ragas* were easily adapted to these colouristic interpretations; we have seen how the *ragas* symbolize definite modes of emotion (*bilaval* = joyful; *marwa* = agitated; *malakosh* = peaceful, et cetera). The *ragamala* painters excelled in metamorphosing Indian poetry and music in visual art, thus fusing three arts into a poetic–musical vision; the painters painted music. In Indian art Walter Pater's dictum that 'All art constantly aspires towards the condition of music' is both understood and put into practice.

China and Tibet *Introduction / Rhythm / Melody / Harmony / Instruments / General Considerations: religion: Confucianism, Taoism, Buddhism; Peking opera, Tibet; dance in China and Tibet; epic song*

When music and courtesy are better understood and appreciated, there will be no war.   CONFUCIUS (551–479 BC)

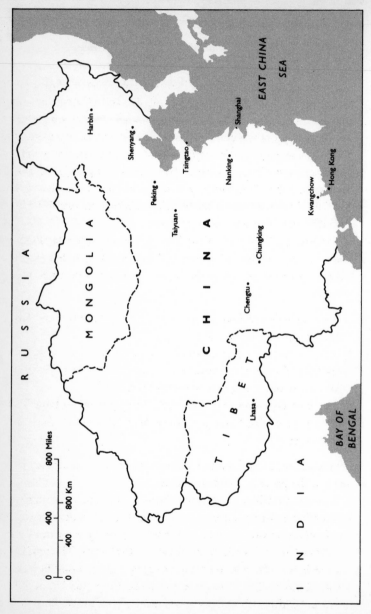

China and Tibet

Introduction

China, or more correctly, the People's Republic of China, has a territory slightly bigger than the United States of America and a population of 1,166 million, a fifth of mankind. It is composed of twenty-one provinces and five autonomous regions, which include Tibet. It is also one of the world's oldest civilizations. For over four thousand years China was ruled by a series of dynasties of which the last one, the Ching dynasty, came to its end in 1911 when Sun Yat Sen's National Party overthrew the Chings and established the Republic of China on 1 January 1912.

Since the publication of Yang Yin-liu's book *Jonggwo Inyueh Shyy Gang* (*Outline History of Chinese Music*) in 1944, it has become customary to divide the music history of China into three broad periods:

A from pre-history through the Shang (1700–1100 BC) and Chou (1100–246 BC) dynasties;
B Chin (246–209 BC), Han (209 BC–AD 220), the Three Kingdoms and the Northern and Southern States (AD 220–605), Swei (AD 605–618) and T'ang (AD 618–906) dynasties;
C the Five Dynasties (AD 906–960), Sung (AD 960–1279), Yuan (AD 1279–1368), Ming (AD 1368–1644), Ching (AD 1644–1911) dynasties.

To the above, a fourth period, covering the twentieth century from 1911 to the present, could be added.

Yin-liu based this periodization on his survey of how the influence of Confucius (Kung Tu-tzu, *c.* 551–479 BC, but better known by the Latinate version, Confucius) fared during the enormous time span from Confucius's death to the twentieth century. This scholastic approach, in which Confucian teaching figures prominently, is justifiable, as he, like Plato, gave educational and moral importance to music. Chinese theorizing about music, even before Confucius, is permeated with the significance of music and with the idea that good music has the power to uplift morally, and has a quality which goes beyond the aesthetic and touches on cosmology and science. One of the functions of music was to reflect and maintain the harmony between the male principle (yang) and the female principle (yin). Music was not seen as a primarily aesthetic phenomenon but as an integral part of nature itself. Accordingly the pentatonic (five-note) scale has profound significance in classical Chinese thinking. These five notes correspond to other things as well, for instance the planets: Saturn, Venus, Jupiter, Mars, Mercury; colours: yellow, white, blue, red, black; directions: centre, north, south, east, west; basic elements: earth, water, fire, metal, wood; the five virtues: benevolence, justice, propriety, wisdom and sincerity. The number itself is divisible as male = 3 and female = 2. Jung's view that number five was the number of 'natural man' is Chinese in origin, as the Chinese interpreted number one as the body, number two as the two arms, and plus two, the two legs of a human being. 'May the fivefold luck enter' was written on ancient Chinese doors on New Year's Day. Like the Om in India, the sound of all sounds, the beginning of creation, was also seen by the Chinese as the *Primal Sound*. The name given to the foundation tone of Chinese music, *Huang Chung* or 'yellow bell' ('yellow pitch' would be closer in practice, as it was not always played on a bell, but more likely on a bamboo pipe), referred not only to music but to the ruler and to divine power. The reference to the colour yellow has its significance as the colour of the imperial court as well as the symbol of sacred wisdom. From its earliest references, music in China was seen as a symbol of extra-musical attributes such as power, wisdom, the harmony of the state, standard measurements (i.e. capacity, length, weight). All of these were based on the measurements of sound. Thus one finds that to this day Chinese music is overwhelmingly programmatic, extra-musical and emphatically colouristic in approach. In a Chinese classic from the first century BC, *Yüeh-chin*, the bell is evaluated not so much for its intrinsic value as an instrument of sound, but rather for its value as a reminder of majesty and military power. Accordingly the ruler's reaction to its sound is that it reminds him of his army officials. There are numerous passages which illustrate that music, by way of association, had a role to play even in matters of statesmanship. In Chinese thinking, that is Confucius-influenced Chinese thinking, ritual, and therefore music, had a major role to play in government. As Chinese society had no divine lawgiver it was of paramount importance that man-made codes of behaviour were worked out and strictly adhered to by using and imitating various models. Among several such models, the *Book of Songs* (*Shih Ching*), allegedly compiled by Confucius himself, stands out. The oldest of the main body of these poems (3000 in all) may date back several hundred years before Confucius. In the *Book of Songs* there is a selection of 305 poems of dynastic hymns, odes, folk songs and love lyrics. The main reason for selecting these, beautiful as they are as literary works, was for their educational as well as practical importance in the pursuit of government positions and in their use as a vehicle for diplomatic exchange. A knowledge of these poems was believed to ennoble thoughts. Some of these poems, moreover, were written in a popular song style, which government officials used to refer to in order to analyse their content, thus gaining an insight into the mood of the ordinary people in the provinces.

As Confucius stated in his *Analects*: 'One is roused by the Songs, established by ritual, and perfected by music.' And he also stated: 'If one can govern a country by ritual and deference, there is no more to be said . . .' 'If a man is not humane, what has he to do with ritual? If a man is not humane, what has he to do with music?' The ritual, the sacrifice (*li*), the sacred and the secular were seen by Confucius as united activities in life. It is of interest to note that the ancient Chinese character for music is identical to the word for enjoy. A pleasing coincidence? The Chinese were fully aware of the joy music can give and the impact it had on the emotions, but even more significant were the ritualistic associations which music represented not only in terms of moral education but also in fostering the harmonious relationship between ruler and the ruled: the art of governing. Cosmic events were marked by musical rituals, which a ruler was meant to support for the good of everyone concerned. As Confucius stated in his *Analects*, 'if the ruler loves ritual, then the people will be easy to employ'. Thus we see that good music was something which educated people, regulated society and was used to give ritualistic framework to government and to keep in harmony with nature. The *Huang Chung*, the fundamental pitch from which all pitches were derived, was seen to be sacrosanct and not to be lightly tampered with. There was a deeply felt belief that any change to the *Huang Chung* would bring disaster to China itself. Yet, according to Yang Yin-liu, during the period from the thirteenth century BC to 1911 there were about thirty-five changes of pitches ranging from c' to a'. One of the main reasons for these changes was the custom of the emperors to call for musicians and astrologers to recalculate the *Huang Chung* according to favourable predictions, thus tuning, as it were, the emperor's reign with the natural order of the universe. Any disasters which had befallen China, especially from the Mongolian invaders, were not, of course, connected to the changes of the fundamental pitch but rather to man's insatiable desire to conquer and dominate one another. With all fairness to the 'Mongol' dynasty under Genghiz Khan and his grandson Kublai Khan (Yuan dynasty, 1273–1368), music flourished, as they loved it, and it was during this dynasty that the Chinese opera and music drama were created in both northern and southern China.

China's isolation, however, even from its neighbours, was considerable. Its relationship with the North (Mongolia and Manchuria), from which it was regularly invaded, was the main reason for building the Great Wall from the north of Tianjin to Lanzhou and the north of Lanzhou. It is likely that this one-sided encounter with the world was a major contributing factor in the long-standing belief that those from outside China were barbarians. Significantly any cultural influence which has affected China came from west of its borders, largely from India. It is telling that the legendary figure Ling Lun (see p. 151) was sent to cut bamboo pipes on the western frontiers of China.

Rhythm

Anyone who listens to Chinese music will notice that its rhythm is somewhat predictable and regular. All the possible variations which may occur are based in 2/4 or 4/4 patterns (the nominator 3 appears only as triplets). Free rhythm can be observed in the opening and closing recitatives of Chinese classical operas, but asymmetric rhythmic patterns, such as are to be found in Africa, Arabic countries or in the Indian subcontinent are alien to Chinese musical thinking. 'Square rhythm', usually in moderate speeds, seems to be the classical approach in China. This may be a reflection of the influence of Confucius, who required music to be contemplative and peaceful and was against all dramatic effects such as crescendo, decrescendo and, above all, loudness and speed, in complete contrast to the Western tradition.

It is evident that the rhythmic pattern of 2/4 time dominates not only China but to a certain extent the Far Eastern world. Curt Sachs, the German, and later American, musicologist, suggests that one of the reasons for this may be the less accentuated differences between the sexes. He states: 'The body of "Yellow" man is hairless, short, and often graceful, light-footed, slim; and – with the exception of archaic dances like those of the court of Japan – the eastern dancer, in all his vigour, has ideals of motion which in closeness and restraint are very similar to those of the female sex.'[1] Plato, as ever, perspicaciously observed in his *Laws*, 'Both sexes have melodies and rhythms which of necessity belong to them; and those of women are clearly enough indicated by their natural difference. The grand, and that which tends to courage, may be fairly called manly; but that which inclines to moderation and temperance may be declared both in law and in ordinary speech to be a more womanly quality.' These generalizations, limited as they may be, nevertheless throw some light on the striking fact that Chinese rhythm is square and predictable. How far it is also affected by the fact that in Chinese language both metre and dynamic accents are lacking, that that poetic rhythm is numerical rather than metrical, are matters of debate. So is Confucius's deintoxicating approach to music, which is likely to have contributed to the relative rhythmic monotony of Chinese music. Be that as it may, the lack of rhythmic drive in Chinese music should not be seen so much as a loss but as a fundamental characteristic.

Melody

Theories in music always follow what is already 'realized' in practice. When we talk about scale systems, it should be borne in mind that scales are abstractions of melodies and not vice versa. The broad similarity of the twelve notes (the Chinese *lü*) within the octave, which corresponds to the Pythagorean calculation of pitches, was a theoretical explanation of pitches. What was practised on the other hand were the pentatonic scales: C D F G A (C); C D E G A (C); and what became more common, F G A C D (F). The bracketed notes are the octave repetitions. Two more notes were from time to time used as 'passing' or 'changing notes'; these were the sixth and seventh *lü* notes: thinking in C these would be F♯, and B. In notation therefore the above would be like:

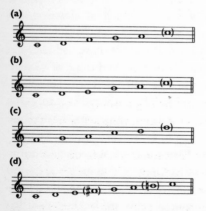

Fig. 1

The working out of these pitches, as is so often the case, was linked to a legend. In this case it was a most informative legend concerning the origin of Chinese music in about 2690 BC. The emperor Huang-Ti sent a legendary figure, Ling Lun, to the western borders of China in order to cut bamboo pipes from which the basic pitches (*lü(s)*) of music could be calculated. He proceeded to cut a series of bamboo pipes which he organized in an order giving him first the *Huang Chung* (yellow bell or sound) for foundation. All the other pitches were calculated in alternating the lengths of the pipes by 2/3 and 4/3 ratios. The pitches thus gained are:

Fig. 2

The first five pitches represent the basic pentatonic notes (*wu sheng*) of Chinese music which are named according to their position in the scale thus:

Fig. 3 *kung shang chiao chih yü*
     (do) (re) (mi) (so) (la)

Musicians were able to transpose (to begin from any of the notes belonging to the twelve pitches) by starting with *kung* at any chosen pitch.

The 'Hymn to Confucius', a ceremonial piece in his honour, is probably one of the oldest pieces in China. There are six verses set to a pentatonic melody of great serenity and restraint. The final lines are uttered in offering sacrifice for the good of the people and for the protection of Confucian teaching.

(Very slowly)

Fig. 4 Hymn to Confucius

The 'Entrance Hymn to the Temple of Confucius' or, as it is sometimes referred to, the 'Entrance Hymn for the Emperor', is another noble example of ancient pentatonic melody from a time well before Christ.

(Slow)

Fig. 5 The entrance hymn to the temple of Confucius

The final melodic example is a lament, called 'Smoke Flower', written in popular music style and sung by an abandoned woman with great simplicity and sad acceptance. Note that in all three melodic examples the rhythmic patterns were either 2/4 or 4/4.

Fig. 6

Harmony

As in Chinese thinking, one single note is in itself an experience of harmony which can trigger off other extra-musical harmonious references. The Chinese concept of harmony is entirely different from the Western approach to this subject. A pentatonic scale is already a representation of harmony. The melody based on it is harmony. Thus the simultaneous superimposition of pitches, that is the vertical aspect of music, for its own sake as it were, is not considered to be an essential feature of Chinese music making. Nevertheless, as in African, Arabic or Indian music, there are certain simultaneously sounding pitches which clearly indicate harmonic implications and procedures. These are shown in Fig. 7.

Fig. 7

Octave

(a) When an octave is either sung or played by two or more voices, instruments or in combination.

Fifth

(b) Same as above, with an interval of a fifth.

Fourth

(c) Same as above with an interval of a fourth.

Third

(d) Same as above with an interval of a third.

Sixth

(e) Same as above with an interval of a sixth.

Second

(f) Seconds or their inversion (seventh) may occur as 'passing notes' or 'changing notes'. When this happens, a momentary 'dissonant' harmonic clash is the resulting sound.

Colour harmony

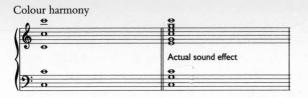

Actual sound effect

(g) Colour harmony is a characteristic feature of all music, but it has particular relevance to non-Western music. Its principle is based on the acoustical fact that, according to their particular harmonics, all instruments have their characteristic sounds (i.e. violin, trumpet, piccolo, et cetera). When these instruments are played in unison, that is the same melody, the total harmonic effect is not so much that they are in unison, but rather that they maintain their independent colours, thus producing colour harmony. Non-Western ensemble music is often based on this colouristic phenomenon, as a melody is frequently reinforced by one or more accompanying melodic instruments which duplicate the melodic line. It is the same and yet different. It offers colouristic, painterly variation, relying on melody and colour. The large Chinese orchestras with their varied instrumental colouring compensate by the presence of upper harmonics for the lack of harmonic procedures.

It cannot be sufficiently emphasized that the starting point of non-Western music is melody and therefore the approach to sound is fundamentally linear. Chinese music, moreover, is emphatically extra-musical, programmatic. Fig. 8 illustrates this point.

—	autumn	spring	summer	winter
earth	metal	wood	fire	water
yellow	white	blue	red	black
centre	west	east	south	north
Saturn	Venus	Jupiter	Mars	Mercury
do = c	re = d	mi = e	sol = g	la = a
kung	*shang*	*chiau*	*chi*	*yü*

Fig. 8

Chinese compositions are thus dominatingly illustrative works with poetic programmatic titles and references.

To a Western ear the Chinese harmonic procedure is rather similar to the 'parallel organum' technique of the European Middle Ages (*circa* tenth to thirteenth centuries). It is worth noting that this style has been seriously reconsidered in the West by several twentieth-century composers since Debussy. Finally a popular homophonic device is to accompany the main melody with rhythmic punctuations on a percussive instrument. This not only provides rhythmic interest but also adds to the performance colour and texture, as Fig. 9 illustrates.

Fig. 9

Instruments

In the highly organized, orderly world of traditional China and in the structured symbolism of its music, the instruments were also neatly arranged to form a coherent invocation of associations. The profound preoccupation with the symbolic interpretation of the feminine yin and the masculine yang and their inner balance was also expressed in symbols. The Chinese established eight possible signs which they believed symbolized eight basic permutations of complementary opposites in the dualistic universe. The establishing of these eight symbols is attributed to Fu Hsi, a mythical first emperor of China (*c.* 2500 BC). The principle of the *I Ching* (Oracle of Changes) is based on these symbols. Confucius himself stressed in his *Analects* that 'If some years were added to my life, I would denote fifty of them to the study of the oracle, and might then avoid committing great errors.' In the eight signs yin is represented by the broken line − −; the yang is represented by an unbroken line —. The combined yin-yang symbol, *ta ki*, represents a balance of the forces in the universe which are nevertheless interdependent, as they each contain within themselves part of the other.

Fig. 10

Fig. 10 is the symbol of *ta ki* in which yin and yang are encircled and function interdependently in the *cosmic egg* of balance and harmony; separate, yet one in essence.

It is by no means an accident that the number eight was reached in working out the eight signs. It is worth recalling that the Muslims speak of seven bells, but of eight paradises, as God's mercy is greater than his punishment. In Persian literature, *Hasht bihisht*, the 'Eight Paradises', are recurrent images in, for instance, Sa'di's *Gulistan* ('Rose Garden'), which is divided into eight chapters, the very number into which, in Iran as well as in Muslim India, gardens are planned and divided. In China eight is also a highly significant number. Under Buddhist influence they too speak of the eight symbols of Buddhism, but also of the eight precious items of Confucianism. The life cycles of man are interpreted in the following

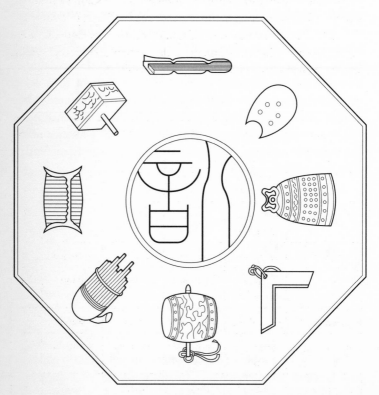

Fig. 11 (a)

manner: milk teeth at eight months; the loss of them by eight years of age; puberty is calculated at $2 \times 8 = 16$; sexual drive is weakening at 64 years (8×8). The eight immortals in China are usually represented: Chang Ko-lao on a donkey, Chung-li Chi'üan with a fan, Han Hsiang with a flute, Ho Hsien-Ku with a magic lotus flower, Lan Ts'ai-ho with a basket of flowers, Li T'ieh-Kuai with gourd and bat, Lü Tung-pin with the sword, and Ts'ao Kuo-chin with castanet-sounding wooden blocks. There can be little doubt that in the *I Ching*, the $8 \times 8 = 64$ is based on the belief that this number and its permutations are associated with good fortune and perfection. The importance of the number eight in Chinese thinking is reflected in its ordering of musical instruments. Fig. 11(a) illustrates the eight classical instruments of China inside an octagonal frame. Fig. 11(b) names these instruments in the context of their associations and attributes as related to the eight symbols.

sonorous stone (chime)	fuller	active	stone	heaven	NW
bell (chime)	youngest daughter	joyful	metal	dampness	W
zither	second daughter	fire	silk	fire	S
panpipes	eldest son	arousing	bamboo	thunder	E
tiger box	eldest daughter	gentle	wood	wind	SE
drum	second son	dangerous	skin	water	N
mouth-organ	youngest son	immovable	ground	mountain	NE
flute	mother	responsive	earth	earth	SW

Fig. 11 (b)

China's theories concerning instruments date back at least 3000 years. It is China which developed and used considerable varieties of musical instruments and which influenced its neighbouring countries. In its classical music we encounter a rich variety of all three main types of instruments: percussion, string and wind instruments. Here is a selection of the most representative of these bearing in mind the eight instruments which the Chinese themselves have emphasized (see list in Fig. 11(b)).

Percussive instruments (lithophones and membraphones)

Lithophones

(a) Chime (or sonorous stone) The Chinese chime (*Pien ch'ing*) is made out of sonorous stones which are struck with beaters. The stones are roughly L-shaped on the longer side. They are the same size (about 30 cm), as the pitches are determined by the thickness of the stones. There are sixteen slabs in all, which are suspended in two rows above each other within a rectangular standing frame. The upper set of eight L-shaped slabs are tuned to the male, the lower to the female pitches. Out of the twelve *lüs*, six have male (the odd numbers) and six have female (the even numbers) attributes, as numbers too have male and female attributes. Roughly the tuning would correspond to $F_\sharp$ (male) – G (female) – $G_\sharp$ (male) – A (female) pitches and so on. Confucius apparently played the chime and to this day in Confucian temples they are in use. Mencius, a Chinese philosopher (372–289 BC), said, 'A concert is complete when the large bell proclaims the commencement of the music, and the sonorous stone proclaims its close.' This statement underlines the practice of using the chimes with bells, or bell chimes.

(b) Struck bells In one form or other, bells have been known in China for at least 4000 years. The two types used in China and in the Far East in general are the struck bells and the bell chimes. The Chinese struck bell stands on a decorated stand and is struck with a striker. The sizes of these bells vary from moderate to gigantic, like

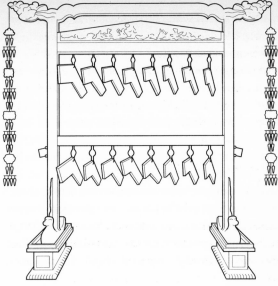

(a)

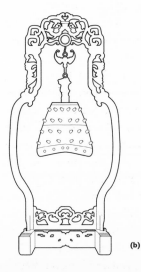

(b)

Fig. 12 Lithophones, idiophones and membraphones

wood in the form of a crouching tiger and mounted on a box-shaped platform which may act as a resonating box – the reason for calling it the tiger box. The spine of the tiger (*yü*) is emphasized in order to enable the player to scrape it with a bamboo split to its middle in twelve switches.

It is a Confucian ritual instrument, indicating the end of a Confucian service. But there is more to this simple instrument and its scraping stick, as scraping has creative sexual connotations and the

(e)

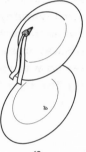

(f)

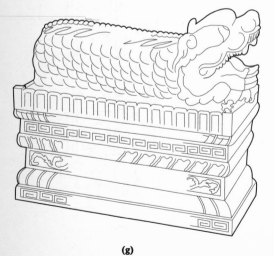

(g)

Fig. 12 Lithophones, idiophones and membraphones – *continued*

split bamboo rod is known to be a symbol of life not only in Asia but in other parts of the world as well.

Membraphones

Of the many drum types available in China, two stand out in popularity: the barrel drum and the *pan ku*.

(h) Barrel drum This is perhaps the most popular type of drum used in China. As we have already discussed this type of drum in an earlier chapter it is sufficient to say here that it is played with either one or two drumsticks. The sound of the Chinese barrel drum can be altered by striking it at various points from the edge towards the centre of the stretched skin, that is the head of the drum.

(i) *Pan ku* This Chinese drum is made of six wedges of wood which are held in position by a metal hoop over which a skin is stretched.

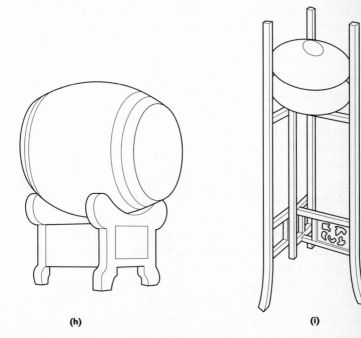

(h)   (i)

Fig. 12 Lithophones, idiophones and membraphones – *continued*

It is a single-headed small drum of about 25 cm in diameter. It has a dry and sharp sound with great penetrating power. For this reason it is played by the leader of the orchestra who can determine the nature and tempo of the composition. It is used in popular orchestral music and theatre orchestras. The *pan ku* can be substituted with either the clappers or with just wooden sticks or wooden blocks. In fact these are often played together with the *pan ku*.

Although membraphones are in plenty in China, the preference on the whole is towards lithophones.

Chordophones

The eight materials for sounds (*pa yin*) is yet another example of how the Chinese like to classify in an orderly manner more or less anything worth classifying. The eight materials from which instruments can be made are: earth (pottery), stone, metal, skin, wood, bamboo, gourd and silk. The Chinese are particularly partial to instruments belonging to the 'silk' category, that is to those string instruments which have silk strings. Of those the most popular are: the *p'ip'a* (lute) and *ch'in* (zither).

(a) P'ip'a The *p'ip'a* is a lute with frets on the belly and a relatively short neck. Its back is rounded, but shallow. The four strings which are usually tuned e' a' b' e² are held by slim laterally positioned tuning pegs. Its compass is e^1–e^4. There are other *p'ip'a* types, such as one with two silk strings (*nun-hu*), but it is also possible to find one with thirteen strings. The player holds the instrument on his thigh in an upright position and plays it by plucking the strings with his fingers. The two-stringed *nun-hu* is played with a bow.

(b) Ch'in This instrument belongs to the zithers but, as opposed to other Chinese zithers, it has no bridge. Its seven strings are tuned C, D, E, A, c, d. It appeared in the late Han dynasty and as such it is perhaps one of the oldest string instruments of China. The classic position of the instrument when played is to be in front of the player horizontally on the ground, a table or on the performer's knees. The player plays with his right hand by plucking the strings while

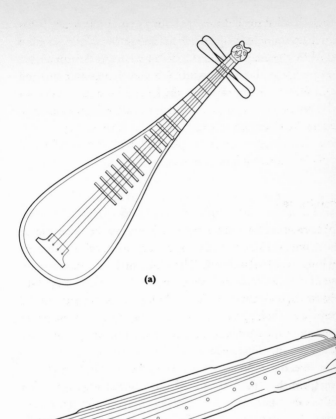

(a)

(b)

Fig. 13 Chordophones

the left glides from one position to the next and presses the strings to obtain the required pitches. To the Chinese the *ch'in* is a symbol of musical culture and civilization itself. For this reason it is associated not only with Confucius but with the very intellectual life and standing of China. Numerous paintings depict scenes in which a bearded wise man is seated with his beloved instrument, the *ch'in*, in a contemplative mood.

Aerophones

(a) Ti-tzu or just ti Originally the *ti-tzu* was an end-blown flute with variable finger holes, but it changed into a side-blown flute made of a lacquered bamboo stick with six finger holes plus a membrane-covered hole as well as some vent holes. The membrane-covered hole gives a reedy quality to the tone of this fine instrument.

(b) Sona This is a Chinese oboe usually made of wood, but there are some which are made of metal. It has seven frontal finger holes and a rear thumb hole. It is a double-reed instrument often used in ensembles of theatre music for accompanying military scenes, as its original use was in military contexts. It has a characteristically wide, trumpet-like end (bell).

(c) Sheng (mouth-organ) The *sheng* is a free-reed instrument, that is an instrument where the pitch is produced by the player blowing into a wind chamber through which the air travels into a set of pipes controlled by the player by covering the finger holes with his fingers. When the holes are open, air escapes through them but when they are covered, the air is channelled right up the pipe where the free reed is placed and makes it vibrate. The length and thickness of the pipes will determine the pitches. The use of these mouth-organs was first referred to in China over three thousand years ago. In terms of sizes there are small, medium and large ones, but also gigantic mouth-organs of about ten feet in height. The pipes number seventeen and are arranged in a circle. They are of five different lengths. Some of the pipes (four of them) are not for making sounds, but are there purely for the sake of symmetry.

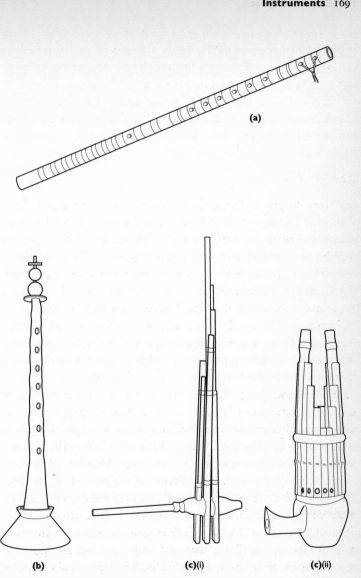

(a)

(b)　　　　(c)(i)　　　　(c)(ii)

Fig. 14

General Considerations

Religion

Apart from Christian converts, and after thirty or more years of suppression of religion under Communism during this century, the three most influential religions in China are Confucianism, Taoism and Buddhism.

Confucianism

We have already encountered Confucius in connection with education, government and music. We will now examine him as a moral teacher as well. Confucius was born in 551 BC in northern China and died in 479 BC. As he failed, during this troubled time, to gain an administrative post, he took up teaching. His method of discussing problems of his day – for example, education, government or family duties – was by debate rather than by lecturing. The account of his teaching can be found in the *Analects*, which contains a collection of his discussions and sayings. Perhaps the most important aspect of his teaching is his emphasis on filial piety, a veneration of the ancestors, a concern for people and that life should be governed by propriety or gentlemanly orderliness. The concept of *li*, that is rites, which in Confucian terms means 'good manners', together with the moral code *shu*, that is 'What you do not want done to yourself, do not do to others', can sum up the gentle moral principles of Confucianism. His teaching was eventually further promoted by two of his great successors Meng Tzu (known as Mencius) and Hsün Tzu (*c.* 312–238 BC). It was they who spread Confucianism and who further elaborated his ideas.

Confucianism is not strictly speaking a religion, as a Confucian may not have to believe in or worship any god; it is therefore rather a way of life with strict moral and social codes of behaviour.

Taoism

Taoist teaching was for a long time attributed to Lao Tzu (b. *c.* 604 BC), but it has been strongly disputed as his name means 'Old Master', which could have been given to a number of teachers following Confucius. Be that as it may, the *Tao Te Ching* (*The Way and Its Power*) is one of China's most influential books in which the original Taoist ideas can be traced. It is an anthology of compressed passages probably dating from the fourth century BC. The word *Tao* means a way or path, referring to the way of nature. A Taoist follows the way of nature as symbolized by the way of a watercourse. Taoists seek to obtain oneness with the eternal through the power of mystical contemplation and ritual prayer. Enlightenment is attained by turning away from society and by turning to the contemplation of nature as well as of death and of how to achieve immortality by using magic and rituals as executed by priests. As is stated in the *Tao Te Ching*:

> Quietness: that is the name of the return to the source.
> Fulfilling that is eternal nature.
> Knowing the eternal is enlightenment;
> But not knowing the eternal brings disaster.

Buddhism

Buddhism has already been discussed in Chapter 3. Here our concern is its influence on China. Buddhist thought entered China in about the first century BC. To begin with it met with resistance as neither the monastic life nor the doctrine of Buddhist rebirth fitted with Chinese ancestor worship and family-orientated filial piety. Nevertheless, in time, the liberal doctrines of Buddhism and the fact that Taoism had some common ground – they both respect quiet and practise meditation – meant that Buddhism established itself in China. Indeed it is there that the Buddhist meditation known as *ch'an* first evolved and eventually became better established as Zen in Japan.

★

The ceremonies of all these religions involve music making of one kind or another especially at festival times, when dancing, sport and ceremonial processions are organized annually. A universally shared festival is, of course, the New Year festival when rituals are performed to drive out evil spirits and houses are cleaned to get rid of last year's ills. In order to celebrate Buddha's birth, enlightenment and death, ceremonies take place in monasteries. There is, of course, fasting, but there is also great merrymaking with processional music, dancing and acting. In all these activities traditional music is played on traditional instruments such as those discussed in the previous section of this chapter. A significant development in this century is the increasing execution of ritualistic activities by 'ritual specialists' rather than by ordained priests who live ordinary lives. Consequently, the demarcation line between folk tradition and professional temple tradition is considerably blurred. As Stephen Jones pointed out in his outstanding book, *Folk Music of China*:

the music of the temples on the mountain has much in common with folk practice at the foot of the mountain. In fact, Buddhism and Daoism (Taoism) often coexist at the popular level: the syncretism of popular religion is highly functional. It is concerned with the propitiation of Heaven, seeking blessing and averting disasters; Buddhist and Daoist deities mingle as part of the large folk pantheon.[2]

In such circumstances it is often the case that the very same lay ritual musician can serve both Buddhist and Taoist ceremonies. Although vocal music is dominant, instrumental music is also common, depending on the ideology of the various sects. For instance, some Buddhists prefer to use only percussive instruments for their rituals; on the other hand, the Taoist sect the *Zhengyis* emphatically cultivate melodic instrumental music.

Peking opera

Chinese classical writings on which we largely base our understanding of the musical life in China up to 1912 suggest that, apart from folk music, music was dominated by court music and exercised in a Confucius-influenced milieu. The main divisions of music, which in many ways are interrelated, were: folk music, court music, banquet music, songs and military styles. To these should be added the Chinese opera, which has evolved during several centuries and has become a national pastime. The Chinese opera is widely known in the West as the 'Peking opera', which, outstanding as it is, is just one among several regional operas in China, each with its peculiar styles. In China, operas are known not according to the names of the composers or librettists, but by their regions.

By now, the Peking opera (*ching-chü*) is largely accepted as being the most characteristic and dominant opera of China. Its history is linked to the Emperor Ch'ien-lung (1736–96) whose eightieth birthday called for a grand celebration. Various theatrical companies travelled to Peking in order to mark that occasion. It was from these visiting companies, largely from the south of China, that the Peking opera style was established. It should be noted that when one talks of performances given by these theatre/operatic companies, one is not talking of operatic performances in opera houses in the Western meaning of the term, but of tea houses, restaurant-theatres, halls or private residential halls. In these places the audience not only took the opportunity to meet socially – that is universal – but went on chatting during performances and chose the programme as they chose their food and drink. The occasional crudity of the shows may have been the reason for banning it in 1798. But despite its vulgarity at times, or perhaps because of it, it remained a popular art form backed by the imperial court. Indeed the Peking opera reached one of its peaks during the last years of the Manchu dynasty, which ended in 1911, and its popularity continued until the end of the republican period in 1949. After that the destiny of the Peking opera followed that of its East European counterparts, which were under totalitarian regimes from the 1930s until the fall of the Berlin wall, that is subservience to propaganda.

Originally the female parts of the Peking opera were played by young boys (*tan*), who were recruited from the provinces, but after the Taiping Revolution (1851–64) the boys were purchased from Peking. The characters played in Chinese opera are not so much distinguished by their vocal range as by their stereotyped roles in the action. There are four traditional characters: *sheng*, *tan*, *ching* and *ch'on*. The *sheng* represents the male characters: *lao-sheng* (old *sheng*) is an old bearded official of the imperial court (baritone); the *hsiao-sheng* (young *sheng*) is a lover, has no beard and his voice is high-pitched (tenor or more likely falsetto); the *wu-sheng* (military *sheng*) is a warrior with acrobatic physical skills and always dressed in a costume with armour, indicating his military standing. The *tan* represents the female roles of which the two most typical archetypes are: *ch'ing-i*, the faithful wife or dutiful daughter with lowered eyes and singing in high falsetto; *hua-tan*, on the other hand, represents the flirtatious, carefree woman. Accordingly her movements and eyes are daringly lively. The *ching* can portray several characters, such as bandits or warriors, but can also portray gods. A characteristic feature of a *ching* is his painted face. The colours indicate the character he is enacting, for instance red symbolizes dignity. The *ch'on* is the clown of the show, wearing white paint round his eyes and on his nose. He is something of the emperor's fool, in a sense that he can say more or less anything in an improvised style, including, of course, jokes.

The staging is very sparse as there are no sets and no front curtain, only a few cloths hanging in the background. What matters is not the staging, but the symbolic meaning of the acting. Every gesture, every movement of the body counts towards the realization of the drama and Chinese audiences are familiar with the meaning of all these movements. In the acting there is an element of the pantomime. The most sophisticated mime-like movements are blended with downright clowning.

Singspiel-like, the music consists of dialogue and singing. The singing is accompanied by an orchestra, which used to sit on the stage, but under Western influences the orchestra nowadays is either in a pit or off stage. The orchestra is divided into string, wind and percussion sections. The 'conductor' is a player of percussive instruments. With one hand he beats a small drum and with the other a clapper. He is the one who determines the beat and tempo followed by the rest of the ensemble. It should be noted again that the rhythm is in simple time, that is 2/4 and 4/4 or very fast 1/4. The music is linear, harmony is completely ignored and dynamic differentiations are minimal.

Perhaps the most popular of the many operatic works are *The White Serpent*, written in 1771, but based on an ancient story; *Lady Precious Stream*, dating from 1850; and *Beheading a Son* and *Thatched Bridge Pass*, both from the nineteenth century as well. The one which became a prototype is *The Water Margin*, based on a novel by Shin Nai-an (*c.* fourteenth century). It is a heroic tale set in the twelfth century and tells the story of a group of outlaws who fought against the tyranny of the ruling class. As always the Chinese preoccupation with courage, heroism, good and bad and the difficulties overcome or at least nobly suffered by the hero(es) and common people alike, dominate this and most libretti.

In conclusion, the Peking opera, or Chinese opera in general, is a fascinating mongrel of diverse stage activities: theatre, musical, opera/operetta, and because of its acrobatic scenes, the circus as well, all adding up to a peculiarly Chinese entertainment.

Tibet

Tibet is a country on a high plateau, surrounded by mountains which include the Himalayas. It borders on Bhutan, India, Kashmir, Nepal and Sikkim. It was independent from 1911, but in 1950 China again laid claim to its territories and Tibet became unwillingly part of western China.

Culturally it has been profoundly influenced by Buddhism, which was introduced there in the seventh century AD. The Tibetan

Buddhists gained political power in the thirteenth century, when Kublai Khan gave power over East Tibet to Sa-skya Lama. From 1642 the Dalai Lamas were the 'natural' rulers of Tibet. This was the case even during the Chinese control of Tibet during the period 1720–1911 under the Ching dynasty. This political and religious tradition, however, stopped after the suppression of the Tibetan uprising in 1959. The Dalai Lama himself had to flee with many of his compatriots to India.

Culturally Tibet has been influenced by India, China and Mongolia. Large Buddhist monasteries were built where religious chants (*dbyangs*) are sung to a very low pitch (E–G) without stressing rhythm and of equal beats. A most remarkable sound effect is sometimes created by an individual monk (Gelgpa sect) who, by singing a fundamental note (two octaves below middle C) and at the same time being able to reinforce the overtones, is capable of producing harmony, that is a chord. This singular vocal technique is known as the 'split' or 'throat' pitch. The chants are often accompanied by drums, metallophones and by long trumpets (*dung-chen* and *rag-dung*) of twelve feet or more in length on which extremely low drone notes are played. These sacred recitations are, of course, aesthetic experiences, especially for a visitor, but for the monks, these rituals are a way of dissociating themselves from the reality of this world with the help of these esoteric sounds and of entering into sacred communication with God. Even the text is deliberately obscured with syllables which may have meanings for the initiated. This is in order to keep reality at a distance from the spiritual. God is approached with a different voice from the ordinary daily utterances. The chants are learned from singing masters who use traditional song books notated in *neumatic* notation. This is similar in principle to the notational method which was used in the West during the Middle Ages. It consists of signs for single as well as for groups of two or more notes.

In sacred music string instruments are never used, but the villagers, when they play their folk music, use folk-fiddles and lutes. The double-reed wind instrument, the *rgya-gling* (shawm) is used in both sacred and secular contexts. When played in a sacred context, however, it is not allowed to play the chant itself, only the preludes or interludes before and in between the chant recitations.

In Tibet there is a long-standing dramatic tradition of both sacred and secular types. The quasi-sacred mystery drama or mystery dance drama is enacted in the monasteries or on the steps leading to the monastery forecourts, where the action takes place. It is a shamanistic sacred ritual for keeping the spiritual as well as human enemies at bay. Its origin goes back to pre-Buddhist times, but the Buddhists adopted the rite as their own. In various versions an effigy made of dough is used as a scapegoat against ills. In other adaptations the last King of Tibet, Lang Darma, who was an enemy of Buddhism, is ritualistically killed by a lama disguised as a shamanistic dancer. These performances involve elaborate costumes, masks, dancing – which includes whirl-dancing and substantial instrumental music as well as chanting choirs representing not only prayers but also celestial or demonic forces.

The secular dramatic performances are based on Buddhist subject matter, that is historical or legendary themes with a strong moralistic emphasis, which are chanted and recited, but also mimed and danced with instrumental accompaniment. The influence of China's operatic style can also be detected in the execution of these secular dramas with their emphasis on good triumphing over evil and with their tendency to make the event spectacular and richly spiced with traditional folk elements. The historical plays and secular dances are dominated by the use of percussive instruments.

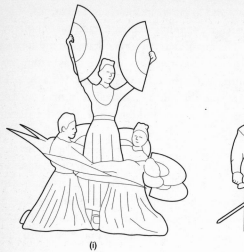

(i)

(ii)

(iii)

(iv)

(v)

Fig. 15

Dance in China and Tibet

China has numerous dances, but the most striking are perhaps those with fans, swords, *bunso* (the brush dance), the long-sleeves dance and the dance of handkerchiefs or scarves.

They all involve great skill in manipulating these objects or materials. For instance, the two types of fan dance, the half-circle fan and the round fan, consist of about thirty basic movements each. In Tibet, influenced by India and China, the dance is an integral part of not only lamaist religious festivities, but also of secular activities, such as the harvesting dance, which is an expression of gratitude to God after a successful harvest. This involves cooking tea leaves and butter in a copper pot which the villagers dance around and sing a thanksgiving. Variations on this thanksgiving theme are performed annually across the country. The *yo* dance is also danced by both men and women in a semicircle formation, to the accompaniment of folk or Chinese fiddle, where they sing about the beauty of nature including the love between men and women. On these occasions, which may last several days, a tent is erected where food and drink are kept for the participants. Apart from music and singing, theatrical shows are also performed during the daytime, leaving the evening for music and dance. The *yo* dance is traditionally danced on New Year's Day as well as in May and August. The sword dance is popular in many countries; Tibet is no exception. The Chinese and Tibetan versions are characterized by dynamic jumps and by the skilful handling of large swords. Costumes are exotic, with fascinating colours, long-sleeved blouses and jewels. Men wear sheepskin skirts with little bells attached to them, thus producing tinkling sounds from the slightest movement.

Epic song

Finally, a few words must be given to the Tibetan epic-song tradition, which is based on a manuscript entitled *Ge-sar sgrungs* (*The History of Ge-sar*) and which has been referred to as the '*Iliad* of Asia'. Monks are allowed to read it, but it is only the traditional *bard* or *travelling singer* who performs it by heart. The story told is about Ge-sar, the hero who kills many tyrannical rulers as well as demons and various monsters. By doing these heroic deeds he defends and revenges his country. No wonder that the Tibetans still believe that one day he will return in order to do justice to Tibet. During his performance, the singing bard is virtually in an exalted state and his performance is listened to by the audience with total devotion for many hours a day over a period of several weeks. The bard usually sings solo and without any accompaniment. The performing style fluctuates between recitative and singing according to whether the text is set to prose or verse.

As we have seen, Tibet has its own musical voice well worth cultivating and defending. Ironically both China and Tibet are under the same Western pop music onslaught, which is a contributing factor in slowly undermining not only ancient traditions, but also monolithic regimes. Confucius expressed in his *Analects* the zest of a timeless conflict: 'The Master said: "I hate the fact that purple is displacing vermilion, I hate the fact that the sounds of Zheng are ruining elegant music . . ."'*

---

* Note that vermilion was the correct ritual colour. The purple displacing it was seen to be wrong. So was the music from the state of Zheng, which was polluting the sound of traditional music.

The Far East *Introduction* **Japan** *Background / Rhythm / Melody / Harmony / Instruments / Ensembles: Gagaku, Bunraku, Kabuki and Noh; General considerations: religion: Shinto, Buddhism in Japan, Zen* **Indonesia: (i) Java; (ii) Bali** *Background / Rhythm / Melody / Harmony / Instruments / Theatrical ensembles and music / Bali*

Dying cricket –
how full of
life, his song.
BASHO (1644–94)

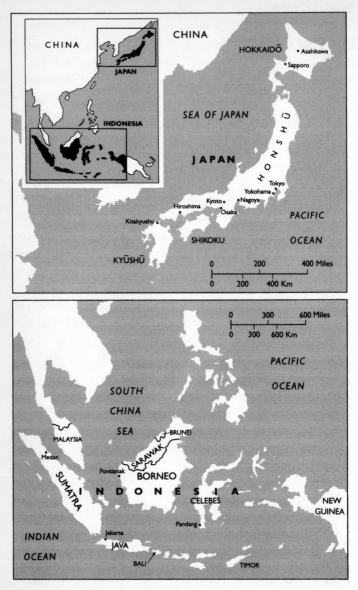

The Far East: Japan and Indonesia

Introduction

The Far East, excluding China already discussed in the previous chapter, consists of vast territories and autonomous countries which, though substantially influenced by Chinese, Indian and Arabic civilizations, are markedly distinct cultures, both musically and otherwise. In general parlance the term Far East refers to countries in East and South East Asia. In this chapter a representative selection of these countries has been chosen for discussion to give the reader a feeling of the rich variety which the Far East represents in musical terms. Those selected are Japan and the Indonesian islands of Java and Bali.

Contrary to previous chapters, where a major culture was considered in each one, in this chapter, two cultures will be considered. The main structure, as outlined in the Preface, will nevertheless be broadly adhered to for each of the three areas in this final chapter. This should enable the reader to find information in conformity with the previous chapters: that is, rhythm, melody, harmony, instruments, et cetera will be discussed in that order.

Japan

Background

Agreed by both native and Western scholars, the history of Japanese traditional music has been conveniently divided into four periods. These all correspond to changes in Japanese society and reflect that differences of styles were largely brought about by geographical conditions and the effects of religion and politics. The chart in Fig. 1 gives the reader an overall view of these periods.

	Music	Dates	Political	Society
1	Period of native music	up to 6th century	—	Primitive
2	Period of international music	7th–10th centuries	Asuka, Nara Heian (early)	Clan system and governmental control
3	Period of national music	11th–17th centuries	Heian (late) Kamakura Muromachi Momoyama Edo	Feudal system ,, ,, ,, (Tokugawa shoganate)
4	Period of modern internationalism	1868–present	Meiji	Industrial revolution, capitalism, democratic development

Fig. 1

Another, perhaps the most important, factor which shaped Japanese music was the influence of China, which first came via Korea and eventually directly from China itself as the dominant regional economic and cultural power. This took place during the Asuka period (AD 552–645). The introduction of Buddhism in the fifth/sixth centuries via China also had a profound effect (see p. 217). During the fifth century, the Yamato clan succeeded in unifying the country. The ancestry of the emperor was linked to the sun goddess, hence the origin of Japan as the country of the sun. By the ninth century, Japan had found its own cultural identity. From powerful families emerged a military class system known as the *samurai* whose influence affected the whole of the social structure, including the emperors, who were swayed by the views of the *samurai*. A *samurai*, Minimoto Yoritomo, became the founder in 1192 of a military government, the shogunate at Kamakura. This military-dominated style of government was maintained until 1868. The power of the Kamakura shogunate was severely undermined by the two Mongol invasions of Japan via Korea in 1274 and 1281. Miraculously Japan was saved by typhoons on both occasions. This made the Japanese believe in their divine protection. The expenses spent on defence, however, ruined the Kamakura shogunate. What followed was three hundred years of rivalry between warring shogunates. In the sixteenth century a *samurai*, Oda Nobunaga, eventually succeeded in uniting Japan again. The ambitious invasion of Korea by his successor, Toyotomi Hideyoshi, however, was not only a failure but laid down the seeds for hatred and suspicion between the two countries to this day.

Tokugawa Ieyasu, having defeated his rivals at the famous battle of Sekigahara in 1600, became the Shogun in 1603. He ruled from a village called Edo, which in time developed into what is now the capital of Japan, Tokyo. His government was entirely controlled by the military, or more accurately, by the police. Confucianism, with its emphasis on loyalty to the master(s), became the basic ideology. Religions, including Christianity, which gained a foothold in the sixteenth century, were more or less eradicated, foreigners were by and large expelled and, as in contemporary totalitarian regimes, natives were not allowed to visit other countries. As in Renaissance Europe, the merchants gained power as money lenders. Although they were looked down on, as they were low in the social hierarchy, their money was in great demand. The feudal *samurai* were at the top of the hierarchy but were vulnerable financially and became dependent on the merchants. In Arai Hakuseki (1656–1726), however, the Edo period found a philosopher–statesman, who, inspired by Confucius, based his government's activities on musical principles and on following rites. He insisted on re-establishing classical values and that music in Noh plays return to ancient tradition. The Edo period was inward looking and isolationist.

During the Edo period of isolation native art nevertheless, or perhaps because of it, flourished and was firmly established. Meanwhile Western interests started to put increasing pressure on Japan to open its doors, as it were, for trade. In 1854 an American naval officer, Matthew C. Perry, in the port of Edo, forced the Japanese government to end their traditional isolation. The split of interests between the 'modernists' and 'isolationists' led to a civil war and to the end of the hundreds-of-years-old shogunate power. In 1868 the emperor's power was restored in the hands of Emperor Meiji. It was he who decided to rename Edo Tokyo, and it was during his reign that fact-finding Japanese went to the West to learn about Western values and technologies. With prodigious speed and ability they modernized themselves. A Prussian-based constitutional monarchy with a parliament was established, but an imperialistic appetite, as a solution to all internal problems, emerged with relentless brutality. A few dates for reminders will suffice: the defeat of China in 1895, followed by Russia in 1905 and Manchuria in 1931; by 1937 Beijing, Shanghai and so on were all occupied; and by 1941 the whole of Indochina. To crown it all, Japan, now an ally of Hitler, bombed the American fleet at Pearl Harbor in December 1941. Tragic as it was, the atomic bombs dropped on Japan put an end to its military omnipotence. Since then it has turned into one of the world's most powerful economies. Culturally it has developed along double lines, that is traditionalism mixed with Western avant-gardism in the arts, including literature and music. It is a fascinating mixture which on occasion reminds one of the concept of Oswald Spengler, who in his monumental historical work *The Decline of the West* wrote about 'pseudomorphosis', that is false development or false growth, which can and did take place in the history of the world, when a culture or civilization only superficially absorbs another and remains spiritually fundamentally unchanged by it.

Folk music

Japan is an archipelago with four main islands: Honshu, Shikoku, Kyushu and Hokkaido. Its geography and its long history have enabled it to evolve rich regional folk traditions with, nevertheless, sufficient common ground to make general points. For instance, folk-dance songs are mostly in regular rhythm (for example, 2/4, 4/4, rarely in 3/4); non-dance-based songs are, however, mostly performed in parlando-rubato style, that is freely executed semi-spoken (recitative) style; there is a marked tendency for melismatic (decorative) style with the voice in high register and sung with an intensively tight throat technique; the melodies are largely pentatonic based (for example, D, E, G, A, B); the songs, when not sung unaccompanied, are frequently accompanied by a three-stringed *shamisen* (lute). As in other countries, in Japan the subject matter for folk songs covers children's songs, songs of courting couples, agricultural rites, drinking songs and so on. The classical syllabic structure on which the folk poems are based is often 5 + 7 + 5 + 7 + 7 syllables. This syllabic pattern is so deeply associated with the folk-song tradition that its name *waka* is synonymous with 'Japanese song'.

A strange custom and sound effect is created when two singers sing into each other's mouths via their half-closed hands. This kind of duet is called *rekukkara*, which, to my knowledge, is unique to North Japanese folk tradition. Melodically it is interesting to note that the Japanese tendency is to stress not so much the tonic note of a scale but rather the notes below or above the tonic. By and large the forms of Japanese folk songs are mostly in binary (AB) or ternary (ABA) forms.

Rhythm

In Japan, as in China, the common times dominate. Beats of 2 in *koto* (see p. 203) and *shamisen* music (see p. 202), 4 for Gagaku (see p. 207) and 8 for Noh plays are the norm. In folk music, children's songs and Buddhist chants, triple time (3/4) may occur.

Additive rhythmic patterns, such as 2 + 4, appear both in Japanese Buddhist chants and in art music. Syncopation, that is the deliberate displacement of the regular beat or accent in a piece of music, is quite frequent and breaks the potential monotony of the regular beats (see Fig. 2).

Fig. 2

A particularly effective device, much used in Japanese music, is the *accelerando*, the gradual increase in tempo. This appears in music all over the world, but the Japanese have made a special virtue of it especially in Gagaku and *koto* music. The same can be said about their use of *relative tempi*, that is the tempo changes within a piece of music, which can be from the very slow to the very fast.

Polyrhythm occurs in Noh plays when one or more drums as well as a flute and singer perform in simultaneous rubato style. The flute, moreover, is generally free rhythmically when it accompanies a singer. All in all the tendency of Japanese instrumentalists is to listen, with the care of chamber music players, to what the other musicians are performing, even when the ensemble is large. The result is that great refinement and subtlety, combined with flexibility, are achieved both rhythmically and otherwise.

Finally, attention should be given to the singular use of silence in Japanese music, which has been developed to a high degree of artistic sophistication. In Western music the music of Webern comes to mind in using silence – that is space between one sound effect and another – with such intensity as Japanese musicians are capable of, especially in Noh plays.

Melody

We have already seen that melodies in the Far East are basically pentatonic. It was the Chinese who introduced, during the Heian period, their system of pitch calculations to Japan. Although the system embraces twelve untempered semitones, in practice not all of them are normally used. The seven-note scale pattern can also be interpreted as pentatonic, based with two auxiliary notes between the main pentatonic notes as illustrated in Fig. 3.

(a) c d e f♯ g a b ⟶ (c)

(b) c d e♭ f g a b♭ ⟶ (c)

Fig. 3

Note the characteristic tendency in introducing semitones in the scale patterns, such as f♯–g; b–c; or d–e♭–a–b♭, as in Fig. 3. Fig. 4 illustrates this point in a short melodic fragment.

The Japanese names given to the two most characteristic pentatonic scales are: *In*, which contains semitones (D E♭ G A B♭), and

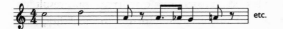

Fig. 4

the *yo* scale without semitones (D E G A B). The *yo* is often used in folk songs while the *in* is more associated with art, *koto* and *shamisen* music. Another interpretation in calculating scale patterns is to build them up in a distance of a fourth apart. This method incorporates the notes of both *in* and *yo* patterns:

c-f-b-e-a-d-g-c

and

c-f-b♭-e♭-a-d-g-c

Fig. 5

A characteristic Japanese melodic opening and a melodic sentence could thus be generalized in the following way:

Fig. 6

Note the numerous syncopations and tied notes.

The most popular overall structure for musical compositions used in Japan is the *jo-ha-kyn*. It is loosely tripartite (ternary) form which is dominated not so much by melodic changes and considerations as by its rhythm. This rhythmic structure broadly falls into the following sections: *jo* = slow introductory opening; *ha* = a build-up of tempi (acceleration) and unfolding; *kyu* = a climactic rush at great speed, followed by a slowing down before the end. This pattern is not only used for entire musical compositions, but also for sections of both vocal and instrumental pieces. It is applied in compositions written for the Gagaku orchestra as well as in the performance of Noh plays.

Harmony

Traditional Japanese music is basically monophonic or heterophonic. Harmonic thinking, in the Western meaning of the term, is therefore not practised. Nevertheless, harmonic moments do occur in Japanese music making. Some of these will now be discussed here.

Consonant and dissonant harmonies

The simultaneous sounding of the intervals of octaves, fifths, fourths, thirds and sixths are part of Japan's harmonic (vertical) vocabulary. So are the clashing sound effects of playing seconds, sevenths and ninths. Interesting dissonant harmony is produced when in an ensemble two instruments play in the manner shown in Fig. 7.

Fig. 7

The consecutive movement of the two parts, b♮ and b♭ produces a dissonant major seventh.

Lute chords

The lute player's arpeggiated chords are other examples of clear
harmonic procedure; for instance Fig. 8 shows a chord on e without
the third, but the upper part (melody), by moving from b (the fifth
of e minor) to a, produces an eleventh which then resolves, so to
speak, to g, the third of an e minor chord e−g−b, or as written,
e−b−e−g.

etc.

Fig. 8

Chords on the mouth-organ

But perhaps the most striking cluster harmonies are produced on
the Japanese mouth-organ, on which five or six pitches can be
played chordally in the manner shown in Fig. 9.

etc.

Fig. 9

The Japanese mouth-organ called *sho* is similar to the Chinese
sheng. The chords played on the *sho* are not harmonic progressions,
in the Western meaning of the word, but rather harmonic pillars
giving support to the ensemble and to the mode of a composition.
Being rather static they create a sense of timeless tranquillity. The
dissonant notes do not seem to undermine the somewhat contempla-

tive or meditative effect these harmonies create; on the contrary, they give a shimmering quality to the chords. It should be borne in mind that in Japanese music chords of two or more notes are mostly for giving emphasis and greater sonority to a piece rather than for the sake of harmony as such. As can be seen from the above illustrations, Japanese music does contain harmonic elements, albeit different from the classic Western concept in its application and importance.

Polyphony

Under this term three distinct musical phenomena are telescoped. Each of these will now be defined in turn.

(i) *Polyphony* proper occurs when two or more distinct melodic/ rhythmic parts are playing simultaneously, as in Fig. 10.

Fig. 10

(ii) *Heterophony* is monothematic polyphony, that is, the main theme is the subject, with some modification, for two or more players in the manner shown in Fig. 11.

Fig. 11

(iii) *Cacophonic polyphony*. Noisy sound effects are legitimately created by Gagaku players who start playing their part one after the other, not in imitation of a theme like, say, in a fugue or canon, but with complete disregard for each other and the ensuing cacophony. The source of this style, as applied to an orchestra, may be linked to the traditional Japanese method of performing accompanied singing, where the singer is somewhat slightly ahead of the accompaniment. The practical reason for this technique must be in order to assure the comprehensibility of the text. The Japanese orchestral musician evolved this discrepancy a step further and nearer to momentarily calculated chaos.

Instruments

Percussive instruments (idiophones and membraphones)

Idiophones

(a) Fan The Japanese fan is often used in both secular and sacred contexts as a clapper-like instrument. It is sounded by striking the fan against the palm of the other hand.

(b) Dragon clapper This is a wooden clapper of which the upper part is shaped like the head of a dragon. By shaking it rhythmically, it gives a dry wooden clapping sound.

A similar, but simpler and undecorated clapper, is the *shaku byoshi*. It is made of two thin pieces of wood which are clapped together during Gagaku and Shinto music performances. Needless to say, there are several other variants of the same thing, like the *hyoshipi* used in Kabuki theatre and also by fire watchers.

(c) Slit drum The Japanese also like the sound of the wooden slit drum, which they carve into the shape of a fish (*mo kugyo* = wood fish). The same instrument is known in China, from where it is likely to have originated, as *mu yü*, and in Korea, as *mo ko*. It is a ritual instrument used by Buddhists in Japan.

(a)

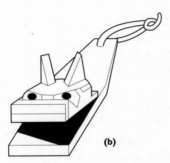

(b)

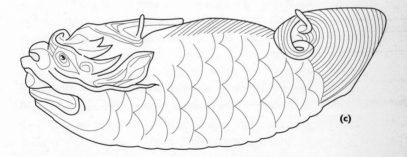

(c)

Fig. 12 Idiophones

(d) Gong Gongs (*shoko*) are very popular in the Far East and in Japan they are part of the Gagaku instrumental ensembles. They are made of bronze and in different sizes and are suspended in decorated frames. The players usually kneel behind the gongs, hitting them with hand beaters. Apart from colouristic effects their main role is to give emphasis to important beats.

(e) Bells Apart from hand bells, there are three characteristic bell types in Japan.

(i) Buddhist temple bell (*ogane*) This is an extremely large bell suspended from a strong beam high above. It is struck with a horizontally suspended wooden beam which is made to swing by a monk via a rope attached to it. This type of temple bell is usually kept in a purpose-built building inside the grounds of a temple.

(ii) Bell chime The Japanese bell chime, like its Chinese equivalent, is characterized by a series of differently pitched bells (sixteen), which are suspended in a frame. The player strikes them with two strikers.

Another bell chime in Japan is the vertically hung bell chimes which look like a series of differently sized bowls strung together upside down, the smallest at the bottom, the largest on the top. The sound is generated by hitting them with one or two sticks.

(iii) Resting bell This is a large bell which is placed rim up on a decorated stand and hit with a stick. There are chime-like resting bells as well which are fixed sideways in a wooden board (*oruguru*). The player plays on them by using two metal rods. This instrument is played in Kabuki music, but it is also a Buddhist temple instrument.

(f) Xylophone Of the many variants of xylophones, the *mokkin*, with thirteen to sixteen pitched slabs placed over a wooden soundbox, is one of the best representatives of this familiar instrument. The player uses two wooden mallets for playing on it. Though it is a pitched melodic instrument, it is often used for rhythmic effects in Kabuki music.

(d)

(e)(i)

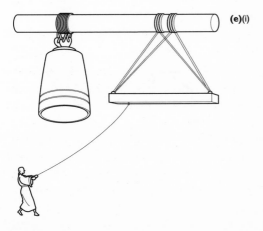

Fig. 12 Idiophones – *continued*

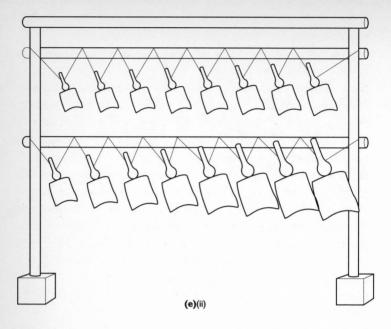

(e)(ii)

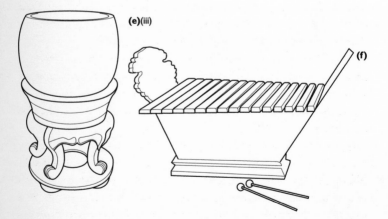

(e)(iii)

(f)

Fig. 12 Idiophones – *continued*

Membraphones

A large number of membraphones are known in Japan, where they are sometimes placed on stands.

(a) Cylindrical drums Of the cylindrical drums, the *okedo*, a double-headed drum, is popular in both folk music and in Kabuki theatre ensembles. So is the *daibyoshi*, 'the great time beater' which, above all, is played in Shinto worship. The shallow cylindrical drum is a much favoured instrument in Noh plays.

(b) Waisted drum The waisted or hourglass drum, for which the generic term in Japanese is *tsuzumi*, is a popular instrument, especially in Noh plays. It is usually made of cherry wood, handsomely decorated and lacquered. The two heads are made of skin and stretched over two iron rings (one for each head). The cords can be gripped with one hand and by tightening or loosening the grip, the tension, and therefore the pitch, can be altered by the player during performance. Assembling this instrument before a performance is a serious ritual.

(c) Barrel drums (i) *Taiko* In folk music, the small and shallow *taiko* is the most popular barrel drum. It has two heads on which the skins are characteristically stitched together with an unusually thick rope. Sometimes it is placed on a holding frame.

(ii) *Tsuri-daiko* The *tsuri-daiko* is a larger barrel drum which is usually suspended in a decorated frame or rests on a stand. The skins are decoratively tacked down and the body is also ornately lacquered. The player uses two sticks, but on one head only. It is a Gagaku instrument.

(iii) *O-daiko* One of the most popular Shinto temple drums is the *o-daiko*. It is a barrel drum of Chinese origin with two nailed heads. Although played in the Kagura orchestra it is primarily a Shinto temple instrument, beaten with two sticks. Generally it stands on a rest. It has, however, two iron rings fixed to its sides which makes it portable during processions.

(iv) *Da-daiko* The *Da-daiko* is the great drum of Japan. It is of majestic size, 5 ft. long with the diameter of the head about 6 ft. It is the Japanese equivalent of the Chinese *tsin ku* and the Korean *chin ko*.

It stands on a suspended frame and is struck with two heavy lacquered beaters, starting with the left hand. It is primarily a Gagaku instrument.

(v) Kakko The *kakko* is a small barrel drum of Turkestan origin. It has two deerskin-covered heads held by wooden or metal hoops and laced together. The heads are played with two drumsticks.

(d) Uchiwa-daiko Finally, a tambourine-like instrument, but without jingles, the *uchiwa-daiko* should be added to our select repertoire as it is a prominent instrument in Buddhist music. It is a single-headed shallow-frame drum with a wooden handle. The player plays on it with a stick.

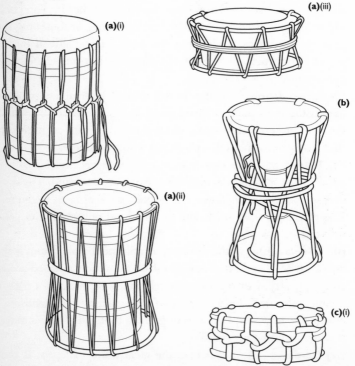

Fig. 13 Membraphones

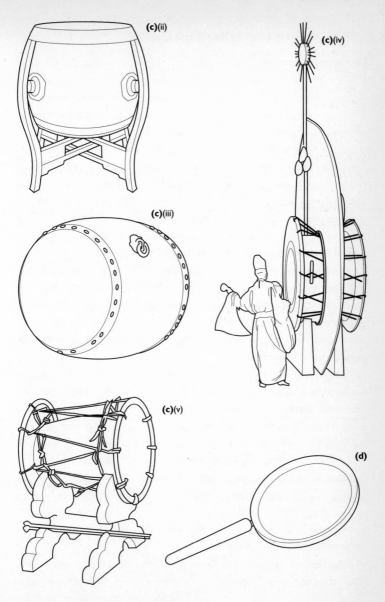

(c)(ii)

(c)(iv)

(c)(iii)

(c)(v)

(d)

Fig. 13 Membraphones – *continued*

String instruments (chordophones)

(a) Lute (folk lute) It was in the seventh century that the Chinese *p'ip'a* was introduced to Japan. Thus the Japanese flat lute, *biwa*, is a close relation to *p'ip'a*, which it resembles in both shape and size. There are, of course, differences between the sizes of Japanese *biwas*, which may be smaller or larger. Normally a *biwa* is made of two parts; the back is carved out of a solid piece of wood. This hollowed-out back is made into a soundbox; the front covering is glued over the soundbox and contains two sound holes. Usually it has four silk strings fixed between the L-shaped neck and the tailpiece of the pear-shaped instrument. The strings are plucked with a rather large plectrum. As the use of the plectrum can be quite forceful, the upper part of the instrument is often reinforced with an extra strip of wood or other suitable material such as leather or lacquer. The strings can be tuned in five ways (for example, e–b–e–a; g–a–d–a; f♯–b–e–a). As the strings are plucked in an arpeggiated way, the four pitches produce chords. For this reason it is frequently used as a rhythmic instrument as well. When a melody is played on it, it is mostly played on the top string.

(b) *Shamisen* The Japanese *shamisen* is the equivalent of the Chinese *san hsien*, which was introduced to Japan in 1560. It is a long-necked lute with three strings stretched over the neck and a skin-covered belly. The Japanese version is square in shape. The player plays on it with a characteristically large plectrum (*bachi*). As it is an accompanying instrument, its tuning is rather flexible. The most frequently used tunings are: b–e–b; b–e–a; b–e–b or b–f♯–b. It is a simple instrument but very popular for solo playing and singing, for backing narrative styles and, of course, in accompanying folk songs. It should be noted that the *shamisen* player is invariably the singer as well.

Another lute type used in Japan is what is called the 'moonshaped lute' after the word *getsu* (moon), now known as *gekkin*. Its full-moon-shaped body has a very short but stylishly decorated neck and four tuning pegs to which the silk strings are attached. This instrument is also of Chinese origin.

(c) Koto The *koto* is a long zither which is laid horizontally on the floor, on a low table or held horizontally across the knees. It has thirteen silk strings which are placed over movable bridges. The thirteen strings give a compass of two octaves from ♯ below middle c. The player uses three plectra on his right-hand fingers (thumb, index finger and middle finger). The left hand controls the strings by pressing them down behind the bridges. This pressure can change the pitches upward a semitone or a tone. Although of Chinese origin, it is the Japanese who have evolved the *koto* into something of a national instrument. It can produce pure and most delicate sounds.

As the Japanese are singularly interested in using noise for musical/dramatical effects, the *koto* is sometimes used for that purpose, when the strings are not played by plucking them, but rather by scraping or scratching them. This creates a most effective shimmering but noisy sound. There are several ways of tuning the thirteen strings of which perhaps the most popular is shown in Fig. 14(a).

Fig. 14 (a)

A well-known opening pattern on the *koto*, showing a chordally used empty fifth, is illustrated in Fig. 14(b).

Fig. 14 (b)

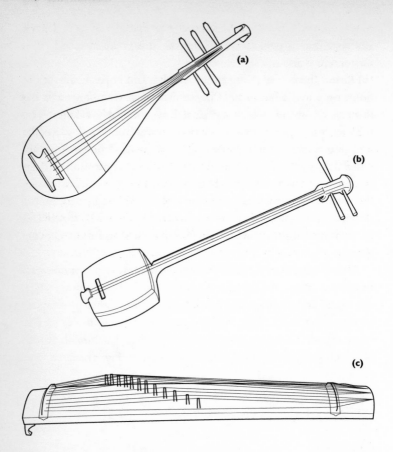

Fig. 15 Chordophones

Wind instruments (aerophones)

(a) Shakuhachi *Shakuhachi* is an ancient bamboo flute of Chinese origin. It is made of an unusually thick bamboo into which four finger holes are cut in the front and one thumb hole in the back. It is a simple instrument which has been popular since the sixteenth century among travelling monks (*komuso*).

It should be noted that the generic term for flute in Japan is *fuye*. Consequently many flute types appear under various compound names of *fuye*.

(b) Cross flute The *Noh-kan* is the cross flute of Japan. It is made of bamboo and is lacquered red inside and black outside and has seven finger holes. As its name suggests, it is used in Noh ensembles.

(c) Sho Since this remarkable wind instrument was already discussed on p. 192, here it is sufficient to say that this Japanese 'mouth-organ' consists of a wooden wind chamber of lacquered wood. The cup-shaped wind chamber is covered by a plate made of horn. The seventeen bamboo pipes are set through the cover. The player blows air through the mouthpiece, which is attached to the wind chamber. It is a delicate instrument whose sound is just audible. Its great fascination, as we have seen, lies in its harmony-producing sound effects.

The cross section of the wind chamber and the pipe is illustrated in Fig. 16.

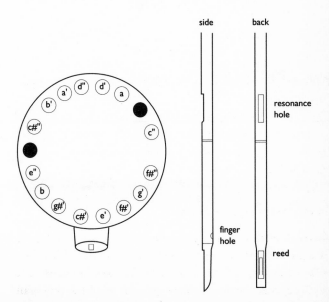

Fig. 16

(d) Oboe The *hichiriki* is a short cylindrical oboe made of bamboo. It is a double-reed instrument, the reeds being inserted in the top of the pipe. It is made from lacquered bamboo and bound with bark. The range of notes is about g–a'.

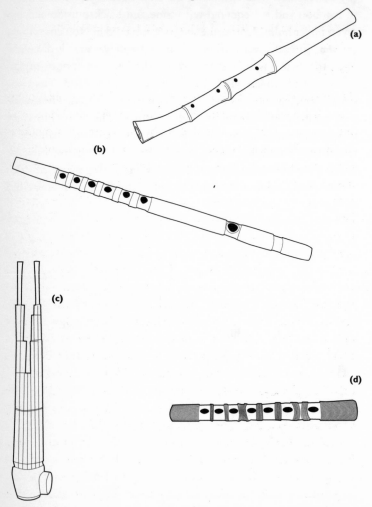

Fig. 17 Aerophones

Having discussed the most characteristic Japanese instruments we now turn to see their place in Japanese instrumental and theatrical ensembles, the Gagaku, Kabuki and in Noh plays.

Instrumental and Theatrical Ensembles

Gagaku

The literal meaning of *gagaku* is 'elegant music', that is music of the court. It was established in the eighth century and has been presented and practised ever since. It is likely to be the oldest surviving music of Japan. The term Gagaku is also used for defining orchestral music in China and Korea, the two neighbouring countries which introduced it to Japan. It was under their influence that the Japanese established the Imperial Music Bureau in 701. From then on the Japanese evolved their own Gagaku style which reached its peak during the Heian period (894–1092). The present-day Gagaku is largely a revival of that classic period. The two main categories of the Gagaku are a pure instrumental ensemble called *kangen*, and an ensemble accompanist of dances, *bugaku*. In accordance with the Japanese idea that left is superior to right, both *kangen* and *bugaku* are further subdivided into left (*shaho*) music, which is of Chinese or Indian origin, while the right (*uho*) music represents the influences of other countries, largely of Korea. The instruments used for *kangen* are flute, oboe, mouth-organ, zither, lute, side drum, gong and big drum. The *bugaku* is the same, but without the zither and lute. The right music differs from these by not including the harmony-giving instrument, the *sho*; by using a different flute (the cross flute of Korean origin: *koma fuye*); and instead of the side drum, a large hourglass drum (*san no tsuzumi*) of Chinese origin, but introduced to Japan by the Koreans. Both the *kangen* and *bugaku* can also be joined by a singer, who will sing court songs at banquets and at other court ceremonies. The Gagaku is also used for Shinto ritual music.

In general the rhythmic patterns are expressed on the percussion by varying strong (s) and weak (w) beats in the following popular schemes: swww, swsw, swsww. The melodic parts are usually played by the wind instruments, often in heterophonic styles. On occasions in the right (*uho*) style of music, the two wind instruments may play two different parts simultaneously (see p. 193). The strings may play melodically, but often their function is percussive and therefore rhythmic. As has already been stated, the most popular form for Gagaku music is the three-part structure: slow introduction (*jo*), moderate (*ha*) and fast ending (*kyu*). Fig. 18 shows a schematized seating plan for a Gagaku ensemble.

Fig. 18 Gagaku ensemble

There are three traditional Japanese theatrical styles which are so closely linked to music that they cannot be separated, and they will be discussed here in turn.

Bunraku (puppet theatre)

The proper name for puppet theatre in Japanese is *ningyo foruri* (*ningyo* = doll; *foruri* = narrative style of vocal music with *shamisen* (lute) accompaniment). The name *bunraku* was given to puppet theatre after the name of one of its main creators, Uemura Bun-rakuken, who was an outstanding developer of this genre in Osaka in 1872. It is one of the most popular art forms of Japan. In a way it is unfair that the name of this art form is monopolized by one of its creators as there were already several masters well before him in the seventeenth century.

One of the most striking aspects of this art is that the puppeteers move about on the stage and manipulate the puppets in full view of the audience. The manipulators are dressed in black and are often hooded as well so that they blend into the background. For the musicians, there is a specially elevated platform on which they are usually also in full view of the spectators on the left-hand side of the stage. There are two types of drama: five-act and three-act. The five-act dramas are based on historical sagas concerning the *samurai*; the three-act dramas are about contemporary events based on ordinary people's activities and their problems concerning the authorities, love, loyalty, et cetera.

The puppet's actions are made intelligible by the narrator singer who, with the help of words, explains the actions on the stage and usually represents all the characters in the story, whether peasant, merchant or *samurai*, et cetera. It is at this point that the *shamisen* player's role comes to full force, not only because the music enhances the theatrical action, but because the accompaniment of the narrator and his own vocal recitative, which at climactic movements may develop into a passionate song, are all essential parts of the whole theatrical experience. The purely instrumental parts played on the *shamisen* are subordinated to the duet-like collaboration between narrator and accompanist. In a *bunraku* performance there can be several narrators and *shamisen* players. Whether this is so depends on the dramatic intensity of the story and action. It is a Japanese custom to allow players of lesser standing to perform small and less important parts of the play. For larger and more significant parts, however, it is the more experienced musicians who take over. For the final scene of the drama it is the best narrator and *shamisen* players who are called to perform. Thus in every performance, there is a hierarchy of performers taking part determined by age and ability.

Kabuki

Another popular theatrical art form of the Edo period (1603–1868) was the Kabuki. The original meaning of the term *kabuki* meant someone behaving and dressing in an unusual manner. However, the word *kabuki*, based on three Chinese characters, now denotes song, dance and theatre.

The history of the Kabuki goes back to the late sixteenth and early seventeenth centuries when a female dancer called Okuni introduced a Buddhist folk-song-based dance drama. Originally it was performed by women alone but, as women were not permitted to perform in front of an audience, it was banned. The genre, nevertheless, did continue by employing young men. In turn they were also banned on grounds of immorality among the boys. Eventually the young boys were replaced by adult men. From the 1650s onwards, the Kabuki established itself as a main Japanese theatrical entertainment. Theatres were built in which the two styles of Kabuki, the forceful for the Samurai class and the more sophisticated for the well-to-do merchant class, were regularly performed. By then the fusion of theatre and dance was well established and remains so to this day.

Originally the drama could take a whole day. This has through time been shortened considerably. The influence of puppet dramas can be detected in the two story types, one concerning ordinary people, such as peasants and merchants, while the other category is represented by the *samurai*, their families and the historical legends concerning their activities. The milieu is, of course, feudal and concerns love, loyalty and aspects of moral conflicts. Dances are part of the dramatic development and are meant to give diversions and interest to the performance. On occasion, in order to give some prominence to a well-known dancer, extra dances are created to please the dancer and his audience.

As in the puppet theatre, in the Kabuki theatre the hierarchic system concerning the participants is also applied. The Kabuki involves both men and women performers.

The Kabuki is characterized by having a turntable stage in the centre of the main theatre as well as other movable platforms. An especially interesting feature of the Kabuki stage is its extension in the form of a long stage which is positioned running down into the auditorium at the left side, or sometimes on both sides. The effect is that some of the actors can walk from the main stage into the audience, thus enhancing the dramatic impact by practically being among them. This theatrical equivalent of a catwalk is called *hanamichi* or 'flower way', as traditionally it was used by the audience to give offerings of flowers to celebrated actors.

Music is an integral part of the performance: it provides, above all, atmosphere, it contributes to the dance and pantomime sections as well as giving sound effects to the spoken parts, and it marks interludes and preludes between and before dramatic actions. The much-loved *shamisen* is in great demand in Kabuki performances, not only as an accompanying lute but also to fill in, as it were, when the actor is not speaking.

The musicians are on the stage to be seen by the audience. There is, however, another ensemble placed to the left on the stage who are not visible as they are behind a bamboo or wooden screen. According to the genre of Kabuki theatre, other seating arrangements can also be followed; for instance, musicians might sit in a long row at the back of the stage. Be that as it may, the audience gets a spectacular view of actors, puppets, dancers and musicians, not forgetting the colourful staging. In many ways the music's function is not unlike that of film music: it enhances with programmatic sound effects the unfolding of theatrical events, whether this be passionate love or a sudden shower.

Noh

The Noh or No play, which means 'perfect art', is one of the most glorious manifestations of Japanese theatrical art. It is the Japanese answer to Wagner's idea of *Gesamtkunstwerk*, a synthesis of literature, theatre, dance and music. As in the *bunraku* and Kabuki theatres, music is of fundamental importance in the realization of a Noh play, which incorporates the very essence of Japanese traditional music. It is the long tradition of the Noh which has influenced the development of theatrical and musical genres such as the *bunraku* and Kabuki.

The Noh was established under the patronage of the Shogun Ashika Yoshimitsu in the fourteenth century, who approved of the innovative theatrical activities of Kiyotsugu Kannauni, an author and actor (1333–84?), and his son Zeami Motokiyo (1363–1443?). They were influenced by such early theatrical forms as the *sarugaku*, of Chinese origin.

The term *sarugaku* means 'monkey's show or performance' and it refers to the monkey's ability to imitate as actors imitate human life on the stage. Indeed, during the two founders' lives the name for their theatrical innovation was *sarugaku-noh*. *Noh* means ability. Thus the genre was called 'monkey's performance ability'. In time, the word *sarugaku* was dropped and the *noh* remained to denote the genre.

It was during the Edo period (1603–1868) that the Noh style became formalized in its quasi-ritualistic form, appealing more to the initiated cognoscenti than to the general theatre-goers. Of the 2000 dramas written by the two founders and later by several others during the period of the fourteenth and sixteenth centuries, only 200 have survived.

As we have seen, actors have a strictly hierarchical system in Japan, which is applied to Noh players as well. There are three main classes of performers: the principal actor (*shite*), who acts, sings and dances, is the main, most well-rounded performer, the very centre of the action; next to him is the second principal actor (*waki*); thirdly, there is the comic actor (*kyogen*). The dialogues and monologues are highly stylized, using immensely intensive intonations. The acting is also so formalized that it enters the realm of dance. The principal actor is the only one who wears splendiferous costumes and usually a mask. The rest of the participants are rather subdued in comparison.

The dramas, which are often based on subjects which are close to what is known in the West as morality plays, are concentrated pieces in one or two acts. When the drama is in two acts, the principal actor may act two different roles. For instance, he may be a woman in the first act and a man in the second act. The plays are themselves classified according to subjects. For instance, a play may be a demon's play, a woman's play, battle play and so on. The comic actor's role is mostly to play a comic intermezzo between acts or between two Noh performances. His text is spoken while the principal actor's is either recited or sung. As in most Japanese theatre, Noh plays are performed by men only.

The stage consists of a main stage (*hon-butai*) and an entrance ramp (*hashigakari*) on the left side of the stage. Both of these are covered with a roof; the one on the main stage is held up by four pillars, which gives the stage a temple or altar-like appearance. This increases the intensity and solitary beauty of the performance. An interesting device is the use of large clay pots which are placed under the stage for creating echo effects and for reinforcing sounds. Apart from a small curtain at the back of the entrance ramp, there is no curtain and the minimum of scenery. What passes for scenery is symbolic. So is most of the acting, which leaves a lot to the creative imagination of the audience, who are intellectually participating in the realization of the drama. They decipher signs which are conveyed to them. The symbolic nature of Noh is perhaps its more characteristic feature.

All the participants are visible on the stage: the instrumentalists are placed at the back of the stage; the chorus are seated on the right of the stage; the assistants are to the rear of the musicians on the left-hand side. Part of the audience faces the main stage, the rest are seated at the left between the main stage and the entrance ramp.

Fig. 19 gives an aerial view of the Noh stage to orientate the reader when the opportunity occurs to attend an actual performance.

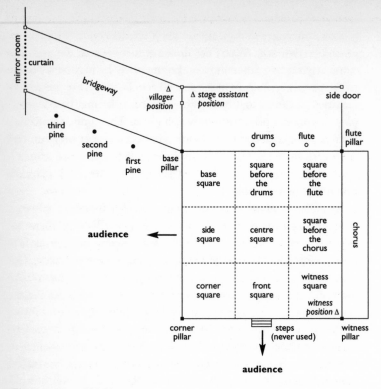

Fig. 19 Plan of Noh stage

Noh play and music

The number of musicians participating in a Noh play is small and chamber music-like. One can expect eight members in the chorus, which includes the head of the chorus, called *ji-gashiva*. He leads the chorus discreetly, without the narcissistic gesticulations we are accustomed to in the West. The accompaniment is provided by three or four instrumentalists, usually three drums and a flute. Their playing style is characterized by punctuating silence with single sound effects. The actors provide the solo singing, monologues and dialogues. The recitative-like singing is sometimes embellished with decorative passages. The singing, however, is nearer to monodrama (i.e. one character dominates the stage in turn), than to opera in general or aria in particular. The Noh is a musico-dramatic experience but not an operatic one in the sense of, for example, Verdi or Puccini.

Listeners may find that there are two styles of singing in a Noh play, soft (*yowagin*) and strong (*tsnyogin*). In soft singing there are three central notes: low, middle and high. These are a perfect fourth apart (b(ge)–e(dru)–a(jo)). There are, of course, other notes up and down the scale, but these three represent a central force which is borne in the performer's mind. A piece of music may end on either a low note or high note, but never on a middle note, as this gives an unfinished feeling. In the strong singing style there are only two central notes a minor third apart (for example, f♯'–a'). As there are only two central notes at a shorter distance from each other this version of a scale pattern is more restricted. In the soft style, as can be seen, each note is a fourth apart, while in the strong style it is a minor third. The intervals between those notes representing the two styles determine whether one is singing in the soft or strong style.

Rhythmically the sung text is based on phrases of 8, 12 and 16 syllables, of which the most popular pattern is the 12-syllabic structure (7 + 5). When this structure is adapted to 8 beats, the ingenious solution is to do the following:

1	2 3	4	5 6	7	8 9	10 11	12
1	2	3	4	5	6	7	8

Fig. 20

Rhythm in any music is either strict (*giusto*) or free (*rubato*). Freedom, however, should not be interpreted as anarchy, but rather as disciplined flexibility. The Japanese Noh players are masters of both.

As far as the three or four instruments in the ensemble are concerned, three of them are drums (one barrel drum, two hourglass drums) and one a transverse bamboo flute, known as *fue* or *nohkan*.

It is the only melodic instrument in the quartet (or trio if one of the drums is dropped).

It was Zeami Motokiyo, the founder of Noh, who established that a Noh play should constitute noble elegance and charm within the framework of extreme concentration and symbolic expression. The Noh is one of the great theatrical innovations of mankind.

General Considerations

Religion

In Chapters 3 and 4 we have already discussed the natures of Buddhism, Confucianism and Taoism. Of these, Buddhism and Confucianism affected Japan's spiritual and social life profoundly. In the nineteenth century, Christians made a renewed attempt to convert the Japanese to their faith. This attempt had a very modest success. Statistically, however, Buddhism represents 73 per cent of the population and Shinto, Japan's own religion for over 2000 years, 87 per cent. Which shows that they profess both religions.

Shinto

The word Shinto was coined from the Chinese *shen* (gods) and the word *tao* (way) at the time when Buddhism was introduced to Japan. It was meant to distinguish between Buddhism and the older Japanese religion, 'the Way of the Kami'. The central theme of Shinto is the belief in the mysterious forces of nature, the *kamis*, which manifest themselves in millions of ways, in plants, animals, seas and mountains, et cetera. It combines oneness with nature, reverence for tradition and loyalty to the reigning dynasty as descendants of the sun goddess, Amaterasu. The Meiji rulers developed the theme of loyalty by stressing obedience to the point of subservience and militaristic devotion to the emperor. This aspect of the traditional Shinto was dropped after the end of the Second World War. Shinto combines in the veneration of nature an emphatic feeling of awe and wonder and a cultivated sense of the divine in life. There can be little doubt that the Shinto preoccupation with nature is based on an early agriculturally oriented fertility cult. This is evident in the Shinto's veneration of sacred trees, planting ceremonies, harvesting festivities, the pilgrimage to the sacred Mount Fuji and not least the pilgrimage to the shrine at Ise of the most important *kami*, the sun goddess Amaterasu.

Shinto has no scriptural literature, but it has a mythology recorded in the eighth century AD. There are two texts (*Kojiki* and *Nihongi*) in which Shinto mythology tells that the age of *kami* began after the cosmos emerged out of chaos and when the sun goddess Amaterasu-Omikani, the most important *kami*, emerged. Humanity's history started when the grandchild of Amaterasu, Ninigi, descended to the lower regions of Japan and when the great-grandson, Jimmu Tenno, the legendary ruler of Japan, became the ruler of the unified country in about 660 BC.

Of the thirteen Shinto sects, five groups seem to summarize their activities:

(i) *Pure Shinto* (veneration of ancestors and loyalty to the emperor);
(ii) *Mountain sects* (Shinto sects who believe in gods living in sacred mountain places);
(iii) *Purification sects* (believers in physical and ritual purity);
(iv) *Confucian sects* (those who combine Confucianism and Shinto);
(v) *Faith-healers* (who believe that illness and evil are spiritual deformations and encourage purification rituals to remedy these mental and physical aberrations).

Buddhism in Japan

Buddhism was introduced to Japan via Korea between 550 and 600 AD, when the Korean nobility sent to the Japanese imperial court envoys and missionaries with gifts and Buddhist scriptures. They succeeded in making the emperors believe that Buddhism had the powerful charm of securing national stability and general welfare.

For a period of over a thousand years Buddhism became the state religion of Japan. Fortunately, as Buddhism practises tolerance, the Shinto shrines were not disturbed by the Buddhist priests and though they reinterpreted Shinto beliefs according to Buddhist doctrines, the Shinto rites were also largely preserved.

Religions have the tendency to branch out into sects. Out of the numerous Buddhist sects in Japan such as Tendal, Shingon, Jodo, Nichiren and Zen, Zen has had a major impact on Japanese life and thinking.

Zen

It was Eisai (1141–1215), a Japanese Buddhist monk, who introduced Zen and tea-drinking from China to Japan. Then another priest, Dogen (1200–1253), spread it and emphasized the importance of a work ethic and discipline during one's journey towards self-realization and the discovery of one's own Buddha-nature. In Zen the importance of meditation is stressed and in order to achieve enlightenment (*satori*) the *koan* questioning technique is practised. The riddle-like – sometimes to the point of seeming to be nonsensical – *koan* questions are meant to derail, as it were, the logical rational thinking of the questionee in order to help shift him into that of transcendental wisdom. A higher level of insight is aimed at, far beyond rational logic. A well-known Zen question is 'What is the sound of one hand clapping?'

Zen can mean several things for many people. For instance the most popular images are: the tea-ceremony; the calm serenity of the sand-garden; archery; flower arrangements; the 'orderly spontaneity' of doing things; and one's attitude to life in general. It is not of insignificant interest that at the time when Noh was developed, Zen, with its liking for riddles and allusions as well as its preference for seemingly illogical or anti-logical techniques, was more forcefully exercising its influence on Japan and that the founders of the Noh were themselves influenced by the spirit of Zen. Likewise Buddhist temple ritual is influenced by Zen, in, for instance, the use of the large bell (*ogane*, see p. 196). So too it is a Zen tradition to hit a wooden board with a mallet when summoning the monks to the main hall for meditation.

All through their history the Japanese have demonstrated a singular ability, in religion, philosophy, the arts and, in this century, in science and technology, to absorb diverse influences and to mould these influences to their own image with stupendous originality and determination.

(i) Java; (ii) Bali

Background

Indonesia's large population – over 184 million inhabitants of multi-ethnic backgrounds – lives in a spread of several thousand islands. The origins of Indonesia can be traced back to the Malay kingdom of Srivijaya, which included not only the Malay peninsula but also part of Western Java and Sumatra. The Malay kingdom flourished during the period between the seventh and twelfth centuries. The Srivijaya and eventually the Majapahit kingdoms, which by the thirteenth century dominated Java, were influenced by both Buddhism and Hinduism. These religions could have established themselves, but Islam, via India, arrived in the thirteenth century and within two hundred years, with the sole exception of Bali, which succeeded in remaining Hindu, it established itself as the main religion of the archipelago.

The ethnic constitution of Indonesia is based on the Malay race, which can be broadly divided into three main groups: the Hindus, who are mainly rice growers in Java and Bali; the coastal people, who are followers of Islam; and lastly the various minor tribal groups. The Chinese are the largest of the non-indigenous groups and are officially obliged to adopt the Bahasa Indonesian language.

In the sixteenth century Indonesia was occupied in turn by the Portuguese, the British and the Dutch. From 1602 to 1798 it was ruled by the Dutch East India Company. Then it became a colony of the Netherlands which, apart from a brief period during the years 1805–16, lasted uninterrupted until the Japanese invasion in 1942. The joy of getting rid of the Dutch colonialists with the help, ironically, of another colonialist force helped the cause of the Indonesian Nationalist Party, which was awaiting the opportunity for a take-over. After the defeat of Japan in 1945 the party's leader, Dr Sukarno, declared Indonesia's independence. Four years of messy conflict followed between the Dutch and the Indonesians, but in 1949 Indonesia was granted independence. The details of the dramatic complexities of the social, political and economic conflicts and confusions which have taken place since with plots, military take overs, executions, et cetera are beyond the scope of this introductory information.

What concerns us here, however, is the cultural constitution of Indonesian society, which can be summarized as being synthetic. Contacts with Hindu, Buddhist, Islamic, Chinese and Western elements have shaped its present hybrid and yet markedly individual cultural identity. Even Islam, with its inflexible ideology, seems to have blended into Indonesia, albeit via its artistically more lenient Sufist representation, which happened to be the dominating force of Islamic expansion, above all in Java. Sufism's more flexible attitude towards the arts had a fruitful encounter with the indigenous forms of arts, which it has enriched rather than oppressed. Indonesia's and above all Java's ability to accommodate diverse interactions and colonizations without losing their identity is similar to India's own remarkable ability to assimilate quite formidable intrusions. Thus, as Sumarsam pointed out in his book, *Gamelan: Cultural Interaction and Musical Development in Central Java*:

Nineteenth-century Javanese court culture should be viewed not only as the consequence of an 'inward focus' of court activity, but also as an 'outward expression' of court attempts to accommodate the diversity of society. More importantly, the development of Javanese culture should be understood as the result of complex interactions in the multi-class and multi-ethnic population of Java: Javanese (aristocrats and common folk), Dutch, Indos, and Chinese. Such interactions involved competing and conflicting models of culture, religion and ideology. The heterogeneous court culture was the result of a cultural consensus between the colonizers and their Javanese subjects.[1]

This 'cultural consensus between the colonizers and their Javanese subjects' took place three times, with the Hindu, Islamic and Western encounters. In each case the Javanese ability to accommodate vastly different ideologies and cultures made these encounters positive. It is significant that the Islamization of Java was mellowed by the fact that Islamic influence in Java came via India and was thus modified by Hinduism, which was more to the inclination of the Javanese. The dominating presence of Sufism, already stressed on p. 220, made the absorption of Islam much smoother because, as we have noted, Sufism is more tolerant towards both music and dance, which have fundamental importance in Javanese culture.

By the end of the nineteenth century and first half of the twentieth century, Indonesia not only learned how to cope with Western ways of thinking, but at the same time developed its natural pride not so much against but in conjunction with the European influences. As Sumarsam summed it up,

In this period, the Europeans and European elements became prominent. This was the pinnacle of development, such that the Dutch national anthem had to be played together with 'Gendhing Sri Katon' (the signature piece of the King Paku Buwana) whenever Paku Buwana appeared in his court chamber; in a religiously significant court event, the court musicians for European music played a repertoire from a genre of European popular music. This was the period of *kaélokan* (mysterious, fantastic, and strange), in which Javanese traditional forces lived side by side with the secular, modern Western world.[2]

It was also the period when the traditional gamelan (*gamel*: hammer; a reference to the hammer-like sticks which are used to play on the metallophones) music of Java was projected by the Indonesian nationalists as being the most appropriate musical expression of the nation.

Rhythm

By and large and in conformity with the general tendency of the Far East, Javanese and Balinese rhythm is dominatingly square. What is striking, however, is the layering and interlocking techniques applied to their music which gives one of its most complex and intoxicating characteristics. Let us examine these in more detail.

Fig. 1

Although layering is to do with the nature and size of instruments, it also affects the rhythmic subdivision of the music. The basic principle is that a large and a low-sounding instrument will have less frequent notes to play. Conversely small and higher-pitched instruments will play notes in greater frequency. Thus in relation to each other, some instruments will be playing more or less numbers of notes. To illustrate this point, Fig. 1 shows the rhythm of four unspecified instruments: one, low pitched and large; one, middle ranged and medium sized; a small high pitched and an even smaller and higher pitched.

What we can observe in Fig. 1 is not polyrhythm, which is after all the simultaneous combination of different rhythmic patterns (for example, 2 with 3 and 5, et cetera . . .), but the technique of layering the rhythmic density or frequency of notes in a given metric unit. In our case 4/4. The proportionate relationship between all the sounds is self-evident, yet the overall effect is strikingly independent and therefore polyphonic.

The next point to be observed is what is known as interlocking. Again a practical example is likely to illustrate the principle better than words (see Fig. 2).

etc.

Fig. 2

The bracketed notes clearly show that the melody is identical, yet a kind of monothematic polyphony is created by virtue of using more notes in the upper part. In fact, the two parts are interlocked by both their metric interdependence and their pitch relationship. We witness 'variation in unity'.

These two most characteristic features of Javanese and Balinese rhythm are, among other aspects of Indonesian music, what give it its elemental vitality and complexity. No wonder that Western audiences of the late nineteenth century were bewildered when they heard Balinese music for the first time in Paris. Its impact on twentieth-century composers, such as Debussy, was significant. One could postulate that to a considerable degree modern Western music has evolved as it did because of its fruitful encounter with non-Western musical styles.

Melody

It doesn't take long before an attentive listener of Indonesian music, above all Javanese and Balinese music, notices the preponderance of the place of the major third in its melodic structure. Indeed, in western Java singers may perform with two separate major third tetrachords (for example, b–c'–d'–e', g'–a'–b'–c'). Another familiar sound is the pentatonic or near-pentatonic scale patterns, such as c' d' e' g' a'.

As neither the cycle of fifths nor the Pythagorean divisions of the strings are practised by traditional Indonesian musicians, the scales are learnt through imitation of instinctive and traditional patterns rather than scientifically constructed. As the instruments are dominatingly idiophones, a certain pitch discrepancy is tolerated and considered as normal.

Moreover, in order to accommodate several modes on the idiophones, a flexible scale pattern has evolved. This scale pattern consists of the following seven notes: E F G A B C D. It enables the players to play most of the popular modes including, of course, the pentatonic scale. In modal terms it is, in fact, the equivalent of an incomplete Phrygian scale.

Three examples of the Indonesian melodic style are shown in Fig. 3(a), (b) and (c).

(a)

(b)

Fig. 3 (c)

Note that Fig. 3(a) is pentatonic while (b) is similar to the lower half of a C major scale. The notes utilized in these two melodies correspond to the seven-note collective scale pattern outlined above.

It is the ostinato rhythmic and melodic repetitions and variations of these types of melodies together with the layering and interlocking techniques played on largely idiophonic instruments which give Javanese and Balinese music its characteristic sound quality.

With reference to tempo (speed), according to J. Kunst in his book *Music in Java*, in some regions of Java up to seven tempi names can be found: extremely slow, very fast, slow, fairly slow, moderately quick, quick and fast.[3] Even more subtle divisions can be detected in western Java but, equally, fewer can be found in the east of Java, where only five grades are in use. This is in striking contrast to the Chinese conservative tradition concerning dynamics. This is not an indication that all music in China is peaceful or restrained; it is, however, less agitated and varied in terms of dynamic differentiation in contrast to that of Indonesia.

Before the discussion and illustration of the Javanese and Balinese orchestral practice and plan, as known by its generic name gamelan, we first turn to the discussion of those individual instruments which are part of the gamelan ensemble.

Instruments

Indonesian music is overwhelmingly percussive. Apart from the folk fiddle (chordophone) and the folk *shawm* (aerophone), Indonesian music is performed on a wide range of percussive instruments of which the gongs and xylophones or xylophone-like instruments in various sizes tend to dominate and give the characteristic metallic percussive tone of the gamelan ensemble.

Percussive instruments (idiophones, metallophones and membraphones)

Idiophones
(a) *Anklung* This most elegant, fragile instrument is a bamboo rattle (or sliding rattle). It is made of two or three bamboo tubes, tuned at an octave, which are suspended vertically in a delicate bamboo frame while their lower parts are positioned flexibly in the groove of a horizontally positioned bamboo. When shaken to and fro, or when the rim of the horizontal bamboo is hit, it produces a subtle and pleasant sound.

It is often played in groups where each is of a different size and together form the notes of a pentatonic scale (for example, c'd'e'g'a').

(b) Clappers Three clappers stand out as being the most popular:

(i) *Kemanak* First there are clappers made out of metal, called *kemanak*. They are banana shaped with two thin handles. They are often used in ensembles accompanying dances.

(ii) *Loutar* The *loutar*, from Bali, is a clapper with two or more, often several, sounding parts, either made of wood or metal, which when shaken or flicked, make sharp clapping sounds.

(iii) Clapper bell Thirdly there is the clapper bell, which can be made out of decorated wood such as the one used in Bali, or from metal such as those made not only in Java and Bali, but also in Burma and Korea.

(c) Jingle The frame jingle of Bali is one of the most characteristic-looking instruments, as the frame on which the bells or jingles are hung is broadly in the shape of a Christmas-tree. Both the bottom or the top of the 'tree', as it were, can be used as the handle for rhythmically shaking the jingles.

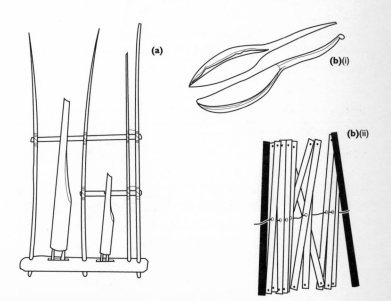

Fig. 4 Idiophones

(d) Gongs Basically a gong is made of a metal disc which is struck with a beater. The early gongs were just flat bronze plates, but this evolved into a substantially bulging surface or at least with a raised and centrally positioned boss. Contrary to the vibration of the bell, where the vibration is dead in the centre but very active around the rim, the gong vibrates most intensively at its centre and gradually fades away towards its rim.

Although an instrument known worldwide, gongs in general are to be found in South-East Asia, where its most popular form is not so much the suspended version, but rather the horizontally positioned individual gong or the similarly positioned series of gong chimes.

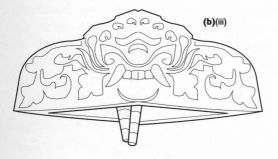

(b)(iii)

(c)

Fig. 4 Idiophones – *continued*

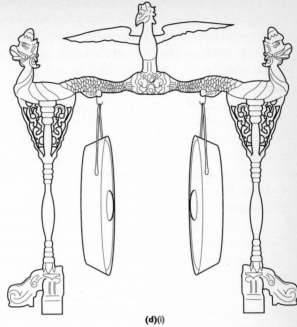

(d)(i)

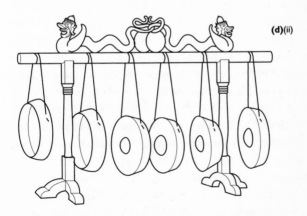

(d)(ii)

Fig. 4 Idiophones – *continued*

(i) and (ii) Suspended gongs Beautifully ornamented stands of suspended gongs can be found in all of South East Asia, but perhaps the most lavishly decorated ones are from Indonesia and above all from Java. In Fig. 4(d)(i) and (ii) are two examples from Java, one with two hanging gongs, *gong ageng*, and the other the multiple hanging gongs.

(iii) Kenong The *kenong* is an unusually deep-rimmed gong which rests on crossed cords which are themselves attached to a highly ornate square table-like stand. This is a large horizontal gong to be played on singly. It is a rather high-pitched gong which, intriguingly, is considered to be male.

The term *kenong*, however, also refers to a *set* of horizontal gongs which will be discussed next.

(iv) Gong chimes Gong chimes are popular in China, Thailand, Burma, Borneo, Sumatra, et cetera, but it is the Javanese group chime which seems to have left the deepest impression on Western travellers.

They are known as *bonang* and there are several variations, both in shape and in pitch, the most obvious being: large, *bonang panembung*; medium, *bonang barung*; and small, *bonang panerus*. The most popular is one which consists of two rows of five, six or seven gongs. The one with six groups covers a two-octave compass. The player strikes them, usually an octave apart, with two padded sticks as he sits in front of the longer side of the frame. Here too, the high-pitched gongs are considered male while the lower ones are seen to be female. The *bonangs* are an essential part of the gamelan ensemble.

(e) Cymbals Like the name of the gong, the various names given to cymbals, in particular in Bali, such as *chengcheng* or *rinchik*, are onomatopoeic words which make the names of the instruments instantly memorable. Whatever shape the Indonesian cymbal may take, its basic principle is the same: a cymbal in each hand is struck against another pair of cymbals on the ground.

(f) Xylophones The xylophones of South East Asia are splendiferous instruments not only in terms of their sound quality and versatility, as they are both melodic and rhythmic instruments, but also in terms of being objects of art, as the body over which the bars (slabs) are placed is decorated. They can be cradle-shaped or, as in

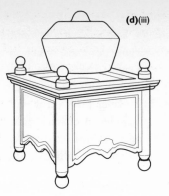

(d)(iii)

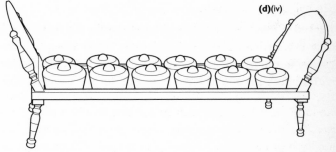

(d)(iv)

(e)(i)

(e)(ii)

Fig. 4 Idiophones – *continued*

the case of the Javanese *gambang*, peacock-shaped with carved and brightly coloured plumage. The slabs of a xylophone are made of hard wood and it has a varying compass, which in modern makes may cover up to four octaves (c'–c⁴). The traditional gamelan xylophone rarely goes beyond twenty-one keys (slabs), that is about two octaves or more. The player plays on it with two disc-type beaters fixed to two long handles. A characteristic feature of both Javanese and Balinese playing is playing in octaves (*gembyangan*) and in regular rhythmic and melodic patterns, which give a trance-inducing quality to the sound.

Metallophones

The metallophones are basically xylophone-like, but with metal (usually bronze) rather than wooden slabs. They are an ancient percussive instrument, as they were already known in China in the seventh century AD and in Indonesia from the ninth century AD.

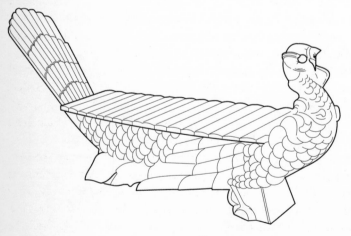

(f)

Fig. 4 Idiophones – *continued*

They are immensely important in Java and Bali as they form the largest part of the gamelan ensemble in both islands. They provide the melody of the gamelan. The resonators are mostly cradle-shaped and highly ornate, decorated with dragon heads and tails.

(a) Saron The Javanese generic name for the metallophone is *saron*. As is the case with horizontal gongs, the *sarons* are also divided into three broad categories: large, *saron demung*; medium, *saron barung*; and small, *saron panerus*. The compass of these metallophones is usually one octave, but there are also multi-octave *sarons*. The popular single-octave *saron*, according to its tuning system, may be *pelog* or *slendro*. Together they represent eighteen types of basic tuning, but beware, as there are hardly two gamelans which could share the same tuning structure. Local traditions and individual and/ or group preferences overrule scientific theories. The *pelog* tuning style is visually observable, as the instrument will have seven bars, whereas those tuned in *slendro* are likely to have five, six, seven or eight to twelve bars.

In terms of musical notation, the *pelog* system is based on the following pitches: d' e♭'(+) f'(−)' g♯(−)' a' b♭' c"(+) (d");★ the *slendro* system, which is the oldest, shows a clear pentatonic structure: c' d(+)' f' g' a(+)' (c"). The two systems represent a complementary relationship, as one is chromatic and the other is diatonic/pentatonic. However, it should be noted that the main difference between these two scale systems is not so much the number of notes (in practice, out of the seven-note *pelog*, only five are used at any given time), but rather the intervallic relationship within the scales which gives the characteristic melodic quality to each.

(b) Gender The *gender* differs from the *saron* by the slabs (or bars) being placed over individual bamboo resonators. The slabs (or bars) are thinner than those on the *saron*. As a result the sound is rather thinner or muted and in a mellower way complements the *saron*, whose tone is louder and more emphatic. At this point it should be

★ The (+) sign indicates sharper and the (−) sign indicates flatter pitches than it is possible to write in Western notation.

noted that the Indonesians think of musical expression in terms of dynamics, that is 'loud' and 'quiet' instruments.

It is likely that it was the *gender* which, during migration, may have reached Africa, as the African *marimbas* are more or less identical to the Indonesian *gender*. The possibility of this migration was suggested by the great ethno-musicologist, Jaap Kunst. It is difficult to verify, but it is certainly a possible theory, especially in the light of Madagascar's Indonesian affiliation.

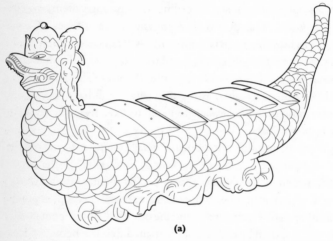

(a)

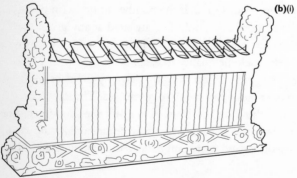

(b)(i)

Fig. 5 Metallophones

There are two types of *genders*, the large-sized, low- and middle-range gender (*gender baring*); and the small-sized, high-to-middle-range gender (*gender panerus*). They are both important members of the gamelan. Their placing in the gamelan ensemble is illustrated on p. 239.

Drums (membraphones)

(a) Cylindrical drum Cylindrical drums are very popular, especially in Bali. They are made in different sizes and are played on both sides by the player, as they are double-headed drums. Normally they are placed on the laps of the players.

(b) Conical drum As it is a one-headed drum it is either placed on the floor or held sideways.

(c) *Kendang* This is a two-headed, but asymmetrical, drum with the heads held by leather loops laced in a Y pattern. It is usually placed on a stand enabling the player to use both hands. It is the *kendang* player whose responsibility it is to keep a steady tempo and also to change tempo towards the end of the performance. There are four types of *kendang*: large, medium, small and little.

(d) Frame drum The frame drum is a single construction of one or two membranes stretched over a shallow frame, which is usually

(b)(ii)

Fig. 5 Metallophones – *continued*

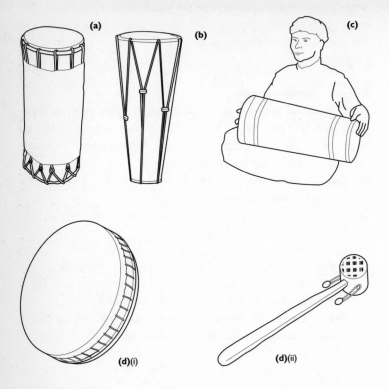

Fig. 6 Membraphones

circular. The Javanese *terbang* is one of this type of tambourine-like instrument. A much more interesting frame drum, originating from China, indeed it is only played by the Chinese settlers in Java, is the *klontong* or *kelontong*. In Bali it is known as *ketipluk*. It is a miniature double-headed barrel drum fixed to a handle. In addition two hard little pellets are attached to either side of the heads by cords. When shaken, these pellets hit the drum heads, creating a dry percussive sound effect.

String instruments (chordophones)

Folk fiddles or spike fiddles are popular string instruments in Asia and in the far-eastern countries of China, Japan, Thailand, Cambodia and Indonesia, including, of course, Java and Bali, where each country has its fiddle variants. One of the most characteristic and popular of these in Java is the *rebab* or spike fiddle.

(a) Spike fiddle This is an elegant two-stringed instrument which was introduced to Indonesia by the Muslims. It has a heart-shaped shallow body with strikingly elongated horizontal pegs and spike. The pitches are produced both by the position of the player's fingers on the strings, and by the pressure which he puts on them. The bow is tied loosely. It is a very important melody instrument, as its function is not only to lead the melody but to mediate, as it were, between the instrumental and vocal sections of the ensemble. Of the two spike fiddles which form part of the gamelan, one is tuned to *pelog*, the other to *slendro* (see p. 233). Note, however, that only one plays at any given time in the gamelan ensemble; they never play together.

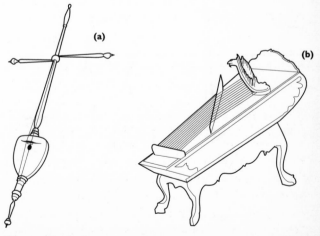

Fig. 7 Chordophones

(b) *Celempung* **(zither)** This is a plucked string instrument with thirteen (sometimes fourteen) pairs of strings which run between tuning pins. It is, of course, a melody instrument which is plucked with the thumbnails. Visually it is easily recognizable as it looks like a small coffin placed on a downward-sloping frame (which is often a resonator as well), with longer legs at its head and shorter at its feet. There can be as many as three *celempungs* in a gamelan.

Wind instruments (aerophones)

(a) *Shawm* *Shawms* are of Middle Eastern origin, but they were established in China, Tibet and India as well as in Indonesia. The Javanese version is similar to that of the Tibetan version, but much more ornate. It is not played in the gamelan ensemble.

(b) *Suling* This is a Javanese cross flute with six finger holes. It is an end-blown flute made of bamboo. Like the spike fiddles, there are two *sulings* in the gamelan ensemble: one for the *pelog*, the other for the *slendro*. The *sulings* are the only wind instrument used in the orchestra.

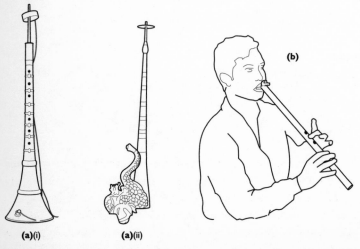

(a)(i)   **(a)(ii)**   **(b)**

Fig. 8 Aerophones

The human voice

Finally the peculiar use of the human voice should be mentioned, as it is applied as an instrument, that is both female (*sindenam*) and male (*gerongan*) singers function as rhythmic and melodic lines as part of the 'instrumentation' of the gamelan ensemble and not as vocal solos accompanied (backed) by the orchestra, as in the West.

To complete this section the layout of a gamelan ensemble is shown in Fig. 9 (i) and (ii).

Fig. 9 (i) View of gamelan ensemble

Theatrical Ensembles and Music

It should be borne in mind that Indonesian theatre, above all that of Java, Bali and Sunda, is a fusion of several art forms, particularly drama, dance, puppet theatre, staging and music. Indeed music has a fundamentally cohesive importance in traditional Indonesian theatrical performances. For instance, the use of the scale patterns *slendro* and *pelog* (see p. 233) clearly defines Hindu and Muslim

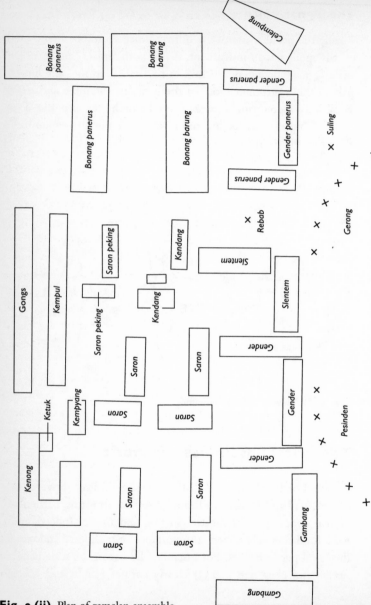

Fig. 9 (ii) Plan of gamelan ensemble

influences: tales of Hindu origin are likely to be performed musically by using the five-tone *slendro* scale, whereas the Muslim-influenced tales will be executed in the seven-tone *pelog*. Music also affects the overall performance in terms of structure, by signalling beginnings, changes, stops and endings. It can also determine character types in the theatre, as they may be associated with certain notes or patterns of the *slendro* or *pelog* scales.

Traditional performances are largely improvised by both the players of the play and the musicians participating in it. The inter-action of the two groups is an essential part of the success of the performance, which thus combines the expected (the tradition) with the unexpected (the newly found improvised expression or variant).

The *dalang* (puppeteer or storyteller) or *pantun* is not only a storyteller but a singing bard as well, who often improvises songs in order to enhance the general mood of the play. Moreover, we have seen that in Indonesian thinking music and musical instruments are broadly grouped into soft and loud categories. Similarly Indonesian actors not only have archetypal characters – such as aristocrat, aesthete, warrior, royalty, clown, which appear both in puppet theatre (*wajang*) as well as in dance dramas (*topeng*: masked dance) – but they may fall into two broad categories: the refined (*alns*) and the rough (*kasar*).

Another characteristic feature of the Indonesian version of *Gesamtkunstwerk* style is its length. A performance may last not only several hours, but a whole day and night, if not beyond. For instance a *wajang* in general begins at 9 p.m. and ends at 5 a.m. During these marathon performances members of the audience may choose to eat, sleep or select a favourite scene, then depart to be with friends, and return again later, perhaps with children who are interested in seeing the clown's performance, et cetera. These theatrical 'shows' are community events to be enjoyed by all and sundry either fully or in part according to preferences to topics, taste and time. The expected and the unexpected are experienced by those who partici-pate in a truly festive spirit.

Wayang

Of all the spectacular plays and dances it is the *wayang*, the Javanese puppet and shadow plays, which are likely to present the outsider with a dramatic and musical experience which is unlikely to be forgotten easily. It is worth stressing that the meaning of *wayang* is puppet. But the meaning goes well beyond the restricted sense of the word, as it contains plays, whether performed by puppets or human beings, as well as the shadow puppets. These are made of leather and, being flat, represent in a two-dimensional form a highly sophisticated dramatic art form. Among several possible variants, two types of traditional forms can be distinguished: the *wayang-kulit* (the word *kulit* refers to leather); the *wayang-golek* (which is the three-dimensional puppet show and which does not need the canvas that is essential for the *wayang-kulit*); and thirdly the *wayang orang* or *wong* (this is a human dance-theatre).

The music accompanying the *wayang* is the gamelan ensemble which, as we have seen, is dominated by percussion, that is metallo-phones (*gender*), xylophones (*gambang*) and drums (*kendang*). The melody is projected by the flute (*suling*) and by the folk fiddle (*rebab*).

The music is based on two different but nevertheless complemen-tary scale patterns, the *pelog* and the *slendro* (see p. 233). This means that basically there are two of each instrument in order to enable the ensemble to play these scales. It is the sensitive interrelationship between these two scale patterns which gives the gamelan one of its characteristic sound qualities.

The mode of a gamelan performance is determined by the degree of the selected pitch on which the music is based (e.g. d e g a c is similar, yet different from c d e g a). The chosen note on which the scale pattern is based is called *patet*. It is the interplays and changes in the melodic (*gending*) modes that can express the necessary atmos-pheres required in the numerous episodes of a *wayang*.

In a good performance everyone's contribution is important; nevertheless, one can hardly exaggerate the significance of the puppeteer (*dalang*). It is he who is the selector of the script, producer, performer, singer and conductor of the gamelan.

No wonder that the training of a *dalang* starts in childhood and that it takes many years of apprenticeship to become a master. Not only is the *dalang* something of a universal artist but until quite recently he used to be seen as a priest, as the *wayang* is not just an entertainment but a cathartic spiritual experience. The mystery of making the puppets or shadow puppets *alive* involves a sense of the ritualistic in which the stage turns into a temporary sacred temple with the *delang* as its high priest.

In order to help the reader to envisage the stage and some of the gamelan instruments which may take part in a *wayang-kulit* performance, a simplified diagram is shown in Fig. 10.

(ii) Bali

This final section will outline briefly the differences between Javanese and Balinese music.

The similarities should by now be obvious, as we have touched upon several topics which are interchangeable between the two islands. For instance, the Old Javanese language is to this day in use in Bali. Musical instruments as well as ideas concerning music and puppet theatre are likely to have originated in or at least were influenced by Java. Mantle Hood, the eminent scholar of Javanese music, in his study *The Evolution of Javanese Gamelan*, suggests that some of the Balinese gamelans are continuations of the east Javanese tradition. There is indeed evidence of cross-fertilization of ideas in terms of both rhythm and instrumentation.

An important break between the two islands was already referred to in the introduction to this chapter, where it was pointed out that Bali did not succumb to Islam, but remained Hindu. India's profound appreciation of the arts in general and music in particular has permeated Balinese culture also, where art is practised to such an extent that in Balinese villages practically everybody is a potential artist or

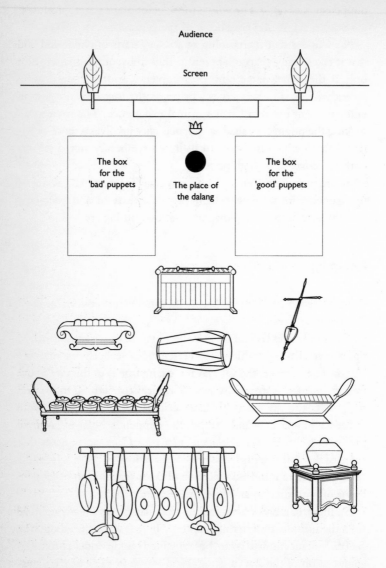

Fig. 10 (i) Plan of *wayang kulit* ensemble

Fig. 10 (ii) View of *wayang kulit* ensemble

at least some kind of craftsman. It is telling that in statistical terms more gamelans can be found in Bali per capita than in the rest of the Indonesian archipelago. The communal aspect of the Balinese approach to the arts and music is perhaps best illustrated by the fact that although one man may and must be the leader of the gamelan ensemble, the performers are invited to contribute their own ideas about the piece to be performed. These suggestions are then incorporated into the eventual performance. Thus we witness a collective compositional style.

In comparison with Java, Balinese performing style is more vigorous, with greater dynamic contrast and orchestral brilliance. One of the likely reasons for the quivering sound effect of the Balinese gamelan is its tuning tradition. The Balinese tune their instruments in pairs, but with one instrument always being slightly higher pitched. This creates what is called 'acoustical beats', which gives a shimmering, throbbing quality to the gamelan. This acoustical phenomenon, combined with the virtuoso execution and rhythmic precision of the trance-inducing repetitions, sudden halts and frenetic continuations of the largely pentatonic melodies played on percussive instruments are those ingredients which give the gamelan its unique colour.

In Bali, dance music dominates the gamelan; this is not the case in Java, where dance-inspired music may be performed by the gamelan without the participation of dancers.

Male and female choral singing is, of course, practised in both Java and Bali, but it is the ancient Balinese trance-inducing choir-dance, called *kecak* – based on the religious ritual known as *sanghyang* and believed to have existed prior to Hindu influence and which was performed to propitiate the gods – that is the most striking vocal sound experience of the island. The *kecak* is sung by a male chorus in which the gamelan interlocking technique (see p. 223) is applied, using the syllable '*cak*' with frenetic rhythmic intensity. The vocal execution includes, moreover, shouts and hisses as well as a mixture of unison singing and complex rhythmic and melodic choral texture executed, when appropriate, at great speed, requiring virtuoso technique. The five-tone *kecak* melodies are usually based on the repetition of a two-plus-two melodic structure in 4/4 time.

In addition the dancer-singers rhythmically raise and shake their arms while swaying back and forth in a state of trance. Once heard and seen it is an experience never to be forgotten.

I wish to conclude by reminding the reader that it was gamelan music which left a deep impression on Debussy in 1889 at the Paris World Fair. Later on, Bartók and Cage were similarly moved, to mention only a few of the twentieth-century masters who have been influenced by it. Indonesia has affected the development of modern Western music with its originality of expression in sound.

Afterword

It would be hypocrisy not to acknowledge that the journey taken in this book was not easy. There were indeed complex and difficult issues to grasp and the reader has more than likely been led through unfamiliar territories. Guiding a reader is not unlike the sherpa's role in leading the climber towards the summit. He can only lead up to the last camp or paths which he is familiar with. From then on it is a lonely struggle to the summit. So it should be. In any subject which is to be properly mastered there is no short cut and easy way. The contemporary tendency to 'sell' difficult topics such as learning Latin, German, mathematics, music, et cetera in the format of *Latin Made Easy*, *German in Three Months* and so forth, under the misleading concept of being 'reader friendly', belongs to the world of dealers who have set out to con the unwary purchaser that it is possible to achieve something without much effort. This introductory book on non-Western music was not easy and the summit ahead is even more difficult. Good luck.

Over and above the books and CDs listed in the bibliography and discography, an excellent book is singled out for further useful and illuminating information, including popular contemporary musical developments: *The Rough Guide to World Music*, edited by S. Broughton, M. Ellingham, D. Muddyman, R. Trillo and K. Burton, also available from Penguin Books. It is hoped that armed with these two volumes a dedicated reader can acquire an under-standing of what was and is going on musically in the world, both in cultural and in technical terms.

Select Bibliography

Dictionaries and General Books

Ahmed, S. Akbar: *Living Islam: From Samarkand to Stornoway*, Penguin, Harmondsworth, 1995.

Apel, Willi: *Harvard Dictionary of Music*, Heinemann Educational Books, London (second edition), 1970.

Baker, Stanley Joan: *Japanese Art* (World of Art Series), Thames and Hudson, London, reprinted 1991.

Brandon, James R.: *The Cambridge Guide to Asian Theatre*, Cambridge University Press, Cambridge, 1995.

Broughton, Simon; Ellingham, Mark; Muddyman, David; Trillo, Richard and Burton, Kim (eds): *The Rough Guide to World Music*, The Rough Guides, London, 1994.

Campbell, Joseph: *The Masks of God: Oriental Mythology*. Arkana, Harmondsworth, 1991.

Confucius (trans. R. Dawson): *The Analects*, Oxford University Press (*The World's Classics Series*), Oxford, 1993.

Courlander, Harold: *A Treasury of African Folklore*, Marlow & Company, New York, 1996.

Craven, Roy C.: *Indian Art*, Thames and Hudson, London. Reprinted 1991.

Denny, Frederick Mathewson: *An Introduction to Islam*, Macmillan, London, 1994.

Diagram Group: *Musical Instruments of the World*, Bantam Books/Paddington Press, London, 1976.

Embree, Ainslie T.: *Sources of Indian Tradition*, vol. 1, Columbia University Press, New York, 1988.

Guillaume, Alfred: *Islam*. Penguin, Harmondsworth, reprinted 1990.

Hall, James: *Hall's Illustrated Dictionary of Symbols in Eastern and Western Art*, John Murray, London, 1994.

Humphreys, Christmas: *Buddhism: An Introduction and Guide*, Penguin, Harmondsworth, 1990.

Hourani, Albert: *A History of the Arab Peoples*, Faber and Faber, London, 1991.

Jenkins, Jean L.: *Musical Instruments*, Horniman Museum, Horniman Museum and Library, London, 1958, 1970 and 1977.

Irwin, Robert: *The Arabian Nights – a Companion*, Penguin, Harmondsworth, 1995.

Keene, Donald: *Anthology of Japanese Literature*, Penguin, Harmondsworth, 1968.

Marcuse, Sibyl: *Musical Instruments: A Comprehensive Dictionary*, Country Life Ltd., London, 1964.

May, Elizabeth (ed.): *Music of Many Cultures*, University of California Press, Berkeley, CA, 1980.

McEvedy, Colin: *The Penguin Atlas of African History*, Penguin, Harmondsworth, 1994.

MacKenzie, John M.: *Orientalism: History, Theory and the Arts*, Manchester University Press, Manchester, 1995.

Owen, Stephen (ed. and trans.): *An Anthology of Chinese Literature*, W. W. Norton, New York, 1996.

Rawson, Philip: *The Art of South-East Asia*, Thames and Hudson, London, reprinted 1990.

Rice, David Talbot: *Islamic Art*, Thames and Hudson, London, reprinted 1993.

Sachs, Curt: *Rhythm and Tempo: A Study in Music History*, W. W. Norton, New York, 1953.

Sachs, Curt: *The Rise of Music in the Ancient World: East and West*, Dent, New York, 1943.

Sachs, Curt: *The History of Musical Instruments*. W. W. Norton, New York, 1940.

Sadie, S. (ed.): *The New Grove Dictionary of Music* (20 vols.), Macmillan, London, 1980.

Sadie, S. (ed.): *The New Grove Dictionary of Musical Instruments* (3 vols), Macmillan, London, 1984.

Said, Edward W.: *Orientalism: Western Conception of the Orient*, Routledge and Kegan Paul, London, 1978.

Said, Edward W.: *Culture and Imperialism*, Vintage, London, 1994.

Sen, K. M.: *Hinduism*, Pelican, Harmondsworth, 1961.

Sykes, Egerton: *Who's Who in Non-Classical Mythology*, Dent, London, 1993.

Tregear, Mary: *Chinese Art*, Thames and Hudson, London, reprinted 1991.

Tyter, Ryall (ed. and trans.): *Japanese No Dramas*, Penguin, Harmondsworth, 1992.

Wellesz, Egon (ed.): *Ancient and Oriental Music*, Oxford University Press, Oxford, 1957.

Willett, Frank: *African Art*, Thames and Hudson, London, reprinted 1995.

Chapter 1 African Music

Agawu, Kofi: *African Rhythm: A Northern Ewe Perspective*, Cambridge University Press, Cambridge, 1995.

Akpabot, Samuel: *Ibibio Music in Nigerian Culture*, Michigan State University Press, Ann Arbor, MI, 1975.

Amenumey, D. E. K.: *The Ewe in Pre-Colonial Times: A Political History with Special Emphasis on the Anlo, Ge and Krepi*, Sedko Publishing, Accra, 1986.

Arom, Simka: *African Polyphony and Polyrhythm: Musical Structure and Methodology*, Cambridge University Press, Cambridge, 1991.

dí Azevedo, Warren L. (ed.): *The Traditional Artist in African Societies*, Indiana University Press, Bloomington, 1973.

Bame, Kwabena N.: *Profiles in African Traditional Popular Culture: Consensus and Conflict, Dance, Drama, Festivals and Funerals*, Clear Type Press, New York, 1991.

Barber, Karin: *I Could Speak Until Tomorrow: Oriki, Women and the Past in a Yoruba Town*, Edinburgh University Press, Edinburgh, 1991.

Bebey, Francis: *African Music: A People's Art*. Lawrence Hill, New York, reprinted 1975.

Blacking, John: *How Musical is Man?*, Faber and Faber, London, 1976.

Berliner, Paul F.: *The Soul of Mbira: Music and Tradition of the Shona People of Zimbabwe*, University of Chicago Press, Chicago, reprinted 1993.

Brandel, Rose: *The Music of Central Africa: An Ethnomusicological Study*, Martinus Nijhoff, The Hague, 1973.

Bravmann, Rene A.: *Islam and Tribal Art in West Africa*, Cambridge University Press, Cambridge, 1974.

Chernoff, John Miller: *African Rhythm and African Sensibility: Aesthetics and Social Action in African Musical Idioms*, University of Chicago Press, Chicago, 1979.

Finnegan, Ruth: *Oral Literature in Africa*, Clarendon Press, Oxford, 1970.

Graham, Ronnie: *Stern's Guide to Contemporary African Music*, Pluto Press, London, 1989.

Jones, A. M.: *Drums Down the Centuries, African Music*, vols. 1, 4 (Studies in African Music, 2 vols), Oxford University Press, Oxford, 1959.

Merriam, Alan P.: 'African Music', in W. Bascom and M. Herskovits (eds), *Continuity and Change in African Cultures*, University of Chicago Press, Chicago, 1959, pp. 49–86.

Nketia, J. H. Kwabena: *The Music of Africa*, W. W. Norton, New York, 1974.

Nketia, J. H. Kwabena: *Music in African Cultures: A Review of the Meaning and Significance of Traditional African Music*, University of Ghana: Institute of African Studies, Accra, 1966.

Netle, Bruno: *Music in Primitive Culture*, Harvard University Press, Cambridge, MA, 1956.

Pound, Michael: *Ethiopian Music: An Introduction*, Oxford University Press, Oxford, 1968.

Rouget, Gilbert: *Court Songs and Traditional History in the Ancient Kingdoms of Post-Moro and Abomey*, in Klaus Wachsmann (ed.), *Essays on Music and History in Africa*, North Western University Press, Evanston, IL, 1971, pp. 27–64.

Sarosi, Balint: *Melodic Patterns in the Folk Music of the Ethiopian Peoples*, Addis Ababa: Institute of Ethiopian Studies, No. 1, Fall 1968, pp. 280–870.

Savary, Claude and Huet, Michel: *Africa Dances*, Thames and Hudson, London, 1995.

Small, Christopher: *Music of the Common Tongue*, Calder, London, 1987.

Soyinka, Wole: *Myth, Literature and the African World*, Cambridge University Press, Cambridge, 1976.

Tracy, Hugh: *Chopi Musicians: Their Music, Poetry and Instruments*, Oxford University Press, Oxford, reprinted 1970.

Wachsmann, Klaus (ed.): *Music and History in Africa*, North Western University Press, Evanston IL., 1971.

Westermann, Dietrich: *The Languages of West Africa*, Oxford University Press, Oxford, 1952.

Chapter 2 Islam and Music

Malm, William P.: *Music Cultures of the Pacific, the Near East and Asia*, Prentice Hall, Englewood Cliffs, NJ, 1967.

Ribera, Julian: *Music in Ancient Arabia and Spain*, Da Capo Press, New York, reprinted 1970.

Sachs, C.: *The Rise of Music in the Ancient World: East and West*, Dent, New York, 1943.

Sachs, C.: *World History of the Dance*, W. W. Norton, New York, 1963.

Shiloah, Ammon: *Music in the World of Islam (a socio-cultural study)*, Scolar Press, London, 1995.

Shiloah, Ammon: *The Dimension of Music in Islamic and Jewish Culture*, Variorum, London 1993.

Shiloah, Ammon: *The Theory of Music in Arabic Writings (900–1900). Descriptive Catalogue of Manuscripts in Libraries of Europe and the USA*, F. Heinle, Munich, 1979.

Touma, Habib Hassan: *The Music of the Arabs*, Amadeus Press, Portland, OR, 1996.

Wright, Owen: *The Modal System of Arab and Persian Music, AD 1250–1300*, Oxford University Press, Oxford, 1978.

Chapter 3 India

Bharata (trans. Ghosh, Manomohan): *Natya Shastra*, Royal Asiatic Society of Bengal, Calcutta, 1956.

Danielou, Alain: *The Ragas of Northern Indian Music*, Barrie & Cresset, London, 1968.

Danielou, Alain: *The Situation of Music and Musicians in Countries of the Orient*, Leo S. Vlschki, Florence, 1971.

Farrell, Gerry: *Indian Music in Education*, Cambridge University Press, Cambridge, 1990.

Goswami, O.: *The Story of Indian Music*, Asia Publishing House, Bombay, 1961.

Holroyde, Peggy: *Indian Music*, George Allen & Unwin, London, 1972.

Jairazbhoy, N.: *The Ragas of North Indian Music*, Faber and Faber, London, 1971.

Kaufmann, Walter: *The Ragas of South India*, Asia Publishing House, Sittingbourne, Kent, 1972.

Kaufmann, Walter: *The Ragas of North India*, Indiana University Press, Bloomington, 1968.

Kippen, James: *The Tabla of Lucknow: A Cultural Analysis of a Musical Tradition*, Cambridge University Press, Cambridge, 1988.

Malm, William P.: *Music Cultures of the Pacific, the Near East and Asia*, Prentice Hall, New York, 1977.

Massey, Reginald and Jamila: *The Music of India*, Kahn and Averill, London, 1993.

Pal, Pratapaditya: *Dancing to the Flute: Music and Dance in Indian Art*, Art Gallery of New South Wales, Sydney, 1997.

Qureshi-Burckhardt, Regula: *Sufi Music of India and Pakistan: Sound, Context and Meaning in Qawwali*, University of Chicago Press, Chicago 1995.

Rawson, Philip: *Music and Dance in Indian Art*, Edinburgh Festival Society, Edinburgh, 1963.

Rowell, Lewis: *Music and Musical Thought in Early India*, University of Chicago Press, Chicago, 1992.

Sachs, C.: *The Rise of Music in the Ancient World: East and West*, Dent, New York, 1943.

Shankar, Ravi: *My Music, My Life*, Jonathan Cape, London, 1969.

Sorrell, Neil and Narayan, Ram: *Indian Music in Performance: A Practical Introduction*, Manchester University Press, Manchester, 1980.

Vatsyayan, Kapila: *Classical Indian Dance in Literature and the Arts*, Sangeet Natak Akademi, New Delhi, 1968.

Wade, Bonnie C.: *Music in India: The Classical Tradition*, Prentice Hall, New York, 1979.

Chapter 4 China

Jones, Stephen: *Folk Music of China: Living Instrumental Traditions*, Clarendon Press, Oxford, 1995.

Kaufmann, Walter: *Musical Notations of the Orient*, Indiana University Press, Bloomington, 1967.

Kaufmann, Walter: *Tibetan Buddhist Chant*, Indiana University Press, Bloomington, 1975.

Lewis, John: *Foundation of Chinese Musical Art*, Paragon, New York, 1963.

Mackerras, Colin P.: *The Rise of the Peking Opera 1770–1870: Social Aspects of the Theatre in Manchu China*, Clarendon Press, Oxford, 1972.

Mackerras, Colin P.: *Chinese Theatre from Its Origins to the Present Day*, Hawaii University Press, Honolulu, 1983.

Sachs, C.: *The Rise of Music in the Ancient World: East and West*, Dent, New York, 1943.

van Gulik, R. H.: *The Lore of the Chinese Lute*, Sophia University, Tokyo, 1940.

Wichmann, Elizabeth: *Listening to Theatre: The Rural Dimension of Beijing Opera*, University of Hawaii Press, Honolulu, 1991.

Williams, C. A. S.: *Outlines of Chinese Symbolism and Art Motives*, Dover, New York, 1976.

Yung, Bell: *Cantonese Opera*, Cambridge University Press, Cambridge, 1989.

Chapter 5 The Far East: Japan

Adriaansz, Willem: *The Danmono of Japanese Koto Music*, University of California Press, Berkeley, 1973.

Garsian, Robert: *Music of a Thousand Autumns: The Togaku Style of Japanese Court Music*, University of California Press, Berkeley, 1975.

Harich-Schneider, Eta: *A History of Japanese Music*, Oxford University Press, Oxford, 1973.

Kishibe Shigho: *The Traditional Music of Japan*, The Japan Foundation, Tokyo, 1981.

Malm, William P.: *Japanese Music and Musical Instruments*, Charles E. Tuttle Company, Rutland, VT, 1959.

Malm, William P.: 'Some of Japan's Music and Musical Principles' in May, Elizabeth (ed.), *Music of Many Cultures*, University of California Press, Berkeley, 1983.

Nitobe, Inazio: *Music in Japan*, University of Chicago Press, Chicago, 1931.

Waley, Arthur: *The No Plays of Japan*, Grove Press, New York, 1957.

Chapter 5 Indonesia: (i) Java; (ii) Bali

Belo, Jane: *Trance in Bali*, Columbia University Press, New York, 1960.

Brandon, James R.: *The Cambridge Guide to Asian Theatre*, Cambridge University Press, Cambridge, 1993.

Becker, Judith O.: *Traditional Music in Modern Java*, University of Hawaii Press, Honolulu, 1980.

Brinner, Benjamin: *Knowing Music, Making Music (Javanese Gamelan and the Theory of Musical Competence and Interaction)*, University of Chicago Press, Chicago, 1995.

Hood, Mantle: *The Evolution of Javanese Gamelan*, 3 vols., Heinrishofen, Wilhelmshaven, Germany, 1988.

Kunst, Jaap, *Music in Java (Its History, Its Theory and Its Technique)*, 2 vols, Martinus Nijhoff, The Hague, 1949.

Lindsay, Jennifer: *Javanese Gamelan: Traditional Orchestra of Indonesia*, Oxford University Press, Oxford, 1992.

McPhee, Colin: *Music in Bali*, Yale University Press, New Haven, CT, 1996.

van Ness, Edward C. and Shita, Prawirohardjo: *Javanese Wayang Kulit: An Introduction*, Oxford University Press, Oxford, 1980.

Sorrell, Neil: *A Guide to the Gamelan*, Faber and Faber, London, 1990.

Sumarsam: *Gamelan: Cultural Interaction and Musical Development in Central Java*, University of Chicago Press, Chicago, 1992.

Sutton, R. Anderson: *Traditions of Gamelan Music in Java: Musical Pluralism and Regional Identity*, Cambridge University Press, Cambridge, 1991.

Taylor, Eric: *Musical Instruments of South-East Asia*, Oxford University Press, Oxford, 1989.

Tenzer, Michael: *Balinese Music*, Periplus Edition, Singapore, 1991.

Select Discography

In more or less any major record shop it is possible to find CDs or cassettes on non-Western music under headings such as: World Music, Folk Music, Oriental Music or under more specific labels as Indian Music or Japanese Music. In bigger cities, moreover, there are record shops which specialize in non-European music. These can be found (they have a tendency of changing addresses) by making enquiries in the standard shops. Regular browsing in record shops is suggested.

In this select discography those CDs are recommended which are not only relevant to the book, but are also relatively easy to purchase.

Finally the reader is reminded that the following companies specialize in non-Western music:

Bärenreiter – UNESCO Collection
Deutsche Grammophon Gesellschaft – Archiv Collection
Elektra/Nonesuch
Folkways
HMV – History of Music Series
Lyrichord
Musée de L'Homme Collection (Le Chant du Monde)
Nimbus
Ocora
Tangent
Topic

Chapter 1 Africa

Africa: *The Music of a Continent*, Playa Sound PS66006.
Central African Republic: *Music for Xylophones*, Le Chant du Monde LDX274932.
Chad: *Music from Tibesti*, Le Chant du Monde LDX274722.
Ethiopia: *Polyphony of the Dorze*, Le Chant du Monde CNR274646.
Ivory Coast: *Senufo (Music for Fodonon Funerals)*, Le Chant du Monde CNR274838.
Kenya: *Music of Nyanza*, Ocora/Radio France C560022/23.
Musical Instruments of the World, Le Chant du Monde LDX274675.
Musical Instruments I–V (Music of Africa Series), Gallstone Publications.
Music and Polyphonic Songs from the Great Forest (Central Africa), Peoples PEOCD776.
Percussion of Africa, Playa Sound PS65004.
Togo: *Music from West Africa*, Rounder CD5004.

Chapter 2 Islam

Bengal: *Songs of the 'Madmen'*, Le Chant du Monde LDX274715.
Classical Chants from Tunisia and the Middle East, ALCD113.
Fasl: Musique de l'empire Ottoman. Ethnic B6737.
Iraq Makamat, Ocora OCR79.
Know the Maqam, Series 4, Renanot, The Institute of Jewish Music, P.O. Box 7167, Jerusalem.
Morocco: *Berber Music from the High-Atlas and the Anti-Atlas*, Le Chant du Monde LDX274991.
Morocco: *Festival of Marrakech*. Playasound PS65041.
Morocco: *Maroc, Anthologies*. MCM (Maison des Cultures du Monde) W.260010, W.260014, W.260016, W.260023.
Morocco: *Ustad Massano Tazi*, Musique classique andalouse de Fès, Octora HM83.
Music in the World of Islam, Recordings by Jean Jenking and Paul Rovsing Olsen. Topic World Series/Tangent Records TSCD901-3.
Musiques de l'Islam d'Asie. MCM W.260022.
Musique Soufi, vols. 1–5. Arion 33655.
Tunisia: *Anthologie du Malouf: Musique Arabo-Andalouse*, 4 CDs, MCM W. 260046.

Turkey: *Turquie, Musique soufi*, MCM W.260021.
UNESCO: *Collection Musical Sources*, Philips.
UNESCO: *A Musical Anthology of the Orient*, Bärenreiter.

Chapter 3 India

Inde du Sud – L'art de la Vina, Playasound PS65048.
Indo-Arabic Variations, Playasound PS65035.
Instrumental Music of Rajasthan – Langas and Manganiyars, World Music Library, King Record Co. Ltd. KICC5118.
Instrumental Music of North India, Anvidis/Unesco D.8021.
Lakshmi Shankar – Evening Concert, RSMC-D-102.
North India: *Mithila: Love Songs of Vidyapati*, Ocora C580063.
Nusrat Fateh Ali Khan: *(i) Chazal & Geet; (ii) Nusrat Fateh Ali Khan Qawwal & Party*, Undo Chazals, Star Cassette.
Rag Lalit (Saringi), Nimbus Records Ltd. N15183.
Qureshi-Burckhardt, Regula: *Sufi Music of India and Pakistan*, CUP, Cambridge, 1986 (this disc is to accompany her book under the same title).
Ramani, Dr N.: *Classical Karnatic Flute*, Nimbus Records NI5257.
South India: *Ritual Music and Theatre of Kerala*, Le Chant du Monde LDX274910.

Chapter 4 China

Chine: Musique Ancienne de Chang'an, MCM W.260036.
Chine: Musique Classique, Playasound PS65048.
Chine: Musique Classique Instrumental, Playasound PS65005.
The Hugo Masters – An Anthology of Chinese Classical Music, CDs 1–4, 13042–5.
Music of Chinese Minorities, World Music Library, King Record Co. Ltd. K1CC5142.
Musique du Toit du Monde – Ladakh et Nepal, Playasound PS65021.

Chapter 5 The Far East: Japan

UNESCO Collection: *A Musical Anthology of the Orient I–VI*.
Traditional and Instrumental Music, Elektra/Nonesuch Records Explorer Series 7559–72072-2.

Gagaku, Ocora C559018 HM65.

Sudanese Classical Music, World Music Library, King Record Co. Ltd. K1CC5131.

Chapter 5 Indonesia: (i) Java; (ii) Bali

Indonesia – Music from West Java, Audivis/Unesco D804.

Bali – le Ramayana, Playasound PS65003.

Kecak and Sanghyang of Bali, World Music Library, King Record Co. Ltd. K1CC5128.

Music in Bali, World Music Library, King Record Co. Ltd. K1CC5127.

Notes

Chapter 1 African Music

1. J. H. Kwabena Nketia, *The Music of Africa*, W. W. Norton, New York, 1974, p. 6.

2. Alan P. Merriam, 'African Music' in W. Bascom and M. Herskovits (eds), *Continuity and Change in African Cultures*, University of Chicago Press, Chicago, 1959, p. 85.

3. R. F. Thomson, 'An Aesthetic of the Cool: West African Dance', *African Forum*, vol. 2, part 2, Fall 1966.

4. In *African Art*, BBC2, May 1997.

5. Kofi Agawu, *Africa Rhythm: A Northern Ewe Perspective*, Cambridge University Press, Cambridge, 1995, p. 6.

6. Marghanita Laski, *Ecstasy*, Cresset Press, London, 1961, p. 190.

7. Marius Schnieder, 'Tone and Tune in West African Music', *African Music, Ethnomusicology*, vol. 3, 1961, pp. 204−15.

8. Victor Zuckerkandl, *Music and the Eternal World, Sound and Symbol*, vol. 1, Routledge, London, 1936, p. 15.

9. Anton Ehrenzweig, *The Psychoanalysis of Artistic Vision and Hearing*, Sheldon Press, London, 1975, pp. 164−5.

10. John A. Sloboda, *The Musical Mind*, Clarendon Press, Oxford, 1985, p. 267.

11. Francis Bebey, *African Music: A People's Art*, Lawrence Hill, New York, reprinted 1975, p. 134.

12. G. Herzog, 'Canon in Western African Xylophone Melodies', *Journal of the American Musicological Society*, II, 1949.

13. Nketia, *Music of Africa*, pp. 177−8.

14. Jack Goody, *Death, Property and the Ancestors*, Routledge, London, 1962, p. 103.

15. 'Breath' by Birago Diop, in Wole Soyink (ed.), *Poems of Black Africa*, Heinemann, London, 1957.

16. K. Oberg, 'The Ankole Kingdom in Uganda', in M. Fortes and E. E. Evans-Pritchard (eds), *African Political Systems*, Oxford University Press, Oxford, 1940, p. 142.

Chapter 2 Islam and Music

1. William P. Malm, *Music Cultures of the Pacific, the Near East and Asia*, Prentice Hall, Englewood Cliffs, NJ, 1967, pp. 54–5.

2. Habib Hassan Touma, *The Music of the Arabs*, Amadeus Press, Portland, OR, 1996, p. 69.

3. Bernhard Lewis, *The Arabs in History*, Hutchinson's University Library, London, 1950, p. 178.

Chapter 3 The Indian Subcontinent

1. Harold Powers, 'A Historical and Comparative Approach to the Classification of Ragas (with an Appendix on Indian Tunings)' *Select Reports* 1:12–78, Los Angeles: Institute of Ethnomusicology, University of California.

2. Philip Glass, *Opera on the Beach: Philip Glass on His New World of Theatre Music*, Faber and Faber, London, 1988, p. 17.

3. Ravi Shankar, *My Music, My Life*, Jonathan Cape, London, 1969, pp. 26–7.

4. Shankar, *My Music, My Life*, p. 21.

5. *The Dhammapada (The Path of Perfection)*, trans. Juan Mascaró, Penguin, Harmondsworth, 1973, p. 51.

6. Regula Qureshi-Burckhardt, *Sufi Music of India and Pakistan: Sound, Context and Meaning in Qawwali*, University of Chicago Press, Chicago, p. xiii.

Chapter 4 China

1. Curt Sachs, *Rhythm and Tempo: A Study in Music History*, W. W. Norton, New York, 1953, p. 60.
2. Stephen Jones, *Folk Music of China: Living Instrumental Traditions*, Clarendon Press, Oxford, 1995, p. 26.

Chapter 5 The Far East: Japan and Indonesia

1. Sumarsam, *Gamelan: Cultural Interaction and Musical Development in Central Java*, Cambridge University Press, Cambridge, 1991, p. 100.
2. Sumarsam, *Gamelan*, p. 241.
3. Jaap Kunst, *Music in Java (Its History, Its Theory, Its Technique)*, 2 vols, Martinus Nijhoff, The Hague, 1949, vol. 1, p. 409.

Index

Abu Bakr, 59
Abu Hamid al-Ghazali, 89
accelerando, 188, 190–91
additive rhythm, 11, 106–8, 188
aerophones, *see* wind instruments
Africa, cultural aspects, 3, 4–7, 46–7
African hand piano, *see mbira*
African music
  functional uses, 5, 21, 47
  harmony in, 22–5
  instruments in, 26–45, 62–3, 80, 234
  Islam and, 62–3
  melody in, 18–20, 25
  rhythm in, 8–9, 12–16
  scales in, 18–20
  tempo in, 16–18
  vocal styles, 20
  see also Arabic music
African traditional religions, 46–7
Agawu, Kofi, 9
akandinda, 51
alap, 116
Algeria, 69, 80
Ali al-Dunya, 89
Amire Khusro, 102
Andalusi ensemble, 87
animals, imitation of, 37
anklung, 226
Anlo Ewes, 23, 37

Arabic music
  and Africa, 62–3
  form in, 69–70
  harmony in, 62, 70–71
  history, 59–63
  and India, 122
  instruments in, 58, 59, 70, 72–87
  melody in, 66–70
  rhythm in, 64–6
audiences, 213, 241
  see also listening
Augustine, St, 20
Aum/Om, 99, 146

Babeme, 42
bagpipes, 84–5, 131
Bahadur Shah II, 103
Bali, 243–6
Balinese music, *see* Indonesian music
bandir, 75–6
Bangladesh, 98
bansuri, 130
barrel drum, Chinese, 165
Bartók, Béla, 16, 50, 246
bayan, see tabla
Bebey, Francis, 47
Bedouins, 59
bell(s)
  in Africa, 28, 30

bell(s) – *cont.*
  in Arabic music, 73
  in China, 160–62, 179
  in dancing, 28, 119–20, 179
  in India, 119–20
  in Indonesia, 227
  in Japan, 196
  in Tibet, 179
  'yellow bell' (*Huang Chung*) in
    Chinese thought, 146, 148, 151
bell chimes, 162, 196
Bharata, 100–101, 139–40
Bhatkhande, V. N., 112, 114
bin, see vina
biwa, 202
bols, 123
bonang, 230
bow, 38, 124
Brandel, Rose, 12
Buddhism, 97, 135–6, 142, 158, 171
  in Japan, 184, 216, 217–19: religious
    music, 188, 194, 196, 200, 218–19
  and music, 117, 172
  and Shinto, 216, 218
  in Tibet, 175–6, 177
bugaku, 207
buka, 59
bunraku, 208–10
Bunrakuken, Uemura, 209
Burundi, 34
al-Busiri, 91
buzug, 80
buzzers/buzz-discs, 43

Cage, John, 246
camel bells, 73
Cameroon, 43
castanets, 80
celempung, 238
chengcheng, 230
chimes, 160, 162–3, 196, 230
ch'in, 166–8
chin ko, 200

China
  history, 145, 148
  and Tibet, 175
Chinese music
  dynamics in, 149, 226
  and Gagaku, 207
  harmony in, 153–6
  instruments in, 160–68, 194, 200,
    202, 203
  melody in, 150–52
  programmatism in, 146, 155–6
  rhythm in, 149–50, 152
Chinese opera, 148, 149, 173–5
  and Tibetan drama, 177
Chopi, 32
choral singing, 91, 246
chordophones, *see* string instruments
Christianity
  in Africa, 46
  Coptic church music, 3, 30
  and dance, 6–7
  in India, 131, 136
  in Japan, 216
Church modes, *see* modes
circle dances, 92
clapper bell, 227
clappers
  in China, 163, 175
  in India, 119
  in Indonesia, 227
  in Japan, 194
clapping, 26, 73, 103
  in *qawwali*, 138, 139
clarinets, 84, 87, 131, 141
colour harmony, 155
communication/language, music and,
  ix–x, 20–22, 47–8, 66, 149–50
composition, 18, 51, 245
conducting, 175
Confucianism, 158, 170
  and music, 164, 172
Confucius, 145, 147–8, 149, 150, 157,
  170

and change, 180
and chimes, 160
and the *ch'in*, 168
Congo, 30, 32, 38, 42, 46–7
contemplation, 117
Coptic Christian music, 3, 30
Côte d'Ivoire, 37
crotals, 73
cymbals, 73, 119, 141, 163, 230

da-daiko, 199–200
daff zinjari, 75
daibyoshi, 199
dalangs, 241, 243
damru, 98, 139
dance
    in Africa, 6–7
    in Arabic culture, 75
    in China, 179
    in India, 98, 119–20, 139–42
    in Indonesia, 246
    in Japan, 187
    Mevlevi circle-dance, 92
    music and, 6, 14, 37, 49, 139–40
    in Sufi worship, 91
    in Tibet, 177, 179
dance drama, 49, 141, 177
    see also Kabuki
darabukkah (goblet drums), 76, 87
darb, 64, 66
Darwin, Charles, 20
dawar, 66
Debussy, Claude, 156, 224, 246
Dervishes, 58, 84, 92
Deva, B. Chaitanya, 131
Devi, 99
dhikr, 91–2
dholak, 139
Diop, Birago, 50
dirges, 49–50, 52
dissonance, 191, 192–4
double-reed instruments
    in Africa, 62

in Arabic music, 84–5, 87
in China, 168
in India, 131
in Indonesia, 226, 238
in Japan, 206, 207
in Tibet, 176–7
dragon clapper, 194
drama, *see* dance drama *and* theatre
drones
    in bagpipes, 85
    in Indian music, 116–17, 118, 127,
        131
drums
    in Africa, 32–7
    in Arabic music, 59, 76–8, 83, 87, 91
    in China, 156, 165–6, 175, 194, 200,
        236
    in India, 122–4, 139, 141–2
    in Indonesia, 235–6, 242
    in Islamic religious music, 91
    in Japan, 194, 199–200, 207, 214,
        215–16
    in qawwali, 137, 139
    and ritual, 52, 142
    Shiva and, 98, 142
    slit, 194
    in Tibetan Buddhist monasteries, 176
    tuning, 122, 123–4, 199
duff, 59, 75
dulcimer, 82, 87
dynamics, 149, 226, 234

ecstasy, 16, 91, 92, 138
Egypt, 72–3
Ehrenzweig, Anton, 21
emotions, music and, 49–50, 101
ensembles
    in Africa, 34, 42
    in Arabic music, 72–3, 82, 87
    in India, 121, 130, 133
    in japan, 207–8, 214, 215–16: *see also*
        Gagaku, Kabuki *and* Noh
d'Erlanger, R., 68

Ethiopia, 38, 40, 73, 78, 80
    Coptic Christian church music, 3, 30
Ewe, 9, 23, 37

fan
    in Chinese dance, 179
    as musical instrument in Japan, 194
al-Farabi, 61, 67
festivals, 85, 134–5, 137, 172, 179
fiddles
    in Africa, 40, 80
    in Arabic music, 80–82
    in India, 130
    in Indonesia, 226, 237, 242
    in Tibet, 176
    tunings, 82
    see also violin
film music, Egyptian, 73
flutes
    in Africa, 42, 43
    in Arabic music, 59, 83–4, 87
    in China, 168
    in India, 130, 141
    in Indonesia, 238, 242
    in Japan, 204–5, 207, 214, 215–16
folk fiddles, see fiddles
form
    in Arabic music, 69–70
    in Japanese music, 187, 190–91, 208
frame drums, 75, 235–6
    see also tambourines
friction drums, 34–7
fue, 215–16
funerals, 49, 51, 76

Gabon, 40
Gagaku, 188, 191, 193–4, 207–8
    instruments used in, 196, 199, 200, 207
gamaks, 116
gambang, 232, 242
Gambia, 52, 62–3
gamelan, 245, 246
    and dance music, 246

Indonesian nationalists and, 221–2
    instruments of, 226–39: melody
        instruments, 233–5, 237–9
    and wayang, 242, 243
Gates, H. L., 7
gats, 116
gekkin, 202–3
gender
    bells and, 162
    and instruments: in Africa, 37, 42, 45,
        52; in Arabic culture, 75, 76, 84; in
        India, 127
    and pitch in Chinese music, 160
    and professional performance, 59, 60
    and rhythm in Chinese music, 149
    roles in qawwali, 138
    see also sexual symbolism
gender (Indonesian instrument), 233–5,
    242
genius, attitudes to, 51
Gesamtkunstwerk, 212, 241
Ghana, 37, 51
Ghosh, Manomohan, 101
Glass, Philip, 107–8
globalization, 92
goblet drums, 76, 87
gong chimes, 162–3, 230
gongs, 73, 228–30
    in Africa, 30
    in China, 162–3
    in India, 119
    in Indonesia, 226, 228–30
    in Japan, 196, 207
Goody, Jack, 4
Granada, 61–2, 69
griots, 52
Guinea, 34
guitar, 80

Haazen, Father, 46–7
hadith, 60, 88
hand piano, see mbira
harmonium, 104, 131–2, 138, 139

harmony
in African music, 22–5
in Arabic music, 70–71
in Chinese music, 153–6
in Chinese thought, 153
colour, 155
in Indian music, 117–18
in Indonesian music, 71, 232
in Japanese music, 71, 191–4, 202,
203, 208
place in music, 18
harp, 40, 59, 78, 126
Hassan Ibn Thabit, 91
healing, 40
hemiola, 12–13, 15
Herodotus, 4
Herzog, G., 48
heterophony, 62, 70, 71, 191, 193, 208
hichiriki, 206
Hijaz, 67–8
Hindemith, Paul, 16
Hinduism, 97, 99, 133–5, 142
in Bali, 242
in Indonesia, 219
Indonesian music and, 239–41
and music, 98–9, 126, 127
Hindustani music, 100, 103, 104, 108,
109, 112–15
classical ensemble, 130
historical awareness, 5–6
hocket, 24–5
homophony, 156
Hood, Mantle, 243
Hornbostel, E. M., 26
horns, 43, 85, 132–3
Huang Chung, 146, 148, 151
huda, 59
Hungary, 50
hymns
Christian, in India, 131
Islamic, 91, 92
Vedic, 100
hyoshipi, 194

I Ching, 157, 159
Ibn Missja, 60
Ibn Surayi, 60
Ibrahim Ibn al-Mahdi, 60
idiophones, 26
in Africa, 26–32
in Arabic music, 73
in India, 119–21
in Indonesia, 224, 226–32
in Japan, 194–6
imams, 89, 90
improvisation, 50–51
in African music, 50–51
in Arabic music, 67, 69
in Indian music, 103, 118
in Indonesian theatre, 241
in *qawwali*, 138
India
and Bali, 243
history, 97–8
place of music in culture, 98–9
Indian music
harmony in, 117–18
Hindustani/Karnatic, 100, 103, 104,
108–9, 112–15
history, 100–104
improvisation in, 103, 118
instruments in, 104, 119–33
melody in, 109–16
rhythm in, 104–9
training in, 99
see also ragas
Indonesia, 30, 219–21
Indonesian music
differences in, 243–6
harmony in, 71, 232
instruments in, 224, 226–38
melody in, 224–5, 232, 233, 242
rhythm in, 222–4, 232
instruments in, 224, 226–38
in Africa, 26–45, 62–3, 80, 234
in Arabic music, 58, 59, 70,
72–87

Indonesian music – *cont.*
attitudes concerning, 52–3; *see also under* gender
in China, 160–68, 194, 200, 202, 203: theories concerning, 157–60, 166
classification of, 26, 72
in India, 104, 119–33
in Indonesia, 224, 226–38
in Japan, 188, 192–3, 194–210, 211
manufacture of, 75, 122–4
in Tibet, 176–7
interlocking rhythm, 223–4, 246
intervals used in music, 67–8, 112
see also pitch *and* scales
Iran, 84
see also Persia
Iraq, 72–3, 78, 80, 82, 84, 85, 87
al-Isfahani, 61
Ishak, 60
Islam, 57–60, 87–92
and Africa, 46, 62–3
and India, 97, 98, 99, 101–3, 122, 137–9
and Indonesia, 219, 220, 221, 237, 239–41
and music, 58–60, 85, 89–92, 99, 221
religous music, 58, 90–92, 132
see also Qur'an
Islamic music, *see* Arabic music

Jabo, 48
Jainism, 97
jalghi baghnadi, 87
jaltarang, 119, 121
Jamila, 59–60
janya ragas, 114
Japan, 183–7
Japanese music, 187
form in, 187, 190–91, 208
harmony in, 71, 191–4, 202, 203, 208

history, 183–4, 207
instruments in, 188, 192–3, 194–210, 211
melody in, 188, 192–3, 194–210, 215
programmatism in, 211
rhythm in, 187–9, 190–91, 208, 215
Java, 220–22
Javanese music, *see* Indonesian music
Jew's harp, 119, 121
jhalla, 116
jhanj, 119
jingles, 28, 119–21, 179, 227
Jones, Stephen, 172
jongo, 51
jor, 116
Jordan, 84
Jung, Carl Gustav, 146

Kabuki, 196, 199, 210–11
Kagura, 199
Kakaki horn, 43
kakko, 200
kamanjah, 82
kangen, 207
Karnatic music, 100, 103, 108, 109, 114, 115
kartal, 119
kecak, 246
kemanak, 227
kendang, 235, 242
kenong, 230
Kenya, 34, 38, 46
kettledrums, 76, 87
al-Kindi, 67
Koran, *see* Qur'an
Korea, 194, 200, 207, 216
koto (Japanese zither), 188, 190, 203, 207
Krishna, 130, 139
Kunst, Jaap, 225, 234
kwitrah, 80

laments, 49–50, 52, 59
language, *see* communication

Laski, Marghanita, 16
layali, 67, 69
Lebanon, 80, 84
Lemba, 45
Lewis, Bernhard, 92−3
Liberia, 48
Ling Lun, 148, 151
lira da braccio, 82
listening, 91, 112, 138
   see also audiences
lithophones, 32, 160−65
loutar, 227
lutes
   in Africa, 40
   in Arabic music, 78−80, 83, 87
   Chinese, 166
   Japanese, 187, 192, 202−3, 207,
     208−10, 211: *see also* shamisen
   sitar and, 125
   Tibetan, 176
   vina and, 126
lyre, 38, 40, 59, 78

Ma 'bed Rathma, 60
Madagascar, 30, 234
madih, 91
Maghreb, 66, 69, 73, 84
Mahayana Buddhism, 135−6
Mali, 7, 34, 40, 52, 80
malimba, see marimba
Malm, William P., 62
Mambuti, 24
manjara, 119
maqamat, 57, 65, 66−8, 92
   and Islamic religious music, 90, 91
     and recitation/cantillation of the
      Qur'an, 89, 90
marimba, 32, 234
Mashoko, Simon, 53
masks, 7
   instruments as, 45
Matanga, 101
mawlid, 90−91

mazhar, 75−6
mbira, 29, 45, 51, 53
melakarta, 114
melody, 18, 20
   in African music, 18−20, 25
   in Arabic music, 66−70
   in Chinese music, 109−16
   in Indonesian music, 224−5, 232,
     233, 242
   in Japanese music, 187, 189−90, 192,
     202, 215
membraphones, 26
   in Africa, 32−7
   in Arabic music, 75−8
   in China, 165−6
   in India, 122−4
   in Indonesia, 235−6
   in Japan, 199−200
memorization, 21−2, 64
Merriam, Alan, 5
metallophones, 176, 232−5, 242
metre(s), 10−11
   in African music, 13, 16
   in Arabic/Islamic, 64−5, 66
   in Chinese music, 149, 152
   in Indian music, 104−8
   in Japanese music, 187, 188
Mevlevi circle-dance, 92
microtones, 67−8, 112
military bands/music, 73, 85, 168
Missa Luba, 46−7
mizaf, 59
mizan, 64
mnemonics, *see* notation
modes
   Indonesian scales and, 224−5
   ragas and, 115, 118
   see also maqamat, ragas and scales
mohras, 116
mokkin, 196
monochord, 40
monophony, 62, 70, 191
morality plays, 213

Morocco, 66, 69, 72–3, 80

Motokiyo, Zeami, 212, 216

mouth-organs, 168, 192–3, 205, 207

mridangam, 123–4

muezzin, 90

Muhammad, 59, 60, 88, 90–91

mukhannathum, 60

music

and communication, ix–x, 20–22

functional uses, 5, 21, 47

and other arts, 6, 37, 48–9, 101: *see also* dance *and* poetry

and the sacred, 61, 66

theories of origins of, 20, 21

transmission of (aural/written traditions), 3–4, 21–2, 51: *see also* notation

music of the spheres/unstruck sound, 98–9, 146–7

musical bow, 38, 124

musical instruments, *see* instruments

musical theory, *see* theory

musicians, role and status of

in Africa, 5, 52, 53

in Arabic music, 59, 60

in Bali, 245

in India, 137–8

Muslim religion, *see* Islam

Nandi, 46

naqarat/kettledrums, 76, 87, 122

Narada, 102

nash atbar, 80

na't, 91

natural sounds, imitation of, 37, 43

nay, 83–4

neumatic notation, 176

ngoma, 37

Nigeria, 4, 34, 43

Nketia, J. H. Kwabena, 4–5, 48

Noh, 188, 189, 191, 199, 205, 211–16

Zen Buddhism and, 218

Noh-kan, 205, 215–16

notation/mnemonics, 64–5, 67–8, 111–12, 123, 141, 176

nubah, 69–70

number symbolism and theory, 146, 157–9, 166

Nyasa, 13

Obert, K., 52

oboes/shawms

in Arabic music, 84, 87

in China, 168

in India, 131

in Indonesia, 226, 238

in Japan, 206, 207

in Tibet, 176–7

obukano, 38

o-daiko, 199

okedo, 199

Okuni, 210

Om, 99, 146

opera, Chinese, *see* Chinese opera

orchestras

in Arabic music, 72–3

in Chinese opera, 175

Gagaku, 191, 194

organum, 156

ostinatos, 16, 62, 225

overtone chanting, 176

padingbwa, 32

paintings, *ragamala*, 142

Pakistan, 98, 132

pan ku, 165–6

Paris World Fair (1889), 224, 246

parkhawaj, 122

Parvati, 99

Pater, Walter, 142

Peking opera, *see* Chinese opera

pelog, 233, 237, 238, 239–41, 242

percussion instruments

in Africa, 26–37

in Arabic music, 73–8
in China, 160–66
in India, 119–24
in Indonesia, 226–36
in Japan, 194–201
performance contexts/situations
in Africa, 5, 21, 47, 52
in Bali, 245
bunraku, 209
Chinese opera, 173
Indonesian theatre, 241
Noh plays, 213
Tibetan epic-song, 180
Perisa, 78, 80, 82, 125, 129
see also Iran
Picasso, Pablo, 7
p'ip'a, 166, 202
pitch(es)
in China, 146, 148, 150–51, 160:
infuence on Japan, 189
in Indonesia, 224, 233, 242
in Japan, 189
notation for, 67–8, 111–12, 123,
176
sensitivity to, 112
see also microtones, scales *and* tuning
Plato, 71, 145, 149
plectra, 202, 203
poetry, 48, 66, 70, 138, 187
see also songs
polyphony, 118, 193–4, 224
polyrhythm, 15–16, 108, 188, 223
pop music/culture, 5, 92, 180
Power, H. S., 103
Praetorius, Michael, 4
primal sound, 98–9, 146–7
programmatism, 146, 155–6, 211
prostitution, 60, 130
puppet theatre, 208–10, 241, 242–3
Pygmies, 20, 24

qanun, 82
qawwali, 102, 132, 137–9

quarter notes (quartertones), *see*
microtones
Qur'an, 58, 88
and music, 59
recitation/cantillation of, 58, 60,
89–90, 92
Qureshi-Burckhardt, Regula,
139
qussaba, 59

rabab, see rebab
ragas, 101, 103, 109–16
colour and, 101
drones and, 116–17
paintings symbolizing, 142
types and characteristics, 102,
109–11, 142
Ramadan, 85
rattles, 119
rebab/rabab, 82, 127, 237, 242
rebec, 82
recording(s), 4
reed instruments
in Africa, 62
in Arabic music, 84–5, 87
in China, 168
in India, 131–2
in Indonesia, 226, 238
in Japan, 206, 207
in Tibet, 176–7
rekukkara, 187
religion, *see* African traditional religions
and individual religions: see also
spirituality
rgya-gling, 176–7
rhythm, 8–12
additive, 11, 106–8, 188
in African music, 8–9, 12–16
in Arabic music, 64–6
in Chinese music, 149–50, 152
in Indian music, 104–9
in Indonesian music, 222–4, 232
interlocking, 223–4, 246

rhythm – *cont.*
  in Japanese music, 187–9, 190–91,
    208, 215
  layering, 223
  notations and mnemonics for, 64–5,
    141
  primacy of, 8–9, 14, 98, 139
  see also metre(s)
Rig Veda, 100, 134
rinchik, 230
ritual, 47, 51, 52, 142, 172
  in Chinese thought, 147–8
  wayang and, 243
Romania, 50
rondo form, 70
Rousseau, Jean Jacques, 20
rubato, 65–6, 188, 215

sa, 111, 112, 117, 122
Sachs, Curt, 26, 149
sacred, the, music and, 61, 66
  see also ritual *and* spirituality
Safi al-Din, 64
Said, Edward W., x
Sama Veda, 100, 134
San, 24
san hsien, 202
sand drum, 73
sanghyang, 246
sansa (*mbira*), 29, 45, 51, 53
santur, 82
Sarangadeva, 102, 112
sarangi, 130
Saraswati, 126
sargam, 111–12
sarod, 116, 127–9, 141
saron, 233
sargaku, 212
Sati al-Din, 67
saz, 78
scales, 114
  in African music, 18–20
  in Arabic music, *see maqamat*

  in Chinese music, 146, 150–51
  in Indian music, 100: *see also ragas*
  in Indonesian music, 224–5, 233,
    237, 239–41, 242
  in Japanese music, 187, 189–90,
    215
  pentatonic, 146, 150, 151, 153, 187,
    189–90, 224
  ragas and, 103, 114
Schneider, Marius, 20
scrapers, 163–5
Senegal, 34, 52, 62–3
sex roles, *see* gender
sexual symbolism, 42, 45, 162, 164–5
shahada, 88
shahnai, 131
shaku byoshi, 194
shakuhachi, 204
shamisen, 187, 188, 190, 202–3,
    208–10, 211
Shankar, Ravi, 99, 110–11, 114, 125
shari'a, 88
shawms, *see* oboes
sheng, 168, 192
Shi'ites, 89
Shinto, 216–17
  and Buddhism, 216, 218
  religious music, 194, 199, 207
Shiva, 98, 99, 127, 139, 141
sho (Japanese mouth-organ), 192–3,
    205, 207
Shona, 51
Siberia, 78
signalling, 43, 48
Sikhism, 136–7
silence, 188–9
singing/singers
  accompaniment of, 40, 62, 130, 194,
    202
  accompanying dance drama, 141
  in Africa, 20, 40, 62
  in Arabic music, 62, 87
  choral, 91, 246

functioning as instruments, 239
in Indonesia, 239, 246
Islam and, 89–91
overtone chanting, 176
singing into duet partner's mouth, 187
see also songs *and* vocal styles
sitar, 116, 124–6, 130, 133, 141
sarod and, 127, 129
slendro, 233, 237, 238, 239–41, 242
slit drums, 194
Sloboda, John A., 21–2
solmization/sol-fa, 111–12, 141
Somalia, 73
songs, 179–80, 187, 190
see also poetry
sound, primal/unstruck, 98–9, 146–7
South Africa, 28, 34, 37, 38, 43, 45
Spain, 61–2, 69, 80
speed, *see* tempo
Spengler, Oswald, 186
spike fiddle, 80–82, 83, 87, 237
spirit world, 43, 45
spirituality, 61, 243
see also African traditional religions *and individual religions; see also* the sacred
Sri Lanka, 131
srutis, 112
stones as instruments, 160
Stravinsky, Igor, 7, 16
string instruments
in Africa, 38–40
in Arabic music, 78–82
in China, 166–8, 202, 203
in India, 124–30
in Indonesia, 226, 237–8
in Japan, 202–3
in Tibet, 176
strings, sympathetic, 125, 129, 130
structure, *see* form
Sufism, 91–2, 137–9
in Indonesia, 219, 221

and music, 58, 61, 66, 76, 91–2
suites, 69–70
suling, 238
Sumarsam, 220–21
sunna, 88, 89
Sunni, 89
sword dances, 179
syllabic notations, 64–5, 111–12, 123, 141
symbolism, 80, 101, 111–12, 142, 146, 155
of instruments in China, 157–60, 162, 164–5, 168
sexual, 42, 45, 162, 164–5
sympathetic strings, 125, 129, 130
syncopation, 11–12, 188
Syria, 70, 78, 80

tabl baladi, 87
tabla, 116, 122–3, 130, 133, 141
taiko, 199
takht, 87
tal/tala, 104–9
tambourines, 75–6, 87, 200, 236
tambura, 116, 129–30, 133, 141
Tansen, Miyan, 102–3, 110
Tanzania, 13
Taoism, 171, 172
taqm, 66
taqsim, 67, 69
tar, 75, 78
tarana, 102
tchalgi Baghdad, 87
tempo, 16
in African music, 16–18
changes in, 188, 190–91
in Indian music, 108–9
in Indonesian music, 225–6
in Japanese music, 188, 190–91
thaats, 112, 114, 115
theatre, 177, 208–16, 239–43
see also Chinese opera, dance drama, Kabuki *and* Noh

theory, musical
  Arabic/Islamic, 57–8, 61, 64, 67, 72
  Chinese, 145–8, 157–60, 166, 173
  Indian, 100–101, 102, 112, 114: see also ragas
Theravada Buddhism, 135, 136
Thomson, R. F., 6
thumb piano, see mbira
Tibet, 175–80
tiger box, 163–5
tiktiri, 131
timbala band, 32
timpani, see kettledrums
Togo, 4
tonality/tonic, 117–18, 122, 151, 187
Touma, Habib Hassan, 69
traditional religions, 46–7
trance, 16, 66, 84, 91, 245, 246
Troubadours du Roi Baudouin, Les, 46–7
trumpets, 42, 43, 85, 132–3, 176
tsin ku, 200
tsuri-daiko, 199
tsuzumi, 199
tuning
  in African music, 29
  in Chinese music, 151, 160
  in Indian music, 103, 112
  in Indonesian music, 233, 237, 245
  see also pitch
Tunisia, 69, 85
Turkestan, 200
Turkey, 65, 73, 78, 80, 84, 85
Turkish crescent, 73

uchiwa-daiko, 200
ud, see lute
Uganda, 30, 34, 51
ummah, 88
usul, 64

variation form, 51, 69
Vedas, 100, 134
Venda, 37
Venkatamukhi, Pandit, 114
vina, 125, 126–7, 141
viola, 87
violin, 82, 87, 130, 141
  see also fiddles
vocal styles, 20, 62, 187
  in Noh plays, 214–15
  in Sufi worship, 91
  in Tibetan Buddhist monasteries, 176
  see also singing/singers

wayang, 242–3
wan, 59
wazn, 64
Webern, Anton, 189
Western music, influence of Oriental music on, 156, 224, 246
Whirling Dervishes, see Dervishes
White, Peter, F., 4
wind instruments
  in Africa, 42–5, 62
  in Arabic music, 83–7
  in China, 168
  double pipes, 84, 131
  in India, 130–33
  in Indonesia, 226, 238
  in Japan, 204–6, 207, 208
  in Tibet, 176–7
Wolof, 62–3

xylophones
  in Africa, 30–32, 48, 51
  in Indonesia, 226, 230–32, 242; see also gender and saron
  in Japan, 196

Yang Yin-liu, 145, 148
yin/yang, 146, 157
Yoruba, 43
Yunus al-Katib, 61

Zafar, 103
Zambia, 37
Zen Buddhism, 218–19
Zimbabwe, 51
Zirjab, 61–2, 80
zither
    in Africa, 40
in Arabic music, 82, 83, 87
in China, 166–8
in Indonesia, 238
in Japan, *see koto*
sitar and, 125
Zuckerlandl, Victor, 20

READ MORE IN PENGUIN

In every corner of the world, on every subject under the sun, Penguin represents quality and variety – the very best in publishing today.

For complete information about books available from Penguin – including Puffins, Penguin Classics and Arkana – and how to order them, write to us at the appropriate address below. Please note that for copyright reasons the selection of books varies from country to country.

In the United Kingdom: Please write to *Dept. EP, Penguin Books Ltd, Bath Road, Harmondsworth, West Drayton, Middlesex UB7 ODA*

In the United States: Please write to *Consumer Sales, Penguin Putnam Inc., P.O. Box 999, Dept. 17109, Bergenfield, New Jersey 07621-0120.* VISA and MasterCard holders call 1-800-253-6476 to order Penguin titles

In Canada: Please write to *Penguin Books Canada Ltd, 10 Alcorn Avenue, Suite 300, Toronto, Ontario M4V 3B2*

In Australia: Please write to *Penguin Books Australia Ltd, P.O. Box 257, Ringwood, Victoria 3134*

In New Zealand: Please write to *Penguin Books (NZ) Ltd, Private Bag 102902, North Shore Mail Centre, Auckland 10*

In India: Please write to *Penguin Books India Pvt Ltd, 210 Chiranjiv Tower, 43 Nehru Place, New Delhi 110 019*

In the Netherlands: Please write to *Penguin Books Netherlands bv, Postbus 3507, NL-1001 AH Amsterdam*

In Germany: Please write to *Penguin Books Deutschland GmbH, Metzlerstrasse 26, 60594 Frankfurt am Main*

In Spain: Please write to *Penguin Books S. A., Bravo Murillo 19, 1° B, 28015 Madrid*

In Italy: Please write to *Penguin Italia s.r.l., Via Benedetto Croce 2, 20094 Corsico, Milano*

In France: Please write to *Penguin France, Le Carré Wilson, 62 rue Benjamin Baillaud, 31500 Toulouse*

In Japan: Please write to *Penguin Books Japan Ltd, Kaneko Building, 2-3-25 Koraku, Bunkyo-Ku, Tokyo 112*

In South Africa: Please write to *Penguin Books South Africa (Pty) Ltd, Private Bag X14, Parkview, 2122 Johannesburg*

READ MORE IN PENGUIN

A CHOICE OF NON-FICTION

Citizens Simon Schama

'The most marvellous book I have read about the French Revolution in the last fifty years' – *The Times*. 'He has chronicled the vicissitudes of that world with matchless understanding, wisdom, pity and truth, in the pages of this huge and marvellous book' – *Sunday Times*

1945: The World We Fought For Robert Kee

Robert Kee brings to life the events of this historic year as they unfolded, using references to contemporary newspapers, reports and broadcasts, and presenting the reader with the most vivid, immediate account of the year that changed the world. 'Enthralling ... an entirely realistic revelation about the relationship between war and peace' – *Sunday Times*

Cleared for Take-Off Dirk Bogarde

'It begins with his experiences in the Second World War as an interpreter of reconnaissance photographs ... he witnessed the liberation of Belsen – though about this he says he cannot write. But his awareness of the horrors as well as the dottiness of war is essential to the tone of this affecting and strangely beautiful book' – *Daily Telegraph*

Nine Parts of Desire Geraldine Brooks
The Hidden World of Islamic Women

'She takes us behind the veils and into the homes of women in every corner of the Middle East ... It is in her description of her meetings – like that with Khomeini's widow Khadija, who paints him as a New Man (and one for whom she dyed her hair vamp-red) – that the book excels' – *Observer*. 'Frank, engaging and captivating' – *New Yorker*

Insanely Great Steven Levy

The Apple Macintosh revolutionized the world of personal computing – yet the machinations behind its conception were nothing short of insane. 'One of the great stories of the computing industry ... a cast of astonishing characters' – *Observer*. 'Fascinating edge-of-your-seat story' – *Sunday Times*

READ MORE IN PENGUIN

A CHOICE OF NON-FICTION

Time Out Film Guide   Edited by John Pym

The definitive, up-to-the-minute directory of every aspect of world cinema from classics and silent epics to reissues and the latest releases.

Flames in the Field   Rita Kramer

During July 1944, four women agents met their deaths at Struthof-Natzweiler concentration camp at the hands of the SS. They were members of the Special Operations Executive, sent to Nazi-occupied France in 1943. *Flames in the Field* reveals that the odds against their survival were weighted even more heavily than they could possibly have contemplated, for their network was penetrated by double agents and security was dangerously lax.

Colored People   Henry Louis Gates Jr.

'A wittily drawn portrait of a semi-rural American community, in the years when racial segregation was first coming under legal challenge ... In the most beautiful English ... he recreates a past to which, in every imaginable sense, there is no going back' – *Mail on Sunday*

Naturalist   Edward O. Wilson

'His extraordinary drive, encyclopaedic knowledge and insatiable curiosity shine through on virtually every page' – *Sunday Telegraph*. 'There are wonderful accounts of his adventures with snakes, a gigantic ray, butterflies, flies and, of course, ants ... a fascinating insight into a great mind' – *Guardian*

Roots Schmoots   Howard Jacobson

'This is no exercise in sentimental journeys. Jacobson writes with a rare wit and the book sparkles with his gritty humour ... he displays a deliciously caustic edge in his analysis of what is wrong, and right, with modern Jewry' – *Mail on Sunday*

READ MORE IN PENGUIN

A CHOICE OF NON-FICTION

Mornings in the Dark   Edited by David Parkinson
The Graham Greene Film Reader

Prompted by 'a sense of fun' and 'that dangerous third Martini' at a party in June 1935, Graham Greene volunteered himself as the *Spectator* film critic. 'His film reviews are among the most trenchant, witty and memorable one is ever likely to read' – *Sunday Times*

Real Lives, Half Lives   Jeremy Hall

The world has been 'radioactive' for a hundred years – providing countless benefits to medicine and science – but there is a downside to the human mastery of nuclear physics. *Real Lives, Half Lives* uncovers the bizarre and secret stories of people who have been exposed, in one way or another, to radioactivity across the world.

Hidden Lives   Margaret Forster

'A memoir of Forster's grandmother and mother which reflects on the changes in women's lives – about sex, family, work – across three generations. It is a moving, evocative account, passionate in its belief in progress, punchy as a detective novel in its story of Forster's search for her grandmother's illegitimate daughter. It also shows how biography can challenge our basic assumptions about which lives have been significant and why' – *Financial Times*

Eating Children   Jill Tweedie

'Jill Tweedie re-creates in fascinating detail the scenes and conditions that shaped her, scarred her, broke her up or put her back together ... a remarkable story' – *Vogue*. 'A beautiful and courageous book' – Maya Angelou

The Lost Heart of Asia   Colin Thubron

'Thubron's journey takes him through a spectacular, talismanic geography of desert and mountain ... a whole glittering, terrible and romantic history lies abandoned along with thoughts of more prosperous times' – *The Times*

READ MORE IN PENGUIN

A CHOICE OF NON-FICTION

African Nights   Kuki Gallmann

Through a tapestry of interwoven true episodes, Kuki Gallmann here evokes the magic that touches all African life. The adventure of a moonlit picnic on a vanishing island; her son's entrancement with chameleons and the mystical visit of a king cobra to his grave; the mysterious compassion of an elephant herd – each event conveys her delight and wonder at the whole fabric of creation.

Far Flung Floyd   Keith Floyd

Keith Floyd's culinary odyssey takes him to the far-flung East and the exotic flavours of Malaysia, Hong Kong, Vietnam and Thailand. The irrepressible Floyd as usual spices his recipes with witty stories, wry observation and a generous pinch of gastronomic wisdom.

The Reading Solution   Paul Kropp with Wendy Cooling

The Reading Solution makes excellent suggestions for books – both fiction and non-fiction – for readers of all ages that will stimulate a love of reading. Listing hugely enjoyable books from history and humour to thrillers and poetry selections, *The Reading Solution* provides all the help you need to ensure that your child becomes – and stays – a willing, enthusiastic reader.

Lucie Duff Gordon   Katherine Frank
A Passage to Egypt

'Lucie Duff Gordon's life is a rich field for a biographer, and Katherine Frank does her justice ... what stays in the mind is a portrait of an exceptional woman, funny, wry, occasionally flamboyant, always generous-spirited, and firmly rooted in the social history of her day' – *The Times Literary Supplement*

The Missing of the Somme   Geoff Dyer

'A gentle, patient, loving book. It is about mourning and memory, about how the Great War has been represented – and our sense of it shaped and defined – by different artistic media ... its textures are the very rhythms of memory and consciousness' – *Guardian*

READ MORE IN PENGUIN

A CHOICE OF NON-FICTION

The Pillars of Hercules   Paul Theroux

At the gateway to the Mediterranean lie the two Pillars of Hercules. Beginning his journey in Gibraltar, Paul Theroux travels the long way round – through the ravaged developments of the Costa del Sol, into Corsica and Sicily and beyond – to Morocco's southern pillar. 'A terrific book, full of fun as well as anxiety, of vivid characters and curious experiences' – *The Times*

Where the Girls Are   Susan J. Douglas

In this brilliantly researched and hugely entertaining examination of women and popular culture, Susan J. Douglas demonstrates the ways in which music, TV, books, advertising, news and film have affected women of her generation. Essential reading for cultural critics, feminists and everyone else who has ever ironed their hair or worn a miniskirt.

Journals: 1954–1958   Allen Ginsberg

These pages open with Ginsberg at the age of twenty-eight, penniless, travelling alone and unknown in California. Yet, by July 1958 he was returning from Paris to New York as the poet who, with Jack Kerouac, led and inspired the Beats . . .

The New Spaniards   John Hooper

Spain has become a land of extraordinary paradoxes in which traditional attitudes and contemporary preoccupations exist side by side. The country attracts millions of visitors – yet few see beyond the hotels and resorts of its coastline. John Hooper's fascinating study brings to life the many faces of Spain in the 1990s.

A Tuscan Childhood   Kinta Beevor

Kinta Beevor was five when she fell in love with her parents' castle facing the Carrara mountains. 'The descriptions of the harvesting and preparation of food and wine by the locals could not be bettered . . . alive with vivid characters' – *Observer*

READ MORE IN PENGUIN

A SELECTION OF FICTION AND NON-FICTION

Junk Mail Will Self

'Each of the essays in this collection of his journalism and cartoons provides a hit of intravenous prose, a rush of silly and psychedelic excitement that slices through the usual cant about drugs and their culture' – *Observer*. 'Virtuoso stuff' – J. G. Ballard

Jennie Douglas Preston

When the Archibald family adopted Jennie, the tiny, orphaned chimpanzee, they discovered that the dividing line between humans and chimps is finer than anyone had previously thought possible. 'Full of humour and irony, this story is all the more moving for not milking the sentiment' – *Daily Telegraph*

Dear Katie Jacky Fleming

An hilarious collection of letters, as seen in the *Independent on Sunday*, in which Agony Aunt Katie gives her inimitable responses.

A Place of Greater Safety Hilary Mantel

Hilary Mantel's award-winning fictional history of the French Revolution. 'She has soaked herself in the history of the period ... and a striking picture emerges of the exhilaration, dynamic energy and stark horror of those fearful days' – *Daily Telegraph*

Accountable to None Simon Jenkins
The Tory Nationalization of Britain

'An important book, because it brings together, with an insider's authority and anecdotage, both a narrative of domestic Thatcherism and a polemic against its pretensions ... an indispensable guide to the corruptions of power and language which have sustained the illusion that Thatcherism was an attack on "government"' – *Guardian*. 'Superbly researched, cogently argued and deeply worrying ... as a documented denunciation, this book is devastating' – *Sunday Times*

READ MORE IN PENGUIN

A SELECTION OF FICTION AND NON-FICTION

Letters and Journals   Katherine Mansfield

These letters and extracts from the writings of one of our most gifted but tragically short-lived writers, Katherine Mansfield, have been selected to represent her work at its best and to demonstrate how the richness and variety of her style and ideas were a direct reflection of her own personality.

Memories of the Ford Administration   John Updike

'Updike is surely the finest chronicler of post-war American life, and what a sad, if sadly beautiful, chronicle he has made. At the centre of all is loss, loss of love, of opportunity, of time itself . . . one of the best things you are likely to read this year' – *Irish Times*

Cider With Rosie   Laurie Lee

In telling the story of his early life in a remote Cotswold village, Laurie Lee gives us a loving and intimate portrait of a country childhood and an unforgettable record of an era and a community that have disappeared.

Dangerous Pilgrimages   Malcolm Bradbury

'*Dangerous Pilgrimages* covers a wide sweep of cultural history, retracing what Malcolm Bradbury calls the "flourishing traffic in fancy, fantasy, dream and myth" between America and Europe . . . the approach is fresh and invigorating, and Bradbury's zest for his subject makes the book a great adventure for the reader . . . Whether exploring Chateaubriand's noble savage, D. H. Lawrence's love affair with Mexico, or the changing facets of 1990s Euro-identity, Bradbury is always lucid and compelling' – *Literary Review*

Famous Trials   Volumes 1–9

From matricide to mutilation, poisoning and cold-blooded murder, this classic series, now reissued in Penguin, contains nine volumes of gripping criminal investigations that made headlines in their day.

READ MORE IN PENGUIN

A SELECTION OF FICTION AND NON-FICTION

A Period of Adjustment   Dirk Bogarde

William Caldicott has travelled to France to uncover the mystery of his brother James's disappearance. Having learnt the grim truth, William also discovers that he has inherited the lease to Jericho, James's Provençal house. 'Highly readable and beautifully observed' – *Sunday Times*

Murderers and Other Friends   John Mortimer

'Brilliantly written, with something new to learn or to enjoy on nearly every page ... the unveiling of his private life, with its crazy elements of disruption and continuity, is endlessly fascinating ... He has made his own distinct contribution to national life ... and it has been an entirely salutary one, full of humanity, good humour and common sense' – *Sunday Telegraph*

Leonardo   Serge Bramly

'Bramly makes it possible for us better to understand Leonardo's greatness. He does this by fixing him in his time, and interpreting his life and work with an unfailing intelligence and sympathy. This is a very fine book' – *Daily Telegraph*

One Hundred Years of Solitude   Gabriel García Márquez

'Reality and fantasy are indistinguishable: a Spanish galleon beached in the jungle, a flying carpet, a cloud of yellow flowers, an iguana in a woman's womb are more real than guerrilla coups, banana company massacres and the coming of the steam-engine ... As an experience it is enormously, kaleidoscopically, mysteriously alive' – *Guardian*

Falling   Colin Thubron

Mark Swabey, a provincial journalist, is serving a prison sentence in connection with the death of Clara the Swallow, a circus acrobat with whom he fell in love. As the grief-stricken Swabey looks back on their brief affair, the exact nature of his responsibility for Clara's death is movingly revealed ... Every sentence is informed by the most intense anguish' – *Observer*

BY THE SAME AUTHOR

Introducing Music

This introductory handbook sets out to extend your enjoyment and appreciation by providing the basic tools for an understanding of music.

'Here is one of those rare things – an instruction book that seems to succeed completely in what it sets out to do ... The author develops the reader's knowledge of the language and sense of music to the stage where he can both follow, though not necessarily read from scratch, a full score, and even make sense of some of the exceedingly complex programme-notes' *Recorder*

'Well organized ... terms are crisply defined and explanations are lucid' *The Times Literary Supplement*

Introducing Modern Music

In this companion to *Introducing Music* Otto Karolyi offers a lively and comprehensive guide to modern music and provides the reader with some technical understanding of what happens when a twentieth-century composition is being performed.

He looks at the ways in which modern music has moved away from traditional ideas of, for example, form, tonality, harmony, rhythm, orchestration and notation. Through careful and detailed explanation of this evolution he illuminates the works of composers such as Stravinsky, Schoenberg, Bartók and many other musical innovators who have broken away from traditional formulae in their composition.

'An elegant, comprehensible introduction to modern classical form' *Guardian*